Rascals

and
Other Good Men

A Woman's Journey

Rascals

and
Other Good Men

A Woman's Journey

A Memoir

Eva Todasco

IBSN-13: 978-1-7381798-3-1 (softcover)
IBSN-13: 978-1-7381798-2-4 (E-Book)
ISBN-13: 978-1-7381798-4-8 (Audio)
LIBRARY AND ARCHIVES CANADA
CATALOGUING IN PUBLICATION
Title: Rascals and Other Good Men / Eva Kvendbo-Todasco
Subtitle: A Woman's Journey
Names: Todasco, Eva, author.
Published by Sweet Maple Press

1st published in 2024
www.evatodasco.com

Canadian Copyright Registration number 1213035
Registration Owner: Eva Kvendbo-Todasco
Cover design and back cover photo by Bob Todasco
Cover photo of Eva in Madagascar in 1976, courtesy of author.
Edited by Joanne Edwards

To Bob, Terry, Maria (Mia) and other wonderful friends who became part of my life and provided inspiration for this memoir. You know who you are. I love you forever.

Rascals

and

Other Good Men

A Woman's Journey

London, 1970

All I ever wanted was to be happy with a good man and family of my own, but men seem to have other ideas. Everything good or bad happened to me after I met Ryan. Thanks to this charming rascal, I feel like I lived my whole life in my twenties. He changed the direction of my life and prompted the writing of these adventures and misadventures.

I'll never forget the first time I met him. It was at my friend's Steven's condo in mid-September when the weather in London was getting cool and damp. Steven asked me to help cook a meal for him and five other men coming to discuss plans for their big safari trip.

I strained to hear bits of their conversation from the kitchen where I'd put a chicken to roast in the oven. Exotic words like Katmandu, Marrakesh, Bombay, and wildlife safaris in Kenya gave me goosebumps and serious wanderlust. I would love to go with them but was still studying and had two more semesters to go. They planned to travel by Land Rover through Europe, Arabia and India, then by ferry across the Indian ocean to Africa. It would be the trip of a lifetime! I was tempted to forget my studies, and had to restrain myself from asking if there was room for one more.

These lively fellows made themselves comfortable sprawled on a plush carpet around the coffee table, clinking beer glasses vigorously and spilling some on the rug. I saw

Steven wince as the beer fell. Each man took a turn toasting their dream venture, followed by boisterous laughter from the others after each toast. All of them had invested money in the trip and were pumped to go.

When I heard Ryan conversing with the others, I liked him right away. His deep, manly voice resonated in the room and dark hair fell in a wave above his forehead. He seemed laid-back yet decisive (a Leo) and very British with his well-groomed beard and glasses. *I love men in glasses!* His role would be to lead this expedition with South Africa as their final destination. Having grown up in the wilds of Kenya, he was well qualified to organize such a trip. It sounded like a huge undertaking. They still had three months to prepare before leaving. We finally had a chance to talk during a break in their discussion.

"What are you doing in London?" Ryan said, hearing my Canadian accent.

"Studying at the Film School," I felt proud to say.

"And where are you staying?"

"At a Bed-and-Breakfast in Earl's Court where the landlady won't let me bathe more than once a week, and every morning she brings me greasy sausages with runny eggs, and milky tea with tons of sugar!"

He laughed at my description of a typical English breakfast. We talked some more. Conversation came easily. He asked me to meet him at his favourite pub next day after class. This thrilled me, and I quickly agreed.

We met at The Lamb and Flag in Covent Garden the following day where he welcomed me with a tall glass of Guinness. It felt good to see his friendly face again. I glanced around this traditional old pub with well-worn floorboards, creaky wooden chairs and tables. There was a tarnished brass fireplace along a wall, and you could smell ice cold beer in the air and warm bodies just come from work. We talked as he lit one of his French cigarettes. Our ashtray was already full of pungent Gitanes butts; he must have been here for awhile. We spoke about our families, and I learned he'd been married before.

"I could *never* marry a Swedish girl again!" Ryan said, having already done so once.

Being of Swedish descent myself, I may have taken this as a challenge. We talked some more and he revealed why he really wanted to meet me.

"I think you're living in the wrong place," he said, measuring his words carefully. "I've got a spare room in my basement flat near Notting Hill Gate. You're welcome to have it, no strings attached. I'd like to offer it to you before putting it in the newspaper."

He surprised me! If I took up his offer, it would be closer to my school. "No strings attached," sounded good. I was confident that he was a gentleman and had to decide quickly. I needed to move somewhere else, but finding a place to live in London was a real hassle for students. You ended up answering adverts and having to share apartments with strangers in any case. I accepted his offer, and was excited to have such an interesting flatmate.

We spent three happy months together before his departure to Africa. He made me feel at home and we got along well. But the apartment was drafty, and our portable heater only radiated warmth within three feet. It was rare to find a flat with central heating in London. On top of that, the electricity shut itself off until you fed the meter with six-pence. You needed a stack of coins at the ready. This is what you saw in old war-time movies!

When I came home after a day of lectures at the Film School, Ryan would be cooking dinner and laughing at some comedy playing on his mini-TV on the kitchen counter. I loved coming home. Ryan became my family. We'd tell each other about our day, and he was always interested in what I had to say. Every now and then I had to remind myself this was only temporary, that he'd be leaving on safari soon and I'd be without him.

London can be a lonely place even though it's filled with people. I was overwhelmed by loneliness during my first semester when I knew nobody and eventually broke down crying to a stranger in the middle of Piccadilly Circus. This kind stranger listened to me and gave comforting advice. He was just an ordinary middle-aged businessman on his lunch break who understood that I needed to talk. I never knew his name and never saw him again.

Being with Ryan now, I felt I had a friend. It made all the difference to know somebody cared and I wasn't alone. He truly was a gentleman and never forced himself on me, but waited patiently until I was ready to bring our friendship to the next level. It was beautiful to wait for intimacy until love blossomed, and blossom it did. He was a warm and generous lover. I knew I'd miss him terribly when the time came for him to leave for South Africa.

Steven invested most of the money for this safari trip and would of course be going along. He was a socialite, born into family wealth. On the day of departure, a news reporter came to interview him. She took names and photos of the whole crew as they stood around the packed Land Rover bursting with provisions. I accompanied Ryan to this farewell celebration. We passed the champagne and clinked glasses for a successful trip. I turned to him for one last tender touch, one last kiss and then goodbye.

I watched them as they drove off. A haunting emptiness came over me. I'd grown *really* fond of him and felt as though part of me were being torn away. The vehicle grew smaller in the distance, and rocked a little from side to side with heavy suitcases tied to the roof. Then he was gone.

Going back to his empty apartment was sorrowful. I think the couple who owned the house didn't want me to live in their basement after Ryan left. They doubled the rent, trusting I would say no.

"Yes, I'll find the money," I said.

"No, you can't afford it!" they both said in unison.

The English are funny people. They insinuate and politely talk in circles instead of coming right out and saying something directly. They could have just told me to find another place. I don't know why they didn't want me to stay there. I asked around at the Film School if anyone knew of available lodgings. Thankfully, one student had a large basement apartment for rent in his big house in Fulham. It had central heating which was a real luxury on bitter cold days. I invited my classmate Annette to share it with me, and soon came another student and his heavily pregnant girlfriend. It was comforting to have a family again, to talk with in the evenings and share meals and friendship with.

At the Film School, egos were at an all-time high. Most of the students were males, and each one fancied himself to be an Ingmar Bergman or Federico Fellini. They usually grabbed the prize roles of director or cameraman while we girls got relegated to producing, continuity or editing. Such were the times; it was a man's world. None of us wanted to be labelled as selfish bitches, so we let the guys have the roles they wanted. Their egos were bigger than ours, and we weren't prepared to fight about it.

I worked on a fascinating project that term. My film unit chose an Israeli called Ilan Tiano (now known as Ariel Orr Jordan) to be our director. He had a brilliant vision for making a documentary about blind people. My role was to act as producer of the film and make all the arrangements. We often worked late into the night on editing, recording or dubbing sound. Sometimes we had an early shoot starting at six in the morning and often worked twelve hours a day. For this project, we filmed the lives of blind students at a physiotherapy school in London. These students came from all over the world to study there. We got to know them well, and through them we gained insight into what it was like to live without vision.

One evening, some of the kids invited us to a coffee party at their residence. It was truly enlightening. Twenty blind students and my film crew sat in a large bedroom belonging to one of them. They were as lively as any other young people enjoying themselves, and didn't let their lack of sight prevent them from having fun. Animated talk and laughter filled the room as they listened intently to each other speak. They heard everything, every little nuance. One of them told us that their artificial eyes were like jewels in their head for *our* benefit---the sighted people. I wished that Ryan was still in London so I could tell him about this project. He would have found it captivating.

We got to know some of the students on a personal level. Our favourites were a couple in love---Greg and Mary from Rhodesia, both nineteen years old. Greg had no vision due to an illness from childhood. He wore sunglasses all the time so as not to scare people. He was tall and slender with brown hair and a goatee. I accompanied Greg to the city on an errand once. He refused to carry a white cane because he didn't want to attract attention or seem disabled. Instead, he preferred to endure the stress of riding the busy subway and crossing streets relying only on sound. I felt his unease as we walked along the sidewalk.

"Let's go in this store," he said, motioning to the door.

Surprised, I asked how he knew which store it was. He said the vibration from that door differed from any other door. I learned something. He also told me that when snow falls, it's a blind man's nightmare because snow muffles all vibrations and disorients them so they can't hear where they are.

One evening, I went to visit Greg and his girlfriend at their residence to ask them some questions for our film. I knocked on the open bedroom door. In the darkness, all I could see were two lit cigarettes at either end of the room.

"Who's in there?" I said, peering into the blackness. "Can I turn on the light?"

A male voice said. "Sorry, we forgot to turn them on. We don't need lights, but you can turn them on. They're for you".

I felt moved by their consideration in providing lights for us, the sighted people, while they lived in permanent darkness.

Greg and Mary were relaxing on top of one bed with a lit cigarette, and another couple lay on the sofa. Then Mary wanted to show me and her boyfriend the shoes she was going to wear to the party that evening. She took them out of her closet and handed them to Greg.

"Oh, they're old-fashioned!" he said when he felt them.

She looked down and fondled them gently. Then she showed me her long blue dress and asked me if it was stained or dirty. I said it was spotless. She flashed a beautiful smile and her glass eyes sparked. Her shiny dark hair cascaded over her shoulders. I felt love for this girl and wanted to hug her. I'd grown very fond of Mary and Greg during our month of shooting the documentary. I found them fascinating, intelligent, and very sensitive. This was my first experience with blind people. They tugged at my heart. I wanted to cry but also to protect them. After finishing with my questions, I left so they could get ready for their social.

We showed our documentary to the film school and also to the officials who gave us permission to film their institution. Our fellow students and teachers loved the film, but it wasn't well received by the officials. They felt it was too edgy. We thought it was great. It was honest and true. Our film was archived for future reference, and we went on to our next assignment.

I often thought about Ryan and wondered where he was in the world. Was his big trip going well? Had he tried to write to me? I missed the warmth and security of his love, and wondered if I'd ever see him again. Thankfully, school kept me busy. Our homework was to watch as many films as possible, and figure out how they were put together. It was heavenly to escape into different worlds. Little did I know that my own world was about to become just as interesting.

News from Ryan, 1971

Picture my surprise when six months later I received a long, loving letter from Ryan asking me to join him in South Africa. He wrote that he missed me and wanted me with him. He spoke of his modern apartment, his job, fabulous income, and the great things happening in his life. But I think he was counting on having more time to convince me to come. That would have enabled him to make all those fabulous facts and figures come true. His letter arrived just as my studies at the Film School ended.

I was really tempted to join him, but now faced a dilemma. I had just enough money to return to my boring, familiar life in Canada, or not quite enough money to fly someplace new and exciting like South Africa. The promise of adventure won by a long shot.

Arrangements had to be made quickly. The charter flight to South Africa was filling up fast, but I was still short $500. So, I withdrew the maximum overdraft allowed on my Canadian bank card. I then wrote to my parents in Canada and told them that I'll be flying to South Africa in a few days and hoped they'd understand, and would they please spot me the $500 at the bank until I could pay them back.

Annette and I threw a big end-of-term party in our basement apartment for our class of thirty students. It was also a goodbye party for me.

"Why on earth would you go to South Africa?" one student asked me. "I wouldn't go near that place if you paid me!"

What a strange thing to say, I thought, not realizing she was referring to the repressive system of government called "Apartheid," in which the country's different races are segregated by law. I naively hoped to get a well-paying job or become rich finding gold nuggets and diamonds which that country is famous for.

Cape Town

The euphoria of anticipation was delicious. I couldn't stop smiling. Waiting for my flight seemed to take forever, but the big day finally came. I flew from London's Gatwick Airport straight to Cape Town, South Africa. And there he was, my darling Ryan, waiting at Arrivals to pick me up. He was tanned and looking good. His face lit up when he spotted me. Six months had passed but it seemed like no time at all. As I drew near, he scooped me into his arms and I was home.

Driving to his apartment, he confessed that he had slightly embellished his letter to me.

"But don't worry," he said with a sheepish smile. "I'm making good progress."

I wasn't sure what he meant and didn't care. I'd finally arrived, ready to live my life with him and experience that happiness we shared in London. As we drove, I noticed the sky was azure blue, a big change from the pale gray-blue of London. We passed large white houses with Dutch style curved facades and massive gardens with palm trees. I tried not to look awestruck, but in truth I was. It seemed that many white folks in South Africa owned mansions with luxurious grounds and swimming pools.

We reached his modern apartment in Rondebosch, a district in Cape Town. Ryan carried my suitcase to his bedroom which we would share. To my surprise, his brother

Colin appeared in the hallway. He lived there too! I never met him before, but he seemed nice enough. He was a younger version of Ryan but more uptight.

One of my handicaps is that I lack a sense of direction. New places are disorienting to me, and I'd be happiest if I could just roll out some red string and follow it home. I gradually got used to my surroundings by circling our building and slowly increasing the radius to include more streets. It was a decent neighbourhood. On one such walk I got lost and sat on a bench to get my bearings. A young black woman came by and helped me with directions.

"If madam would go up that hill and turn on the first right, then madam would find the way," she said.

Confused, I looked over my shoulder to see who she was talking to, but there was only me. Nobody ever called me madam before. She smiled and gently told me that I might be more comfortable sitting on the "Blanke" bench, because the "Nie Blanke" benches were not as nice. Translated, she meant I should be sitting on the Whites Only bench and not the Non White one. In that little park, I also saw public washrooms with the words Blanke and Nie Blanke written on the doors, and was about to use the wrong bathroom. Was this part of Apartheid? Ryan warned me that races were segregated, and it was against the law to have physical contact. I had no idea life was so complicated here!

꙰

Ryan worked in sales and bought himself a white Datsun pickup. His brother Colin soon found a job in retail, and so did I. We settled into a daily routine and the three of us headed to work in Ryan's truck. Life was stable and good. My job was in the lingerie section of Stuttafords Department Store, a fine old store built in 1938 and designed by Harrod's architect to resemble Harrod's in London. I enjoyed people and was a natural saleslady. At Stuttafords, Management allowed their staff to buy items which would then be deducted from our monthly paycheck. I bought a simple handbag and was deducted 40 % of my pay. This left me with very little in the end. My dream of earning lots of money in South Africa vanished, as did hopes of finding diamonds or gold nuggets.

One day as I strolled on a busy sidewalk at lunchtime, somebody pinched my bum! Astonished, I looked around. All I could see were black men walking from one bus stop to another. What should I do, call the police and say a black man pinched my bum? This was a strange country where there were laws about who could or could not pinch one's bottom. I glanced around to see if any man raised his face to see my reaction, but the culprit didn't give himself away. So, I did nothing and kept on walking.

At home, the brothers and I took turns cooking. Ryan taught me how to make a tasty spaghetti with garlic and herbs which became a favourite. He was a good cook. It always surprised me when I encountered a long line of ants parading in single file across the kitchen floor and up the pantry door to the counter for a tiny drop of spilled coke. Insects find their way.

One weekend, Ryan and I hiked up the rocky terrain on Table Mountain, the magnificent flat-topped mountain in Cape Town. The path was flanked by brightly coloured flowering shrubs and fuzzy pink protea flowers. We reached the gaping mouth of an enormous cave called Woodstock Cave, half-way up Devil's Peak. A stream of fresh water cascaded over the cave's entrance from above. This place must have been used by our cave-dwelling ancestors long ago. The interior felt strangely familiar to me. The smoke from ancient fires scarred the rock ceiling, and the stone floor had natural sunken indentations with slabs of flat rock outcrops to sit on. There were at least eight of these sunken hearths with crude seating around what must have been a fireplace. I was immediately attracted to one such hearth, and sat on a rock near the cave's entrance. It was like Déjà-vu! An overwhelming feeling came over me that this had been my seat in a former life. I *must* have sat right here many lifetimes ago, and really believe that I was part of the clan who lived here. It was an eerie yet exciting awareness.

I'd been with Ryan in Cape Town for a month when his mother Bernice and youngest brother Stuart arrived from Kenya to join us. I had not bargained for the whole family moving in! Stuart was escaping his relationship with his common-law girlfriend and their young son. I guess he wanted his freedom. Doubtless his mother didn't approve of the girl and helped him make his getaway.

Bernice was a short, dominating woman who pursed her lips when she spoke. I found her intimidating. After she'd been with us for a week, I got the distinct impression that she resented me. She hardly looked at me or spoke to me. And if she cooked a meal, she'd pass me a plate after serving herself and her sons. I wanted so much for her to like me. I tried to be kind and attentive, but my efforts seemed to have the opposite effect. Ryan told me that I was trying too hard. I heard her and Colin talking about me in the kitchen.

"What's he doing, bringing a woman to live with him here?" she said. "Even though they're sharing a bedroom, she should pay her equal portion of the rent!"

"Yeah, but she's not earning much, and she buys groceries and cooks," Colin piped up in my defense.

Hearing what their mother said about me, I knew she definitely didn't like me. Our relationship would be a rocky one. Next evening, the brothers and I drank too much wine while we thought their mother was asleep in the next room. But the walls were thin and she heard every word we should not have spoken.

"Mom is so damn bossy," Stuart said, shaking his head. "She hates my girlfriend, and she doesn't like our son either because he looks like his mother. She insisted we come here, so here I am." He gave a shrug, then turned to Ryan. "Didn't she interfere with you and your Swedish wife too?"

"Yes, I'm terrified of her!" Ryan said.

Colin and Stuart chuckled when they heard their oldest brother was scared of their mother.

"I don't think she wants you guys to have any girlfriends," I said. "She wants you all to herself so she can control you. She obviously wants me gone."

Their mother left our apartment next morning without speaking to anyone. Her bags were packed and she took a taxi to the airport. She flew back to Kenya. I was not sorry. My hopes of having a loving relationship with my future mother-in-law were gone for good. I wondered what Ryan's ex-wife must have endured.

Winter in Cape Town was the coldest, windiest time of year. The three brothers decided to go deep-sea fishing one night with a group of other men, and hired a small fishing boat with a captain to navigate. I have no idea why they couldn't go in the daytime. They bought a box of bait and bragged about how many fish they'd catch and all the fish we'd have to eat. They were giddy with anticipation.

That night on the ocean it rained fiercely with gale force winds. The morning light brought the brothers home, frozen and exhausted. All they had for their efforts was the box of bait.

"We can always eat the bait," Ryan joked.

Poor Stuart ended up with a terrible cold which turned into pneumonia. He lay on his mattress for three weeks with no energy for anything. The doctor came and gave him antibiotics and we brought him his meals. But he had no appetite; pneumonia sapped all his strength. I've never seen him so helpless. Silly men, going fishing in a storm at night.

Our Relationship

As months passed, Ryan and I argued about the direction of our relationship. By now, he had a new job as a travel consultant with American Express. He revelled in his "duty" as he called it, of having to attend company parties---without me! He said that networking and public relations were essential for the job. I felt sad to find women's phone numbers in his pockets; he was having a ball doing his duty. He said that he couldn't commit to me due to bad memories of his marriage to the Swedish woman years ago. His social life was flourishing but I wasn't part of it. I spent many lonely nights while he was out gallivanting. That's when I opened myself up to dating others who made me feel desired.

At work in the lingerie department, I soon met a dashing air force pilot who needed my help to chose a warm bathrobe for his mother. He was a handsome man with smile wrinkles, blue eyes and blond hair. He seemed embarrassed to find himself in the ladies' section amidst brassieres and under panties. After showing him as many robes as I could in order to prolong our friendly conversation, he selected a fleecy blue one and invited me for coffee in the store cafeteria on my break. We dated a few times, and he made me feel good. He even sent a big bouquet of red roses to our apartment for me. Ryan was not impressed, and things went from bad to worse between us.

Then I heard on the news that three Mercury jets just slammed into Devil's Peak on Table Mountain while practicing for an air show. The weather was cold and damp with poor visibility. Tragically, the jets disappeared in the mist and crashed. Rhodes Memorial shook, and nearby suburbs reverberated with the explosions. All three pilots were killed. I was frantic that my pilot might be one of the victims, and had to find out if he was still alive. The only way was by going to the Memorial Service which was being held in Cape Town's main cathedral.

The church was filled to capacity, but I found a place to stand along the back wall. The pews down the center aisle were decorated with fresh white lilies and greenery. There were at least two hundred air force members and high-ranking officials present, everyone wearing their smart uniforms. The mood was solemn. The great cathedral ached with silent sorrow for the dead men. Then I spotted my pilot seated with his fellow officers---*he's alive!* He noticed me and gave a little nod. My face got hot and I felt my blood flow fast with thankfulness. I couldn't reach him to talk as he walked out with his squadron. I don't think he wanted me to approach him in front of everybody. Perhaps I was his secret. Maybe he was married, although he never said and I never asked. That was the last time I saw him.

How was it okay for Ryan to go to travel parties, meet women, and get drunk? I worried myself sick when he didn't come home. Many times I fished him out of bars and helped him home because he couldn't walk. I had enough and couldn't stand it any longer. Ryan and I split up!

I answered some adverts placed by girls needing a fourth person to share the rent. The first apartment I went to left me appalled. Their beds were unmade and dirty dishes cluttered the sink.

"Excuse the mess," one of the girls said in her strong South African accent, "but the maid hasn't got around to cleaning up yet."

I couldn't live like that. These girls grew up having maids. I thanked them for considering me but would not be accepting. I couldn't imagine waiting around for the maid to do all the work. To me, that was shocking. The second advert was successful. Three English girls who lived in Sea Point needed another female and I fit in nicely. We were all in our early twenties and accustomed to doing our own housework. The building was located right near the beach, perfect for going swimming. Ryan helped me to move my stuff from his place. He was quiet and seemed surprised that I would actually leave him. But he didn't try to stop me.

I quit working at Stuttafords which was too far from my new apartment. I looked around for another job and thought I could always waitress until something better came along. There were several fine restaurants on the main street, the last one serving Italian food. When I asked for work, the owner invited me in to talk.

"I can't possibly put you in a uniform to wait on tables," he said. (I figured he meant that white girls don't do that). "But you can sit here and look after the cash for me."

He usually did that himself, but wanted to give me something to do. After a few days of working there, I felt that I wasn't really needed. I worried about what else I could find. The relief must have shown on my face when he said that he knew of a club where I could work as a Hostess. He made a phone call and gave me the address.

It turned out to be an exclusive gambling club run by a slick Italian called Vincenzo. I didn't know that gambling was illegal in South Africa, but for this special club the police seemed to turn a blind eye.

I spotted Ryan a few times lurking in his truck within sight of my apartment, no doubt stalking me. Perhaps he was worried. One evening I surprised him by knocking on his window to let him know that I knew he was there. He startled when he saw me, not knowing what to say. Having been caught, he mumbled some feeble excuses and finally offered me a lift to work.

I dressed nicely every evening, usually in pretty business clothes. My favourite outfit was a light apple-green suit. My main duty was to welcome the gambling guests with a friendly smile as they entered the reception room. That room was wallpapered in decadent burgundy velvet with gold floral designs. Incoming guests sat on brown leather sofas and smoked cigars while they waited for more people to arrive. Later they retreated to the back room to play cards for money.

I served drinks made by the barman, a kind English fellow who stuttered. He also maintained the tropical fish tank and was Vincenzo's handyman. Sometimes the guests asked me to make snacks such as sandwiches, omelets or coffee for them. Some players even wanted me to stand beside them at the table to bring them good luck. *How silly!* I discovered that gamblers are a superstitious lot. This job was a learning experience for me, not necessarily uplifting.

There were the regulars who came almost every night. I remember one cranky old woman and her son Willy. He was a big blond Neanderthal. I cooked snacks for them which she complained about and sent back for me to fix.

One evening Vincenzo called me into his office. Willy was standing there with his back to me at first.

"I want to show you something," Vincenzo said as he

turned Willy around to face me. I looked down to see the man sporting a thick erection sticking out of his open fly.

"I thought you might like this," Vincenzo said with a smile, as if Willy were some kind of gift.

They both looked at me. I shook my head and left the room. I felt angry and disrespected, but stayed to finish my shift.

Next day was my day off, giving me time to think over what happened. I decided that the unsavoury lifestyle of a gambling club was not for me. I couldn't continue working there. On my next shift, I would pick up my pay (always in cash) and tell Vincenzo that I quit.

The English barman was the first to greet me at the club on my last night. He made me laugh with his story of a rumoured police raid on the evening I'd been away. When the gamblers got wind of police coming, big Willy panicked and jumped out the second story window of Vincenzo's office! The image of that huge man tumbling out the window in fear of a police raid made me roar with laughter. The barman said that two off-duty cops did indeed come by to inspect. They had a drink with Vincenzo and came to a "friendly understanding." In any case, I quit and never went back there.

❧

I had to find another job quickly. The newspaper advertised a receptionist position at the MGM Films distribution office. Happily, I was hired. It took some getting used to, but I learned how to work the ancient plug-in telephone board using cords and plugs. I've only seen that huge contraption in war-time movies. There was even a small theatre on the premises where we staff got to watch films with the Censor Board. They decided which movies should be banned or which would be suitable for distribution to theatres. Some of the movies we looked at were utterly depraved. "Banned!" voted the Censor Board, after watching them with gusto.

My work was mainly in reception, helping customers choose movies for schools or private viewings. MGM had a large selection in the storage room. One afternoon, a handsome black man came in with his buddies. I'd never seen him before, but I suspect that he must have been watching me. He took out a nicely wrapped present and gave it to me, wanting me to open it then and there. I did, and was flabbergasted by its contents. Inside the silken wrapping paper were three delicate see-through ladies' underpants in pink, light blue and soft green. I didn't know how I should react to this intimate gift from a black stranger. This was a test. I knew that a South African girl would have thrown them back in his face, the bloody cheek of him. But I couldn't do that.

"Thank you, they're very pretty," I said at last.

He relaxed and seemed relieved by my reaction. His friends watched and listened intently. I suspect he must have given me those panties on a dare. Then he opened up and started talking to me, while I stood on my side of the counter and he on his. He said that he's traveled to America and Europe where women were nice to him, not like here. He was able to date white girls over there and have a good time. Listening to him, I felt his sadness. He'd proven his point to his friends and said goodbye. He turned to give me a warm smile as he was leaving, and I watched this good-looking, athletic man with broad shoulders walk away. I wouldn't be allowed to date him in this country even if I wanted to.

San Martini Gardens

Ryan found out where I worked and came by to invite me for lunch. He was more attentive, and expressed regret for his past conduct. As time went on, we saw each other more and more. Our dates were friendly and happy, almost like old times. We'd been separated for about three months when he asked me to live with him again someplace new, just the two of us. His brothers had left Cape Town and were no longer in the picture. We still felt love for each other, so I accepted.

Things weren't going that smoothly with the English girls in any case. They were reserved and very proper. Two were secretaries and one was a bank teller, well-behaved and virtuous with no mistakes or bad behaviour. I shared a bedroom with one of them, a pleasant woman. Perhaps they thought my job at the gambling club was inappropriate, and maybe at MGM as well. They weren't too broken up when I moved out.

Ryan found us a ground floor studio apartment in Cape Town called San Martini Gardens. We spent our weekends doing photography and artwork. Our living quarters became our art studio, and it got messy. I accidentally broke lots of wine glasses because I get excited and talk with my hands and things go flying. Not wanting to waste all that exquisite raw material, I thought it might be nice to create glass sculptures reminiscent of the stunning artwork in the Czech pavilion at Montreal's Expo 67. Needing even more glass, I canvassed restaurants and bars to ask for their broken crockery. Soon I had boxes filled with broken glass in the closet. I also hammered together my collection of wooden blocks which became a long wall sculpture. I attached small squares of painted canvasses to represent buildings. This creation became an abstract city, modern and tasteful. It became one of my prized artworks, and was proudly displayed on our living-room wall.

One evening an older woman, all dolled-up, knocked on our door. When I opened it, she stared at me and clutched her pearl necklace. She tried to say something but kept choking on her words. Finally, she managed to ask for Ryan. I called to him in the bedroom that a lady was here to see him. He mumbled an embarrassed apology to her and she left in a huff. How odd, I thought, but we never mentioned it again.

⁓

The harbour in Cape Town was charming. We often enjoyed a beer at an outdoor pub on the wharf and watched seals frolicking around the big ships moored in port. Cape Town can be a windy city, with gusts whipping around so strong that you have to walk at right angles facing the wind to make any headway. Sometimes I wore my long blond hair pinned up and intertwined with a hairpiece. On one such windy day, my hairpiece blew off as we walked along the quay. I wanted to die of embarrassment, and went chasing after it in front of snickering spectators. Ryan was not amused.

⁓

I strolled to work at MGM every day through a lush park with flowering hibiscus trees, and enjoyed the peace that nature always brings me. On the way, I'd drink a coffee each morning at the park's outdoor café. Sitting there, it struck me how much Africans love vibrant colours. I watched the daily parade of bright skirts and blouses make their way to work; brilliant orange or red blouses with bright green or neon blue skirts. So many energizing, beautiful colours. Who says that colours have to be discreet and coordinated?

By now, Ryan was selling expensive stainless-steel cookware in which we prepared delicious four-course meals on a single Coleman flame. The heat in those miraculous pots would continue to cook food even when it was off the flame. We had no stove in the apartment.

One day he came home with the news that he got fired for not selling enough pots and pans. He talked about leaving Cape Town and starting over in Johannesburg. He had already applied for a position at TAP Airlines and felt sure that he'd get it. I suppose he knew from the start that his heart wasn't into selling pots and pans.

I welcomed a change, and gave notice to end my job at MGM. To celebrate new beginnings, Ryan made a dinner reservation at a fine restaurant. But we had a nap and slept past the dinner hour. To compensate, he cooked us a delicious meal of shrimps in wine sauce with steamed Basmati rice, accompanied by a bottle of cold Chardonnay. He really was a great cook. We were happy, or so I thought.

On to Johannesburg, 1972

We packed all our belongings in Ryan's pickup truck, including my oil paints, canvasses, and heavy boxes of broken glass. Ryan was fed up with carting my glass and paints whenever we moved, but they were indispensable to me.

We drove along the famous Garden Route which followed an untamed sea coast. I loved to feel the ocean mist as it sprayed over the embankment. We passed Plettenburg Bay where wild roses grew by the roadside, and sand dunes with tall grasses overlooked the blue expanse of ocean.

Our journey took us through the Bantu homeland called the Transkei. To my amazement, the Africans lived in round grass huts with thatched roofs as they've done for thousands of years. Their cows and goats were herded into pens made of reeds adjoined to their huts. Young girls with lustrous brown skin and dazzling white teeth walked bare-breasted, their firm bosoms bouncing as they walked. Mothers carried babies in blankets on their backs. I was awestruck. Occasionally, screeching baboons chased each other from the tops of hillsides and kept on fighting down past the road, paying no heed to humans or our cars.

We needed to camp for the night. Ryan spotted a suitable farmer's field where he cut through a barb wire fence. I admired his wild spirit. Why shouldn't the land belong to everyone? It's our world after all. Being brought up in Canada, I would never dare to cut through a fence. It would be trespassing---a criminal offense. But not for my fearless Ryan.

We gathered branches to make a fire to grill our lamb chops and brew fresh coffee. He'd thought of everything--- food for the trip and big plastic jugs filled with water. We sat sipping our gallon of red wine and watched fireflies dancing in the night sky. Ryan started to reminisce.

"Back in Kenya, my buddy and I were coming back from a fishing trip and heard somebody moaning in a field of tall grass like this one," he said, looking over at the dry vegetation. "An African woman was giving birth, but the baby was breach and couldn't come out." He took a swig of wine. "We cut her open, brought the baby out and sewed the woman back up with some fishing line. She would've died if we hadn't come by. Thank God we had some whiskey!"

"For the woman?"

"No, for us. We needed it!" he said with a laugh. "Then she got up, picked up the baby and walked away. They don't feel pain like we do."

I winced at the image of that poor woman, and wondered what else he'd seen in his life. After that frightful bedtime story, Ryan pitched our tent and laid out our sleeping bags. He had some marijuana which he produced before bed, he called it Durban Gold. I smoked some for the first time in my life. He told me to inhale and hold my breath. This I did, and started to float above the clouds. Making love was sensational that night. I felt his touch like never before. He drove me wild, and filled me with himself. He was magnificent.

We continued our drive to the large city of Durban

where his brother Stuart now lived. His girlfriend and their three-year-old son from Kenya had finally caught up with him; there was no escaping. I got the impression that Stuart preferred his offspring born fully grown and educated. He had no patience for the toddler. The mood in their home was tense as he stood over the crying child with a ruler and forced him to finish the food on his plate. Ryan and I didn't want to interfere with his parenting so we said nothing, and neither did the child's mother. But I wondered if this was how the brothers were brought up.

After lunch, Ryan continued driving on his own to Johannesburg where he would find us lodgings and finalize his job at the airline company. I remained at Stuart's place for a week and spent most of my time exploring the city, away from them. Durban was hot and humid, the air thick with moisture. I wandered along main street and smelled the pungent aroma of spices from East Indian shops. But my fondest memories were of strolling through the Botanical Garden where birds filled the air with song as they flitted above me, and exotic wild mauve orchids grew perched on trees. I was surprised to learn this is how they grow in nature.

Ryan secured the job with the airline company and arranged for me to fly to Johannesburg. On the plane, I was seated beside a handsome gentleman farmer who wanted to talk. He must have been in his early forties. He spoke about the success of his sugar cane plantation and the business of farming in Natal province. He mentioned his family---his wife and young children, and gave me the impression he wasn't too happy at home. I listened to him because I enjoy when people talk to me so I can learn what makes them tick. But perhaps I listened with too much interest, because he started to lament about the state of his marriage. It seemed like he was going to reach for my hand at any moment.

"All my friends are on their second wives already, and here I am still with my first!"

I wondered if he thought getting a second wife is a right of passage. I didn't like where this was going.

"All I want is a nice, loving woman to be with who fits into my lifestyle," he said.

He kept looking at me, expecting me to say something or maybe even volunteer. Thankfully the airplane touched down in Johannesburg, ending our conversation. I felt awkward and quickly made my escape. But I imagine he planned to go on a quest to find himself another wife. This made me sad. Are wives so easily replaced? Whatever happened to love?

❧

Ryan was at the airport to pick me up. We drove directly to the home of his good friends from Kenya, and stayed with them for a week until he could find us an apartment to live in. It was generous of the couple to house and feed us. Ryan and the husband went to work while I stayed home with the wife. They were originally from Europe, and had two young daughters who were away at school all day. Like many white women, the pretty wife didn't work and had nothing to do but lounge around the pool while the maid cleaned the house. She was bored, I could sense it. A bored pretty housewife does not bode well for a marriage.

One day, a salesman came by and I could tell he'd been there before; they seemed to know each other. She received him in her kitchen where they sat at the table smiling and talking intimately over coffee. I noticed their hands touched. *Not good.* I made myself scarce and went to the pool. I told Ryan about it later, but he didn't want to believe it. They were his good friends.

He soon found us a place and we moved into our own apartment in a building called "Vickers" in Hillbrow, a residential area with high-rise buildings close to the center of Johannesburg. I found it odd that all the buildings had names.

Ryan worked as a travel agent for the airline company and made friends easily. We had some good times in our Vickers apartment, entertaining guests and cooking dinners for them. These were all people Ryan met through his job.

On one occasion, three couples came for dinner. Our high-rise faced another high-rise directly across the street. We girls cooked in the kitchen while our guys stood looking out the window with binoculars, transfixed by some X-rated activity happening in the building opposite us. With all the boisterousness coming from our men, it must have been juicy. They whooped and hollered and didn't want to leave the action to come to the table.

"Oh, yeah baby!" they laughed, slapping their hands on the window sill.

"Look at that, will you?" one of them roared. "Give it to her!"

"Why is it that men always know what goes on in other people's bedrooms?" one of the women yelled at them from the kitchen. "You guys are such voyeurs!"

"And while we're at it," I joked, "why is it that men can urinate together as if it's a social event?"

"Because," Ryan said, "when men piss side by side, it creates a sense of camaraderie!"

We managed to tear our guys away from their fun and sit them down for dinner while the food was still hot. They seemed jubilant and couldn't stop cracking jokes about what they'd seen. Our evening turned out to be lively and loud.

⁓

Late one night, Ryan and I awoke to blood-curdling screams coming from the street.

"Help, help, murder, help!" came piercing shrieks, over and over again.

We looked out the window as did most people living in the two buildings facing each other. One black man with a machete was chasing another African on the sidewalk. It was horrifying. We had no phone in the apartment and couldn't call the police. I felt powerless to help.

"It wouldn't do any good to call the cops anyway," Ryan said, "they'd never come. They'd let them kill each other."

The screams continued until there were no more.

A Job for Me

Somewhere in his busy social life, Ryan met a fellow called Joseph who wanted to start a casting company for models and actors. He needed a receptionist, so Ryan suggested me. I was painting sample portraits at home but not any making money yet, so why not? Joseph seemed happy that I was available, and promised me a decent wage.

Our first task was to set up his office in a big commercial building on Commissioner Street. We shopped for a desk and chairs for the reception area, and the same for his office. Then I placed an advert in the paper. Gosh, people poured in, hoping to land modeling gigs or perform as magicians, singers or dancers. They were on their best behaviour as I interviewed them. It felt weird to have all that power. I didn't like it, and felt uncomfortable holding their hopes and dreams in my hands.

I photographed them in a side room if they didn't have professional photos of themselves already. Ryan and I developed these pictures in our apartment. He'd bought an enormous second-hand enlarger and set it up on our dining room table. We put chemical trays on the kitchen counter to develop the prints in. But first, we processed the film in our darkened bathroom. I knew how to do it, having taken photography in art classes. We managed to print some decent black-and-white glossy photos of hopeful models. Joseph asked us to bill him.

What Ryan didn't know about Joseph when he first met him, was that he had no capital to start his company. After two months, I still hadn't been paid and neither had any of his suppliers.

One day as I sat at my desk in reception, there was a loud knock on the door. Three big guys came in wanting to speak to the boss. I had a feeling their visit wasn't friendly. They barged into his office and closed the door. I heard scuffles and moans, loud voices and the odd thump on the wall. Minutes later they left. Joseph emerged shaken, bloody and blue. He seemed dazed as he stared at the exit, not saying a word. I believe they wanted to scare him into getting a loan to pay the suppliers what he owed them. I stayed there only a few days after that. It would be silly to keep working for nothing, with bullies coming in to beat up the boss.

New Apartment and New Friends

Gilles, one of Ryan's co-workers, knew of a fine apartment available in Hillbrow in a building called "Plettenburg." It was large and quiet. Ryan grumbled about having to move my boxes of broken glass, but did so to keep the peace.

In our new place, we continued to entertain Ryan's friends. He still worked for TAP Airlines and enjoyed meeting people, lots of people. Our social life came entirely from Ryan's contacts in the business. He sometimes came home late and I started finding women's phone numbers in his pockets again. He was very sociable.

One evening, Gilles came to visit us with his cousin Yvonne and her long-time fiancé Normand. All three of them came from old French families in Mauritius, having moved to South Africa for better job opportunities. Yvonne was quiet and beautiful, and spoke with a charming French accent. She seemed preoccupied, deep in her own thoughts. Her warm brown eyes and black hair contrasted nicely with the red dress she'd sewn for herself. Normand was older and looked like the handsome actor Sean Connery. They lived in our building a few floors below us. Yvonne proved to be an excellent cordon-bleu cook and often invited us for dinner. This was the start of a close friendship.

One night Ryan arranged an evening out with our new friends and one other couple. We partied at a fabulous

Portuguese restaurant, and ordered appetizers and delicious ethnic entrées. I loved their pork and mussels, just as I remembered eating them while on holiday at a seaside restaurant in Portugal some years earlier. Bottles of Mateus wine flowed freely and we had a marvellous time. Ryan had organized the evening, so the guys handed over their money for him to pay. After more wine and desert, the waiter brought the bill and laid it on the table beside Ryan. We all agreed to continue partying at the Brazilian club down the road and dance to the tropical beat of the best Basa Nova band ever.

We headed to our respective cars and got in. Ryan started his engine and we were just about to take off when a swarm of waiters surrounded our car.

"Excuse me sir," our waiter said, "but you didn't pay the bill!"

"Of course, I paid! What are you talking about?" Ryan barked back, adjusting his glasses.

"No, you definitely did not!" the waiter insisted, leaning his arms on the open window. Five husky co-workers encircled our car, backing him up.

"Don't be ridiculous!" Ryan said, "I work for TAP Airlines. Here's my card. Give them a call and they'll tell you that I'd never do such a thing. It's bloody insulting!"

Our friends behind us were obliged to wait in their cars for the ruckus to end. I didn't understand how the waiter could make such a mistake. They finally stepped aside, allowing us to drive on. As we drove further, I saw a slow smile appear on Ryan's face. He opened his suit jacket and showed me a wad of money in his pocket.

"We got away with it," he said with a grin. "We can spend it at the dance club."

I wanted to die of shame. He thought he was so smart,

the rascal. But he went down a big notch in my estimation. I felt disappointed to my very core; what he did was so wrong! I didn't know what to say, so I said nothing. How could we face our friends after this?

On Safari

Ryan came home with the news that he quit TAP Airlines and started a safari company with Dave, one of his buddies. Ryan was the wildlife expert and Dave was the financier--- that is to say, he had a wealthy father who arranged a bank loan to fully-equip two new Land Rovers. These fine-looking vehicles were painted green and beige camouflage and bore the company's name written across a map of Africa. They were even fitted with winches in the front to pull them out of rivers or mud. Beaming with pride, Ryan drove his Land Rover home to show me. It was stunning, and still had that new car smell. I was thrilled when Ryan asked me to go with them on their first safari to Botswana for one week.

Dave invited a reporter called Leon Shirley from the South African Broadcasting Corporation to come along and document the trip. We were super-excited! I bought a pair of strong hiking boots, slacks, shirts, and toilet articles. The safari company provided tents for everyone, as well as food and equipment. We were three girls and six guys going on the adventure of our lives!

We left South Africa in the two Land Rovers and headed towards Botswana. At the border crossing, guards asked us to hand in our weapons to be counted. They also asked to see the bullets, and emptied the boxes on the counter to tally them. They tried putting them back into the boxes with the round heads standing, but of course the bullets kept falling over. I wanted to laugh but our guys motioned for me to keep quiet. Ryan, Dave and the others were dead serious and didn't say a word. I quickly understood that we were at the mercy of guards with guns and I mustn't laugh.

Once across the border, we found ourselves in a world of dust and red clay huts, with clay fences built around each hut to create a courtyard. Children played everywhere while donkeys wandered around freely. The back of a bright blue pickup truck was ingeniously hacked off to serve as a wagon hauled by a donkey.

We followed the dirt road towards the town of Maun, the gateway to the Okavango Delta. Great clouds of red dust accompanied our Land Rovers as we drove. On our first night, we camped beside a watering hole called Mara, and watched a glorious pink sunset reflected on the water. Trees growing on the sandy banks were mirrored on the still water.

Ryan parked the Land Rovers close to our tents amid knee-high dried grass. I gasped at the sight of a leopard kill draped on a branch right above our tents and wondered about the wisdom of our location. What if the leopard returns to finish his half-eaten deer? I was not brave when it came to predators.

The guys built a campfire to cook our first meal on. I was relieved when Leon volunteered to do the cooking for the trip. He enjoyed to cook, and took responsibility for preparing our meals with provisions supplied by the company. He set up his table with pots and spices, and then started grilling some nicely-seasoned pork chops while we women peeled potatoes and made salad.

Darkness fell abruptly at 7 p.m. Nights in the desert

were surprisingly cold, but my Quebec ski-jacket kept me warm. Ryan and I lay in our tent listening to the night. Loud menacing roars surrounded us. I imagined the worst---hungry lions and angry, snorting hippos circling our tents. A crackling fire burned in the middle of our encampment. I was too terrified to sleep and asked Ryan to get up and feed the fire every few hours. In the morning, I laughed when I learned those frightful sounds came from our men snoring in their different tents. One of the single men who slept alone confessed that he was just as scared as me, and was grateful when I woke Ryan up every few hours to put more wood on the fire.

I felt dusty and dirty. Every morning, we were each given a ceramic basin of hot water to wash ourselves. I headed for some privacy behind a bush and sponge-washed my body as well as possible. Thankfully I'd brought lots of feminine wipes. We got used to being dusty.

We passed one village where a crowd of Africans were gathered under a tree by the side of the road. A dead cow lay on the ground which the owner was butchering and selling to the villagers. They asked if we wanted to buy some meat, but our safari leaders politely declined the offer. I pictured worms crawling in that carcass and multiplying in the heat.

Further down the main road we stopped our vehicles at a general store and got out to stretch. I wandered across the road when suddenly the rumbling sound of hooves came towards me---a herd of long-horned cattle stampeding down main street! They kicked up the dust as they thundered by. There must have been a hundred large steers---black, brown and white beasts with huge pointed horns. I was held hostage until they passed. Cattle herds displayed a man's wealth, and dowries to the bride's father were often paid with cows or goats. This was to compensate him for losing his daughter's help at home.

Driving farther into the wilderness we came upon a pride of lions, mainly females. They glared at us as they lazed in the sunshine. The big male eyed us from the bushes, ready to defend. I don't know how the other passengers were brave enough to sit openly on the tarps tied to the roof-racks. They were relaxed and took photos while I huddled inside on the back seat. I've only seen lions on TV documentaries in the safety of my living room or in zoos with a strong fence between us, not roaming free and ready to pounce.

Some landscapes we drove through were dreadfully damaged by elephants. Those gentle giants are inclined to eat everything in their path, pushing down trees and thus killing them. Vegetation was dry and barren where elephants had trod.

When we reached an area of white salt flats, we knew that we were terribly lost. To be fair, this was the safari company's maiden voyage, and getting lost was part of the discovery process. We learned that the Makgadikgadi salt pan was once a large lake in the Kalahari basin which dried up thousands of years ago, and now provided animals with much-needed minerals to lick. Our many breaks involved having a beer while sitting on the hoods of the vehicles where the guys all conferred about which way to go. One of them suggested following the stars, but that didn't fly. They decided on a more logical solution.

❧

THUD! We hit something! Ryan slammed on the breaks as we felt the wheels drive over something. He accidentally hit a grown impala doe. She must have leapt in front of the vehicle at the last second. Everyone got out to inspect the animal; it was horrible. She was still breathing and writhing in pain, blood streaming from her nostrils. The guys looked at each other as if to ask "who will do it?" They didn't speak. In the secret man-talk of silence, it seems that Dave was elected. He took out his pistol and shot her in the head to end her suffering.

They weren't going to let this beautiful animal go to waste. Leon set about skinning it right there by the side of the road. He packed the hide in plastic and cut up manageable pieces of the animal to transport to our next campsite. The remainder of the carcass he left for the scavengers. When we pitched our tents and cooked our meal that evening, Leon prepared a tasty stew of venison and vegetables. We quietly thanked the animal for her sacrifice. The origin of our dinner was a sad story, but her death was not a waste.

The next day, we had a river to cross. The water was unusually high and took our navigators by surprise. We drove along the shoreline, trying to find the shallowest place for the Land Rovers to cross. Trees grew on both sides of the sandy banks. Our safari leaders hollered to each other when at last they found a suitable place. It was still submerged, but we could see the rocky bottom through clear water.

"Everybody out! You have to wade across!" said Ryan.

The rushing water came up to our knees as we tried to step on flat stones. The current was swift, but we held each others' hands and formed a human chain. One by one, we passengers arrived on the other side. Ryan was the first to drive his empty vehicle across. It was bumpy and the engine roared, but he made it. Dave's Land Rover was not so lucky.

"I'm stuck!" he shouted.

Ryan frowned as he watched Dave spin his wheels.

The vehicle looked lopsided. One of the Rover's wheels had dug into sand bottom while the other was blocked by a submerged rock. This could be bad. Ryan waded out to Dave and retrieved the thick metal cord from the winch attached to the front of the vehicle. He rolled out this wire while treading back to shore, and hooked it around a tree Then he returned to the vehicle where he stood on the door step to guide Dave over the rocks. The electric winch churned as it pulled the vehicle to safety. Thankfully it went well and both vehicles were intact. But our clothes and boots were wet. This would be a good place to set up camp and dry our soaked garments. We hung our long pants and socks over bushes and placed our boots in the warm sun.

The highlight of our trip was staying overnight at a lodge on Crocodile River. It was primitive but provided communal shower stalls and sinks for washing our dusty clothes. The shower was divine, even though the water was cold. I lathered my hair and body with soap and let the water run for as long as allowed. My dusty jeans soaked in the sink, the water brown from the dirt that came off. We all washed our clothes and hung them to dry on lines in the courtyard.

Next day was the most exciting. We took a boat ride in a narrow dugout canoe on Crocodile River. It was steered by an African who stood up and used a long pole to push us forward through tall reeds on well defined water paths. Made from one tree, this hollowed-out log held two people plus the guide. The dugout ahead of us created gentle ripples as we passed water lilies undulating on the water's surface.

Crocodiles filled this river; that was the thrill of it--- the undercurrent of danger. I was confident our oarsman had good balance and would guide us through. Another couple glided past. They were relaxed and slept in the dugout as their navigator steered, oblivious to the danger below.

Leaving Crocodile Camp, we stopped at a village to check out the local convenience store where I bought a much-needed chocolate bar. But when I opened the wrapper and was about to bite into it, hundreds of tiny crawling worms were already eating it. The live chocolate bar flew out of my hand!

Farther down the road, about two hundred people of all ages sat on the ground chanting and drumming. Curious, we stopped and mixed with the crowd to see what was happening. Women let out shrill ululating cries, while six male dancers adorned with feathers and colourful beads locked arms and kicked their legs in some kind of traditional dance. This was a celebration!

Suddenly, a witch-like woman dressed in black and brown shawls, swooped into the center of the circle. Her arms were fully extended in front of her as if grabbing the air. Her back was bent forward. She made that same high-pitched ululating scream. It turns out she was the official witch doctor and could put a curse on someone or remove a hex. Now seated, she threw bones on the ground from a leather pouch. These she placed in a pattern and screeched again. People feared and respected her. I was told she was psychic and could foresee the future.

This was fascinating, but it was late and we had to carry on. Dave paid the village officials for letting us watch and we were again on our way. We drove in the dark.

"Stop the car!" the guys shouted.

There in the headlights was a family of long-eared African jackrabbits. Boys will be boys, and they jumped out of the Land Rovers to chase them. They had a few beers in them which made it more fun. Peels of laughter ensued as they chased the hares in the headlights, diving into the bushes to grab them.

"He's in here!" one of them shouted as he landed in some thorny shrubs.

"No, he's right behind you, idiot!" yelled another, laughing hard as he fell flat on his butt.

Three guys flew over one another trying to catch the spastic hares which ran in all directions. Breathless with exhilaration, they accepted their defeat and returned to the vehicle. We continued our journey home to South Africa.

Work in the Safari Office

Once back in Johannesburg, Ryan asked me to answer the phone in his office for a couple of weeks until their permanent secretary could start. The office was in the same building on Commissioner Street as the ill-fated casting company, but on a different floor. Thankfully I didn't run into Joseph, and doubted that his company existed anymore.

The safari office was tastefully furnished with wall-to-wall carpets in a deep mustard color. There were two desks in glossy light brown wood, and a couple of plush chairs with a matching sofa upholstered in avocado green leather. Posters of lions and wildebeests hung on the walls alongside a fine zebra skin.

I had met the incoming secretary at a party before I left on safari with Ryan. She was beautiful, and spoke quietly with a posh English accent. Her brown eyes smoldered while short dark hair framed her pretty face. Her tailored dress was elegant and lady-like. I understood why the fellows hired her and watched them trip over each other at the party, vying for her attention. She remained aloof and intriguing, like the Mona Lisa. I wondered which one of them would be the first to bed her.

I worked alone at the office for two weeks while Ryan and Dave drove passengers on safari to Botswana and Rhodesia. They arrived back in time to greet their lovely new secretary who took over from me. Another trip was scheduled in five days. Ryan was away on tour for weeks at a time.

When he was home, he seemed preoccupied and seldom joined me for dinner. I found telephone numbers and love-notes in his pockets or stuck under the wipers of his Land Rover. He never allowed me to see him off when he met a new group of passengers for the first time. Eventually it donned on me that he didn't want me to spoil his chances with the single ladies by letting them know he had "baggage," as I heard him call me once.

He returned from one trip to Botswana quite elated, and spoke enthusiastically about meeting a travel agent named Ruthie. He hoped to book passengers for his safari tours through her agency. He and Dave would take her to dinner the following evening.

Ryan made love to me after he came home from being with her. I could taste the sex of another woman on him. He hadn't washed before bedding me! I knew it, but like a fool I said nothing. A week later came the clap. We both had it. I was not happy.

"Ruthie must have picked it up somewhere," he said, shaking his head.

We went to the doctor together. The nurse come into the office and prepared to give each of us the magic cure---a shot of penicillin. Ryan pulled down his trousers exposing his butt while he grabbed hold of the table so hard that his knuckles turned white with dread. He clenched his teeth, closed his eyes tight and started to shake. I thought he was going to faint. The nurse laughed at the sight of him.

"That's the third one this week," she said. "Big strong men falling like flies at the thought of a needle!

Photo Studio

I needed a job fast. Things were going downhill with Ryan and me. One advert in the paper caught my eye---a portrait studio downtown was looking for a photographer. I could do that. I had some experience and enjoyed taking pictures. The owner was a friendly man with thick lips. The interview went well and he hired me. I found it strange that not many credentials were needed for white people.

The studio was located on the third floor of John Orr's Department Store on Rissik Street. The reception room was large enough for two desks and some sofas, while the photo studio in the next room was where all the action took place. The standing camera we had to use was enormous, the likes of which I'd never seen before.

For each customer, we loaded a large negative which held twelve different poses. This camera took some getting used to, because the image appeared upside down. Peels of laughter came from that room as we girls underwent our training. Everything we saw through the lens was the wrong way up. There was a much smaller cubbyhole off to the side which served as a darkroom where we loaded the film.

A vivacious French-speaking woman called Mimi was also hired. I liked her immediately; she was a Lebanese ball of fire. Her energy lit up the room, with flashing brown eyes which revealed her emotions like an open book. This woman became one of my closest friends. We drank coffee together during breaks, and I was captivated by the stories she told me of her life. In her youth, she had married a Belgian army officer. He eventually retired from the military, and was hired to manage a large plantation in the Belgian Congo. Mimi was the big boss's wife.

Every Sunday, a long procession of African workers dressed in their Sunday best, came to pay them their respects with gifts of live chickens, eggs or something they'd made. The men's shirts were clean, but consisted of brightly coloured patches sewn together to the main seams and collar, thus filling out the shirts which had long since disintegrated. It was a colourful parade which made its way to their home each week. She looked forward to it, and gave them thoughtful gifts in return---items like thread, cloth, sugar or cocoa.

I loved this woman's positive spirit. She came to my rescue when I tripped while carrying our dirty lunch dishes to the cafeteria upstairs. Plates and cups could be heard crashing down the stairs, broken china scattered everywhere. Mimi saw my dilemma and rushed to my side to face the dragon-ladies in the kitchen upstairs. One of them gave me hell and said I'd have to pay for all the dishes.

"You're lucky she didn't break every bone in her body when she fell!" Mimi said angrily in my defense.

The dragon-ladies fell silent. She'd put them in their place and that was the end of the discussion. After that, I would do anything for my new friend.

Mimi became my salvation during that depressing time with Ryan. I learned more about her with each visit to the little house which she rented with her grown daughter in a suburb called Melville. When she quit the photo studio for a better job with an airline, I missed her cheerful company. Fortunately, we still saw each other on weekends and after work. My visits with them made me happy. I felt like I had a family again. I loved those two women and their positive spirit which made others feel so good.

Art Exhibition at Joubert Park

I thirsted for more in my life. On the few days that Ryan returned from his safari trips to our apartment in Hillbrow, a fog of sadness hung over me like a rain cloud. I felt unimportant to him, like an obstacle to his freedom. I hungered to be immersed in something uplifting.

A huge art exhibit would soon take place at Joubert Park in central Johannesburg for four weekends in a row. The call for artists went out and I jumped at the opportunity. This was exciting! I already had some sample portraits which I'd painted. This would be the perfect chance to display them and make a little money. I was blessed with the ability to draw faces. People's unique faces and personalities fascinated me.

Joubert Park took up several city blocks and lay at the foot of Hillbrow. I could easily walk down the hill from my apartment to the park. People relaxed on benches shaded by jacaranda trees. Perfume from their lavender-coloured blossoms wafted in the air. The spray from a nearby fountain created a rainbow in the sun, and pink begonias were planted in a rock garden nearby.

We were fifty artists in all. Each of us staked our claim in this green oasis in the middle of the city. Half of us lined up on one side of a long walkway, while the other half faced us on the opposite side. My display wall measured twelve feet long and was covered with burlap. I hung five portrait samples which I'd painted from discarded photographs belonging to the photo studio---pictures of people who intrigued me. I tried to imagine what they might be like. One of those black-and-white photos was of a gorgeous, sultry-looking woman with long dark hair. I imagined her with sexy, brown, bedroom eyes and slightly darkened shadows beneath her eyes from lack of sleep; that's how I interpreted her in my painting. A group of passing school children huddled around her portrait.

"Hey, look, there's our teacher!" they said to each other, pointing at her.

Next day, that teacher came to see the painting for herself as the children had told her she was hanging in the exhibition. Her eyes grew wide as she stared at her portrait. She turned to look at me and then back at the portrait several times. She wanted to buy it right there and then. But to my dismay, I noticed she had blue eyes and not the sexy brown eyes I'd imagined. Before she could have it, I had to change the eye color. However, as I discovered when correcting it, blue eyes did not go well with the sultry bedroom shadows under the eyes. Her whole complexion needed to be lightened, and she became a paler version of the sensual temptress I had visualized. The changes were successful and she was thrilled. I did not expect a live person to come and claim one of my sample portraits, and hoped I wouldn't get in trouble for borrowing those discarded photos from my workplace to paint from.

There was a big fellow whose metal sculptures were displayed close to my exhibit. He gave me a warm smile and introduced himself as Hennie. He was a welder by day and artist by night. His brute strength allowed him to work with sheets of steel, cutting and shaping them into sculptures. He examined my easel which wobbled when he touched it.

"I think you need a new easel," he said, in his thick Dutch Afrikaans accent. "I can make you a better one and bring it to the show tomorrow."

I didn't realize my easel was so flimsy, and offered to pay for the materials.

"Nah, it's OK. I have lots of extra wood at home," he said with a shy smile.

Strands of sun-streaked hair kept falling onto his forehead. His face exuded goodness. I liked this man and thanked him for his generous offer. He gestured with his hand as if to say "you're welcome," and I noticed a flash of gold on his finger---his wedding ring, *darn it*. The next day he kept his promise and brought me a better easel than my old one. I set it up in my exhibit, grateful for his kindness. He had made me a solid wooden easel which I have to this day. It's been well-used and is very special to me.

A curious crowd gathered around me as I worked on a portrait of my brother from a passport photo. I wasn't used to people watching me paint; it was nerve-racking! The crowd was dead quiet and it seemed like everybody was holding their breath, waiting for my next paint stroke. Onlookers made me feel so pressured to get things right that I accidentally put a pastel in my mouth, thinking it was my cigarette. Some people laughed when they saw how nervous I was.

A tall, lean South African man and his buddy strolled by my exhibition. He looked very familiar... those smile wrinkles, his tanned weather-beaten face and laughing blue eyes. He came closer and stood in front of one portrait, looking as if he wanted to talk to me.

"Do I know you intimately?" I couldn't help asking.

I regretted the words as soon as they flew out of my mouth. He smiled, somewhat surprised.

"No, I don't think so. I would remember," he said.

We chatted a bit and he left with his friend. Not surprisingly, he and his buddy returned fifteen minutes later. He seemed more energized than before and asked if he could invite me for coffee sometime.

"That would be nice," I said, and gave him the number to the photo studio.

I thought about Ryan who hardly ever came home. I needed to overcome the sadness I felt with him. What harm could it do? Harry called and we started dating. He picked me up from work when it rained and gave me lifts to my apartment. Ryan never did that. Harry wanted to make my life easier and was kind to me. Ryan still had my heart, but it was nice to meet a man who treated me with consideration and seemed to appreciate me. Harry's kindness allowed me to feel better about myself, and helped heal my bruised self-esteem. I was attracted to his manly looks and modest personality, and appreciated the attention he gave me. He was so different from Ryan.

One weekend, he invited me to drive to neighbouring Mozambique with him. Those few happy days with Harry went by quickly, but I was struck by the contrast to South Africa. Barges in the capital city of Maputo's harbour were rusty and the beaches unkempt. Buildings were covered in graffiti. Fishermen carrying their nets looked thin in their ragged clothing. There seemed to be more poverty and lack of care for everything. I tried to take photos of the locals but they fled screaming up the hills.

"Why are they running away?" I asked Harry.

"Because they think you're capturing their spirit in the camera."

The Breakup, 1973

Things had been deteriorating between me and Ryan for months. He kept all his contacts from his previous job with the airline company and enjoyed an active social life. He could have his pick of women. And now his safari tours presented even *more* opportunities to troll for women. Single females were eager to sleep with the safari leaders, and fell into their sleeping bags like manna from heaven. He couldn't refuse them, and neither could his partner Dave whose marriage also broke up during this period.

Ryan didn't come home some nights and I was too naïve to express my dismay. I'd never lived with a man before and didn't know to speak up when I was unhappy. Like a fool, I accepted his behaviour, and still found notes in his pockets with women's phone numbers. I should have yelled and screamed and protested that he should respect our love, but I didn't. Things got worse. One evening, a friend of his came to visit us. I asked him privately on our balcony what he thought I should do about Ryan. He went quiet and seemed unsure whether he should tell me or not. Finally, he divulged what Ryan had told him.

"Johannesburg is not a good place to dump a woman."

With those words I knew.

Ryan would be away on safari for two weeks at a time, back for three days, then out again. On the days he was home I hardly saw him. One night he was very late coming home. I had written him a note saying that I love him but can't go on living this way and was leaving him. I left the note on our bed. Then I took a sleeping bag and placed it in the corner of our living room behind my easel and a pile of other stuff. You couldn't really see me. Then I went to sleep.

Around two in the morning, he arrived with his safari partner and some other buddies. First, he went to the bedroom. A few minutes of silence followed. Then he came into the living room jubilant.

"Great, she fucked off!" he said, as he showed them my note.

Then he offered beers all around and they started talking about sex and the women they'd slept with.

"At least I've had someone you haven't had---that redhead from Holland!" Ryan bragged to the others.

Dave noticed me buried in the sleeping bag and motioned to Ryan. The conversation stopped. I'd been found out. Feeling embarrassed that they caught me, I had nowhere else to go but the bedroom. But I'd heard enough.

That week was unpleasant. I found myself crying uncontrollably for no reason. Ryan was home, but the mood between us was chilly. We said very little, and once again that depressing cloud of sadness hung over me.

On the bus to work one day, I burst out sobbing hysterically and felt the other passengers staring at me. I hopped off the bus and almost stepped into an oncoming car which screeched to a halt at the last second. My eyes were so filled with tears that I couldn't see anything. Still crying and shaking, I rushed into the nearest pharmacy and begged for help, something to calm me down. The pharmacist saw my distress.

"I really shouldn't give you anything without a doctor's prescription," he said as he studied me.

"Please!" I said, my body trembling.

He went to the back room and returned with a week's worth of calming medication. I don't know what it was, maybe Valium. Those pills helped me tremendously. My mountains of misery became molehills, and I was able to cope with the problems at home.

Some days later, Ryan invited me to a party hosted by a competing safari company. They were all friends in the business. Ryan said he'd be joining me later, and arranged for one of the hosts to pick me up. The party got started and I waited for Ryan.

He finally arrived with a young lady in tow---a dainty little thing in high heels and a dress. I was stunned, and so was everyone else. Ryan and the girl danced as the music played, smiling and talking to each other while I sat on the sofa watching them, seething inside. My heart pounded and my head raged with anger. I wanted to kill them both! I couldn't stand it any longer and charged up to them.

"I bet you don't know that Ryan's living with me, do you?" I said in a low menacing growl to the girl, "he's not such a great catch these days!"

I barely managed to control my inclination to murder them. She stared at me wide-eyed but kept on dancing while Ryan twirled her around.

"That's for Mozambique," he said to me with a wicked smile as he pulled her closer.

That did it! I must have attacked him. We struggled and pushed each other to the sofa. Still wrestling, I grabbed his spectacles and twisted the wire frame, pulling them apart in the process. I was furious that he could invite me to a party and bring another date. This was his revenge on me. He and the girl left shortly afterwards, to her place I assume. I got a lift back to our apartment with Russell, the party's host. He was reluctant to leave me there alone.

"You going to be OK?"

"Yeah," I said, although I was scared to face Ryan if he returned. I packed a bag and called Harry from a payphone to pick me up. I was leaving Ryan.

Rescued by Harry

Harry invited me to stay with him in his apartment in Benoni, a half hour's drive from central Johannesburg. We drove to work together every day, me to the photo studio and Harry to the automotive garage where he was the supervisor. He was kind and treated me well, better than Ryan ever did. But I was still upset over that nasty breakup. There was a constant lump in my throat.

Harry had some prescription tranquilizers which he said I should try. They worked well for him and kept him calm. So, before we set out for work one morning, I took his two medications which he said should be taken together. By the time he dropped me off at work, I was feeling mellow. I climbed the stairs slowly to the photo studio, hauling myself up by the railing to the third floor. The other girls were already there. I sat at my desk holding my head.

"Didn't you get any sleep last night, Eva?" they teased.

I managed to sit upright most of the morning but couldn't talk much. My words came out slurred and my head was filled with slumber.

Suddenly I remembered my hair appointment at lunchtime to dye my hair blonde. I forced myself out of my chair, and ambled in slow-motion down the stairs to the hairdresser on the second floor. They must have thought me unusually docile. I snoozed for my bleach job, then they woke me up to escort me to the wash basin. It felt lovely to have somebody massage my head. This relaxed me even more and I fell into a heavenly coma. The hairdresser shook me awake and walked me back to the chair for a blonde toner. My eyes were closed and I responded to instructions like a zombie. Back to the wash basin, then to the curlers. I sank into a deep sleep under the dryer. They woke me again, and a sympathetic hairdresser escorted me upstairs to the photo studio. Exhausted, I told the girls what happened. They roared with laughter and let me take little naps in the back room between customers.

My boyfriend Harry was well-endowed and a wonderful lover. All my co-workers had met my handsome new boyfriend. I casually mentioned to the Manageress, a divorced middle-aged woman, that Harry was one of the sexiest men I'd ever met. Her ears perked up.

"Really?" she said, straightening up and looking right at me.

Two days later she started showering me with gifts, I had no idea why. She handed me a package containing three pairs of stylish bell-bottom jeans and T-shirts to match. Then she invited Harry and me for dinner to her big house in a classy suburb. She cooked roast beef with baked potatoes and lots of fresh salad. It was pleasant enough, just the three of us. She smiled a lot at Harry.

The day after, Harry confessed that she'd taken him aside when I went to the washroom and invited him to visit her on his own. *Oh, boy! I never saw that coming.*

"What did you tell her?"

"I said 'No, but thank you. I'm happy with Eva.'"

I was glad that I could trust him. The gifts from her stopped coming.

The following week, the Manageress took her holidays and left me in charge until she returned. I was to be "Acting Manageress" of the photo studio due to my seniority.

A perky young woman called Amy was newly hired by head office to work with us. We had great fun teaching her how to use that enormous upside-down camera. She learned quickly and exuded confidence. After working with us for only a few days, she sat organizing prints at her desk and glanced at me as I walked past.

"Eva, can you please load some film in the darkroom?" she had the audacity to ask me.

"Yes, of course Amy," I said, managing to stifle a laugh.

Loading film was the duty of the most junior employee. Secretly giggling, I headed obediently to the darkroom and couldn't wait to tease her for the words she just uttered. I felt positively gleeful as I anticipated her reaction.

"Film is loaded, ma'am," I said after finishing in the darkroom. "By the way, did you forget that I am the Acting Manageress and you've only been here for three days?"

That poor girl, her face reddened within seconds. That was the first time I've ever seen someone's face turn rosy red so fast.

"Oh gosh, I'm so sorry!" she said as she looked at me with wide eyes, truly embarrassed.

I had my fun and burst out laughing.

"It's okay, I didn't mind. It just shows you're a natural leader," I said, giving her a pat on the back.

She let out a sigh of relief to be forgiven for her gaffe. We were destined to become lifelong friends, and still are to this day.

I was glad my own request for three weeks vacation was approved and looked forward to a break. Harry suggested a week's holiday to Cape Town with his friends and I agreed. It would be refreshing to get out of Joburg for a bit. We met up with his two buddies and their ladies at a campsite in the Cape. There the fellows erected an enormous green army tent for all of us to sleep in. One couple even brought their dog, a big drooling British bulldog with lots of folds who snored and gasped for air when he breathed.

At night, we heard soft moaning coming from the girlfriend of one of his pals as they lay in their dark corner of the tent. We knew what they were doing.

"That guy has the biggest penis in the world," Harry whispered to me. "I've seen him carry a full teapot on his strong dick and walk around with it. He's a legend!"

I closed my eyes and pictured that image in my head. The sounds of pleasuring coming from that couple was motivating for Harry and me. We couldn't help but be inspired.

Next morning after a hearty breakfast of bacon and eggs cooked over the campfire, we drove to Bird's Island near Cape Town, an important breeding ground for white Cape gannets and black crowned cormorants. The nesting birds screeched and dive-bombed me as I wandered among them for close-up photos. I marvelled at how these two species of birds lived harmoniously on one large tract of land. Hundreds of majestic white gannets nested in the middle, while an equal number of sleek black cormorants assembled on the outside rocks. A distinct path of about three feet separated the two species. How very symbolic of apartheid in South Africa, I thought, as I looked at these black and white birds together but apart.

Harry and I did some sight-seeing on our own, passing

through the quaint mixed-race area then known as District Number Six. This neighbourhood was a feast for the eyes. Little houses painted in pastel colours of pink, blue, green and yellow, were joined together in rows and built on hilly streets. A spectacular view of Table Mountain filled the background.

Groups of singing children dressed in costumes danced down the hill. This was their mini-version of the adult festival then called "Coon Carnival," happening all over Cape Town at that very moment. Black men and women wore colourful costumes, painted their faces and danced to the drumbeat of musicians in the street. This carnival was an annual New Year's event, their time to let loose and celebrate.

I walked into the thick of it to take photos while Harry followed close behind with a worried look on his face. He towered above everyone, ready to protect me in case I got trampled in the crowd. I enjoyed getting close and capturing the expressions on peoples' faces. Other white folks watched the festivities from the sidelines too. Harry and I drove back to our campsite exhilarated, my camera filled with great photos.

The following day as the sun burnt through the cool morning mist, we drove to the ocean just off Cape Town. The cold sea was teaming with enormous lobsters. Harry had brought wet suits for us and dressed me up in one so we could swim out and search for lobsters. He said that lobsters taste fantastic on the barbecue. Thankfully I never found one, as I'd have to negotiate with those big claws of theirs. My greatest pleasure was to frolic in the shallow salt water rock pools and play with brown kelp after the tide went out, and to splash cool water on my face.

Our pleasant week in the Cape came to an end. Harry

and I drove back to Johannesburg at night on a dead straight highway through the Great Karroo, a desert with very little vegetation except for cacti and tumbleweeds. Then BANG!!! Harry frowned as he struggled to control the car. One of our tires just exploded. The car veered from side to side, leaving behind a trail of rubber debris.

We were alone on that motorway in the black of night. All you could see were stars and the sliver of a moon. Harry got to work changing the tire while I shone the flashlight. The roar of a truck sounded in the distance, getting closer by the second. We assumed it could see us. Harry was working on the exposed side of the road and squinted at the blinding lights of the speeding truck. But the truck did not see us. Harry leapt out of the way just in time as the truck righted itself and drove past with a loud sucking whoosh. The driver must have dozed off at the wheel; he almost wiped us out!

When you realize you almost died and that pang in the heart had settled, we thanked God and our lucky stars to be alive. We then drove twelve hours through the night without stopping, relieved to be home.

⁓

One night I woke up screaming from a nightmare in which I'd been knifed in the chest. It felt real and painful. I touched my breast but didn't feel any blood. Harry lay beside me and woke up with a start when I yelled. I told him about my frightening dream.

"It must have been voodoo." He said. "A jealous person can collect nail cuttings or hair from their victim and take it to the witch doctor who places a hex on the person to do them harm."

My thoughts went immediately to memories of that witch doctor in Botswana, and I wondered if there was a connection. But who could be jealous of me and want to

71

harm me? Before this, I didn't believe in voodoo. Even now I am still skeptical. It only works if you really believe in it. Thankfully the pain in my chest subsided. Then Harry told me the true story of a witch doctor who put a curse on his friend's maid, telling her that she would die very soon. Three days later, the maid dropped down dead. Such is the power of belief.

One Saturday, Harry invited me and his buddies to the famous Kyalami Formula One Racetrack near Johannesburg where the great and notorious Jody Schechter would be racing his Ferrari. We had good seats partially shaded by the overhang. The sound of race cars was deafening as they roared around the curve in front of us, again and again. You could easily spot Jody who was known on the circuits as the "South African Wildman." He wove erratically in and out of the lanes, passing one car after another. His aggression made him the best. But this noisy driving around in circles was not my idea of a good time. I found the deafening roar unbearable.

Strawberries

I started craving strawberries. My face and body were getting fuller, although I wasn't eating more than usual. Clothes were tighter and my breasts larger. I started to panic when I realized my period was a couple of months late. Then came the shock when the pharmacist told me my pregnancy test was positive. I always wanted children, but this wasn't the right time or situation. My head ached, trying to grasp the ramifications of it all. *Who would the father be---Harry? Ryan?*

Harry already had a daughter. He was divorced from the mother who still clung to him for help. He was sweet and kind and I adored him, but something was missing between us for the long-term. Nor did I care for his rough friends whom he always had in tow. And Ryan didn't want to settle down. He claimed to be still scarred by his previous marriage to a Swedish woman. He had a daughter by her, and it broke his heart not to be part of his little girl's life. She resided in Sweden with her mother. I remember when Ryan and I lived together in Cape Town and had drunk way too much wine, I asked him if he loved me.

"I'm in love with one little person," he answered half asleep (I presumed it was me), "and that is my daughter Melanie."

His words surprised me. I was pleased that she was in

his thoughts although he seldom spoke of her. A parent's love for their child is something I could never compete with, nor would I ever try.

I racked my brain trying to figure out if the father was Ryan or Harry, or… *oh God, no!*

Shameful memories came flooding back to me of a long-weekend in the neighboring country of Lesotho, shortly after my breakup with Ryan. His safari competitors invited me to come along with them for a free trip. Russell and his crew were hired to drive a group of geologists around who were already there on location. I was happy for the chance to see a new country, and gladly accepted.

Russell's four Land Rovers each had a driver, and they invited four female passengers. I didn't know the men well except from meeting them briefly at that ill-fated party where Ryan and I broke up. They enjoyed having girls around and preferred to fill their Land Rovers instead of driving there empty. Or maybe they felt sorry for me after the way Ryan treated me at their party.

I got a lift with a driver who would otherwise have driven alone. We didn't talk much as we drove higher up the Lesotho mountains. He was deep in his own thoughts and completely ignored me for five hours. I didn't like getting ignored, and it put me in a pissy mood. All four Land Rovers stopped when we came across snow on the ground, a good excuse for a snow-ball fight. Having grown up in Canada, snow didn't excite me.

Our vehicles climbed higher and higher. We passed local Africans living in round huts made of stones, the available building material. Their huts were separated from each other by courtyards surrounded by stone fences. Roofs were constructed from a circular framework of boards upon which they carefully laid reeds. Looking around, there was nothing growing but dry shrub grass, so they must have imported the long reeds. I saw a pile of them tied up and ready for laying. A cooking fire always smoldered in the middle of their small yard. Mothers carried their babies tied to their backs. These people kept warm by wearing blankets around their shoulders. It was cool up in those mountains.

We finally arrived at our destination high on a hilltop where a group of buildings were clumped together. There were separate cabins for sleeping, and a large structure for the cafeteria.

We girls were meant to entertain ourselves in the daytime while the fellows drove the geologists around. One day we went horse-back riding, except I got a mule. We rode along a shallow river which the other women crossed easily. My mule came to a dead stop and refused to cross. I got off him and tried to convince him to join the others. The girls laughed as they heard me negotiating with my mule. Suddenly he decided to take off and I had to run after him. Out of breath, I managed to grab the reins and embark with difficulty.

We rode a little farther and then turned back to base camp. Me and my mule lagged far behind the other women on their horses. I was grateful the camp dog followed us and kept me company as my human companions were long gone. I felt uneasy and scanned the brown grass hills. There were no trees growing, only occasional low shrubbery. I half expected a fierce cougar to ambush me at any moment, although I'd been assured that all wild animals in Lesotho had been killed off. Closer to base camp, my mule and I strolled past a group of geologists kneeling in a tight circle on the ground, enthralled by some rocks they were clawing at. I was amused by their collective fascination with rubble.

One evening after our fellows returned to base camp, we ate dinner together in the cafeteria and drank way too much wine and whiskey. I was still upset after my recent breakup with Ryan, but mostly I was angry at the safari driver who had ignored me and hardly said a word all the way to Lesotho. I got drunker and angrier and swore at him for being a jerk. My fury seemed to mystify him, and he looked to Russell for help. I saw Russell shake his head as if to say "don't say anything, she's plastered." Then I vaguely remember Russell supporting me and walking me to my cabin. He put me to bed, but it didn't end there.

Perhaps he was trying to calm me down by having sex, I can't think of any other reason. The rascal had a girlfriend staying with him in his own cabin, and a wife at home in Johannesburg. Anyway, he did it and then left me to sleep off my drunkenness. I felt ashamed. No mention of this was made the next day or ever, like it never happened.

Being pregnant now certainly put a clear perspective on things. Slumped in a chair in Harry's apartment, my future looked bleak. Having a child by Ryan or Harry or the Lesotho safari leader didn't seem like viable options. I'd most likely be raising the child on my own which was a hardship I couldn't contemplate. I wanted a baby to love and nurture, with a good husband in a stable home. Would I ever find the right man? I agonized over what to do. I cherished children, but not this way. If more time passed, I was afraid that I'd become attached to the developing life inside me and change my mind.

Harry found the money while I made discrete inquiries. Somebody whispered the name of a doctor whose office was above a steakhouse. He might be able to help me, but it was all very hush-hush. Abortion was illegal. The doctor could be prosecuted and so might the patient. I climbed the stairs to his musty office with dirty windows above the steakhouse. He was an elderly little man with glasses who had me lie down on the gurney to examine me. He confirmed what I feared was true, that I was indeed pregnant. We made an appointment to have the procedure done next day.

Harry drove me there. We didn't say much on the way. My soul was at rock bottom and I wanted to cry for what was about to happen. I yearned for a baby, but not knowing who the father was, was not a good situation.

After paying cash to the secretary, Harry sat on a hard chair in the waiting room while I disappeared behind closed doors into another dingy room. The doctor covered my nose and mouth with a gas mask---that dreadful familiar smell of ether, the same gas used on me as a child when my tonsils were removed. Through a haze, I vaguely remember him playing around with me down there and saying it was part of the procedure. I don't know what happened next. He woke me up when it was over and said it was done, that I was no longer pregnant. We thanked him and left. This decision would haunt me forever with regret.

"Let's have a steak dinner," Harry said as he put his arm around my shoulders. "You must be famished after all this."

The restaurant below the doctor's office was open, so we ordered two large T-bone steaks with French fries and salad. I started feeling light-headed and knew something was wrong. Harry bit into his steak but didn't get very far.

"I don't feel good, we have to go!" I said, my head spinning.

He helped me out of our booth and paid the cashier near the door. I got as far as the sidewalk outside the restaurant and remember going down. When I awoke, people were standing around me. Somebody brought a chair and a glass of water. Harry's strong arms were holding me up.

"Can you make it to the car?" he said, his forehead wrinkled with concern.

Leaning on him, I stumbled to the car and we drove home. He put me straight to bed. A huge weariness came over me and I slept on and off for days. Perhaps I lost a lot of blood during the surgery, I don't know, the doctor never said. Nor was there a follow-up appointment. This had been a secret procedure which the doctor would deny if anything went wrong. It took one week for me to regain my strength, and that was the end of my holiday. I was expected back to work at the photo studio.

Harry was a good man who had helped me a great deal, especially during my heartaches with Ryan. But we had little in common. He asked me if I'd like to move to Cape Town with him and start over, leaving the sad memories behind. But I didn't feel my future lay with him. I wanted to remain in Johannesburg and find my own apartment. I enjoyed my job, my co-workers, and painting portraits in Joubert Park. Harry and I stayed together while I looked for a place of my own. I never told anyone about that depressing experience.

Cliffton Court

A girl at work knew a guy whose father owned a sprawling white apartment building called Cliffton Court. It was built on a hidden road named Paddock Street. My application was approved, and I moved in with my suitcase, easel and sleeping bag.

From the window of my ground level flat, I saw giant cacti growing on a hill across the narrow road right in front of my place. Cars came whipping down that road to the parking lot below. This charming but ramshackle building was constructed by the owner whom I suspect built it as a hobby. I wondered if he had building permits, but it didn't matter; nothing seemed like it would collapse just yet.

To decorate, I made shelves from orange crates and painted them white. Green spider plants and ivy cascaded from one of the shelves, and I hung floor-length wooden beads over orange curtains from a thrift store. It felt great to have my own apartment and a good job which allowed me to support myself. I was thankful for everything.

Months had passed since my traumatic breakup with Ryan. We were once again on speaking terms. Yes, that lovable rascal came back into my life. His two brothers Colin and Stuart lived in Johannesburg now, and together the three men built me a sturdy wooden bed. I covered my folding garden chairs with sheepskins which I'd bought in Lesotho.

They were soft and still smelled of sheep, but served as comfortable living room furniture.

All the walls were painted clean white. I built myself a table from bricks and a board, and set a vase with soft dried flowers on the window sill. The blooms glowed bright red in the sunlight. In one corner of the living room, I placed a rubber-tree plant and some tall reeds with fluffy heads. It felt good to have plants around me. My windows were kept wide open for fresh air, and revealed the sweet scent of blossoms from jacaranda trees growing nearby.

There was no refrigerator in the apartment. The weather was cool so I put milk, cheese and butter on the window sill. I washed my laundry in the bathtub. It was wonderful to feel free and not dependent on anyone. Friends said they enjoyed the Bohemian atmosphere in my place. I set my easel up in the living room and hung unfinished paintings on my walls to work on. That catchy song Proud Mary by Creedence Clearwater played on my radio and got me pumped as I worked on portrait commissions.

Ryan in Trouble

Ryan had big problems. His safari company was failing. He still bore responsibility for the office rent and unpaid salary for their posh English secretary. His partner Dave had allegedly mismanaged company funds and couldn't make the payments on their bank loan. Then he disappeared and left Ryan to deal with the mess. Their two Land Rovers were about to be repossessed, and there was nothing Ryan could do to stop it.

Another safari company in the city heard about his ruinous situation and invited him to join forces with them. They wanted to meet. Ryan asked me to go with him to this rendezvous. The men genuinely liked him and insisted that he didn't have to go down with his sinking company.

"Come on, Ryan," the chief guy said, "for God's sake, we'll give you a good salary, and you can have one of our Land Rovers and do exactly what you did with your own company. What's not to like?"

"You're one of us," another fellow said. "Don't let this chance pass you by. We can really use you!"

There was a painful silence. Ryan frowned, lowered his head and closed his eyes for a long minute.

"Sorry, I just can't do it," he said quietly.

I pleaded with him to accept their proposal, but he was stubborn and refused everything they offered him. We were all frustrated trying to convince him but getting nowhere. Finally, the men gave up, shaking their heads. We thanked them and left. Ryan was too damn proud and ashamed that he'd failed with his own venture. He didn't want to accept what he thought was their pity or charity. *Silly, obstinate man!*

He still occupied the same apartment in the building where I used to live with him. One evening he asked me over for a visit. It felt ominous---like the end of everything, as if he wanted to convey his final wishes. He sat very still with his eyes cast down, not saying a word for the longest time. A resignation had come over him. I was afraid he would commit suicide.

He showed me the Eviction Notice from his landlord for failure to pay rent. He had no money. It scared me when he talked about giving away all his possessions. His voice was weak as he told me which friend or family member should get this or that item before the landlord took everything in the apartment. Ryan was in trouble.

He was still my friend and I loved him. But I couldn't let him stay with me because of our troubled breakup and past history. I contacted some good friends of ours, Peter and Patricia, who also lived in Hillbrow. They invited him to stay with them for a few months until he got back on his feet, although they already had a crowded apartment with two teenage daughters, one cherubic toddler and a baby on the way. Ryan accepted their gracious hospitality. I think he felt humbled.

Marilyn

Dave's wife Marilyn ended their marriage due to her husband's philandering. She couldn't live with a man who didn't come home nights, plus the rascal allegedly mishandled his and Ryan's company funds and absconded. We became friends, although she never fit in with my other girlfriends. They thought she wore excessive makeup and her stiletto heels were too high. She made herself look too sexy. Her appearance didn't endear her to other women.

I've always held a fascination for painted ladies, and know that it's only paint after all. It's their intention to *allure* that I found interesting. It's amusing how men can be so easily seduced by makeup and sexy clothes. I've honestly witnessed a few men ask their girlfriends to put their makeup on. I suppose men think it adds mystery and excites them more than a plain face.

Marilyn sometimes confided in me about her relationships with men. One time she told me that her boyfriend said he wanted their love to last a very long time. Her eyes lit up and her whole face beamed. But his words were a red flag to me.

"Marilyn," I said, "the guy must be married. No single man would make a commitment like that. He would leave the door open to run in case he felt trapped."

Her blue eyes grew wide with alarm as she stared at

me, trying to grasp what I just said.

"What, you think he's married? Are you trying to destroy me?" she said, refusing to believe me.

As it happened, she discovered that I was right. Her boyfriend was a cheating rascal, hiding the fact that he had a wife and kids. Marilyn would just serve as fluff on the side. She ended the affair before she completely lost her heart.

Marilyn was a secretary, but hoped to do some modeling for extra income. She asked me to take photos of her in my garden at Cliffton Court. We planned that she should stay overnight so I could photograph her in the first golden rays of the sun as it rose over a stone fence in the yard.

When she got up for breakfast, I was delighted to see her with no make-up or heels. She had freckles and was only about 5' 1" tall. She looked like a wholesome little girl of fifteen instead the sexy vamp she chose to portray.

"You look great without makeup," I said, trying to encourage her to wear less. But she wouldn't hear of it.

A New Beau

Through Ryan, I met a fascinating man called Bill who said he worked in insurance. He was handsome, tall and slender, with dark hair and deep blue eyes. He heard that I was in the market for a car, and said he could give me a great price on a used Bentley which he owned. We dated a few times. He was exciting and fun. I was falling for this debonair, charming man.

We had a dinner date one evening, and I was eager to impress him in my pretty new dress which I bought for the occasion. Day-dreaming at my work desk about how our rendezvous would go, my reverie was interrupted by the shrill ring of the phone just before closing time.

"Hi gorgeous, it's Bill here. Sorry, but I'll have to cancel tonight. Work called with an emergency and I've got to go. We'll make it another time soon, OK?"

"Aww, that's too bad. I was looking forward to seeing you."

Disappointed and feeling empty, I called Marilyn and told her my date cancelled on me.

"Never mind," she said. "Come to my place and I'll make us dinner. We'll have a girls' night. I've got nothing going on anyway."

I walked to her apartment in Hillbrow, grateful she invited me over for the evening.

"C'mon in, honey," she said, and gave me a warm hug at the door.

The delicious aroma of Italian food emanated from the kitchen. I felt honoured that she had toiled in the kitchen to cook an appetizing meal for me. The melted cheese on top of the baked lasagna was perfectly crusted, with mince and ricotta cheese between the pasta layers. It looked mouth-watering! How could Dave not have treated this woman like gold?

We sat down at a nicely laid table with silver-trimmed dishes and fine wine glasses. I felt like a privileged guest. She sure knew how to make a person feel good. We ate our lasagna slowly with warm buns and butter, sipped our Merlot wine and talked about girly things.

"Yeah, I've been out with Bill a few times," I said, with a twinge of sadness. "He's in the insurance business and is absolutely gorgeous. I really like him."

"Oh wow!" Marilyn said, a huge smile animating her face. "I've just met somebody too, he's a film producer!"

By now we'd finished dinner and moved over to the sofa, bringing a fresh bottle with us. We were comparing notes on our new boyfriends when there was a knock on the door. Marilyn sauntered over to answer, wineglass in hand.

"Oh, hello James," Marilyn purred. "What are you doing here? Come in please."

A large bouquet of yellow roses preceded the man through the threshold. Then the handsome face. My heart sank, and I felt a pang of envy. It became clear why I'd been stood-up.

"Hi Bill," I said from the sofa trying to stay calm, although still jealous that she got the roses and I didn't. "I thought you had an emergency at work?"

Bill-James looked baffled for a second, but seemed

amused that he'd been found out. Marilyn looked at me dumbfounded, then back to Bill-James.

"You two know each other?" She asked. "Is this the wonderful Bill you've been talking about?"

"None other," I said, staying seated and trying to remain cool.

Bill-James looked sheepishly at the floor, his coat still on and flowers in his hand. I got over my initial upset, and then Marilyn and I started to laugh. This man was a true rascal!

"Well, you're here now, you might as well come in," she said.

He stepped forward cautiously, once he was sure we wouldn't attack him. He brightened up when he understood that we were taking his shenanigans in stride. No use getting mad at him.

"You're so bad!" we both said, chiding him for his deception.

"Actually, let me make it up to you girls and get some take-out chicken for us," he said, wearing a grin of disbelief that his two girlfriends hadn't gone ballistic and thrown things at him.

"Yes, go ahead and get the chicken!" Marilyn said, shooing him towards the door.

We had eaten, but he clearly had not. We let him leave thinking he might want to escape, and wondered what the odds were that he might not return. When he was gone, we shook our heads and wondered how we both could have been so duped. Twenty minutes later, the brave man returned with food. He seemed to enjoy the novelty of his predicament.

It turns out that he also tried to sell the Bentley to Marilyn. Ryan told me later it had come to light that Bill-James was a fraudster and didn't even own a Bentley. He eventually skipped town, we suspect with the money he received from selling "his Bentley" to some poor soul.

Intrigue at the Art Exhibit

Spring arrived, and the time had come for another art show at Joubert Park. Ryan helped me set up my wall on which we hung my portrait paintings. He sat with me for the first two weekends, giving me moral support and talking to customers when I needed bathroom breaks. He seemed to enjoy talking to people and answering questions about my work.

This time, I painted portraits of Africans. My artwork showed my fascination with the black tribes of my newly-adopted country---the beautiful hues of their velvet skin, proud faces and traditional clothing. The first African I painted was a little boy whose photo appeared in a travel brochure from Swaziland. I used it as a reference to paint from, blending many colours for the skin on his back, arms and face. All the colours I needed were in my pastel box---mauve, brown, copper and beige. The portrait turned out fabulous and was one of my favourites.

A young man came to my display and stared at it for a long time. He returned several times to admire it. There's nothing more flattering for an artist than to have someone gaze at our paintings and daydream.

"So, you like that one, do you?" I asked.

"Yeah, I love it," he said, "but I don't have the money to buy it."

It made me happy that somebody loved my work. I took the painting down, rolled it up and gave it to him. He beamed a big smile and thanked me. I was glad to do it, but hoped nobody saw me give the portrait away.

On the third weekend of the exhibition, my friend Yvonne came by with her father Maurice who was visiting from Durban. Maurice had immigrated to South Africa from Mauritius after the death of his wife almost two years earlier. I couldn't help staring at him. There was something fascinating about this older, distinguished man in his dark suit and combed-back gray hair. His warm brown eyes twinkled when he looked at me. He studied my paintings one by one, then turned to me.

"Mademoiselle, you have gold in your fingertips," he said, in the most charming French accent.

His words warmed my heart, and I decided that I like the way French people say nice things. I loved his daughter Yvonne, and by extension was predisposed to love her father too. I sensed that I would be seeing more of this enchanting man.

‿

My African portraits were attracting attention. The painting of an "Old Man Smoking His Pipe," was my most popular painting. He came from the Xhosa tribe in the Transkei homeland, and sat in a field with an orange ochre robe draped over his shoulders. I saw his photo in a library book and used it for reference. I imagined that his wrinkled forehead was imbued with the wisdom of old age and kindness. And so, it seems, did my first client. My Old Man had a buyer within half an hour.

I must confess that after I sold him on the Friday of that weekend, I was so buoyed by my success that I painted him again that night, and worked into the wee hours of the morning. I felt drowsy, but after three hours of sleep and a strong coffee, was ready to return to the exhibition.

That day, a middle-aged couple strolled to my display and looked at my African portraits. The woman fell in love with this newly-hung painting of the Old Man Smoking His Pipe. I raised the price a bit, and to my surprise they bought it. It was the only portrait of mine that was selling. What magic did it have?

When I got home that night, I couldn't help myself and had to paint another. It felt good to make some money. I simply couldn't resist, although I wasn't used to churning them out this fast. I also suspected that what I was doing was a bit unethical.

The following morning, a third Old Man was proudly displayed on my wall. People walked past making nice comments. To my great embarrassment, the buyer of the second Old Man came by and saw another rendition of the painting he'd bought the day before. He stared at it without saying a word and then left.

Minutes later he came back with his wife. They both stood in front of a copy of their supposedly unique painting. I felt mortified, but there was nowhere to hide. The husband nodded with his chin towards the painting as if to ask "what's this?" I felt my face turn red with shame. Mustering as much courage as I could and with my head high but feeling like a crook, I said that I desperately needed the money and this was my best and only seller. The woman seemed slightly happier with that news.

"Well, I still like *mine* better," she said, and they sauntered down the promenade. My fellow artists knew what I'd done. They saw what happened that weekend. But we artists formed a brotherhood of sorts. They understood.

Brave Brenda

Brenda displayed her paintings beside me at the exhibition. Her dramatic African scenery and wild animals came to life on the canvas. We became friends. I loved her easy laughter and positive spirit alongside me. A few days after the exhibition ended, she asked me to go with her to a private zoo. She knew the owner and said she needed new photos of animals to paint from.

Wow, a private zoo should be exciting! We set off in her Jeep and drove an hour from the city. Her friend Pieter was expecting us and greeted us at the entrance to the zoo. He wore a live black panther draped over his shoulders like a fur stole. The big cat was black and shiny, with yellow eyes that pierced mine with intensity. I was getting nervous already. I had a phobia of black panthers from watching a horror movie as a child. He put the big cat down, and I couldn't help noticing the brute strength of this man's arms and legs. His short-sleeved shirt and khaki shorts exposed his well-developed muscles, suntanned from being outdoors most of the time.

Brenda carried her Nikon camera around her neck and was eager to start taking photos. A big smile came to her face when Pieter suggested the cheetah pen first. We walked to the cage where five grown cheetahs approached the fence and eyed us keenly. Sand and small boulders covered the ground in the enclosure so as to resemble their natural habitat. I was definitely getting more nervous.

"Let's go inside the enclosure, ladies," he said.

I absolutely did not want to go into that pen. So, Pieter told me to climb on a little hill just above the area where I'd be safely separated by a fence and able to see everything from my vantage point. From there, I saw the two humans enter the pen. Pieter introduced Brenda to the cheetahs. They spoke softly and crouched low to the ground to make themselves seem less threatening as the big cats circled them. Two more cheetahs were climbing on logs near tufts of elephant grass and sprang down to examine the visitors. A young Bantu boy held the wooden door shut from outside the pen.

"Hey, Pieter, there's an urgent phone call for you!" someone hollered from outside.

"Sorry, I've got to take this," he said to Brenda. "But don't worry, just stay crouched and don't make any sudden moves."

Then he left! He left her alone with seven cheetahs, hissing and growling with their ears back. She must be terrified, I thought. She turned slowly and took close-up photos of their fierce expressions, open mouths and snarling teeth. I could see it all happening and called loudly to her with false bravado:

"Good girl, keep it up, you're doing great!"

But to myself I thought---Oh God, I'm the only one watching! What if something bad happens? My friend Brenda was braver than I could ever be. With Pieter gone, that young black boy was pushing the door to the pen closed with all his might, his face distorted by exertion and his eyes squeezed shut in dread. He was even more scared than I was, because he would be directly in the path of the big cats if the door flew open. My heart pounded as I belted out words of encouragement so Brenda wouldn't feel alone. In fact, she looked exhilarated as she snapped photos of the cats moving around her, baring their teeth and hissing in mock charges.

After what seemed like an eternity, Pieter came back and asked her if she'd taken enough pictures. She stood up slowly and I thought she was shaking. He helped steady her and they left the pen. That was my cue to climb down the hill and congratulate her. I felt like a coward, but on the other hand, I never felt it my mission to be alone with seven wild cheetahs. Library books are safer. We explored the zoo a bit more, but I remember nothing except seeing my friend abandoned in that pen with snarling cheetahs.

We felt elated driving back to her sprawling farm on the outskirts of Johannesburg. Brenda's cheeks were flushed with excitement. She couldn't stop smiling. We climbed the stairs to her art studio in the loft. It was separated from the main house so she could get some peace away from her five children and elderly mother who lived with them. I looked around the big room where unfinished canvasses of wildlife hung on the walls, and tubes of oil paints were scattered on the work table. This was her escape. I felt the love she devoted to her art. How lucky she was to have such a large studio to work in. This was a real art studio.

We bumped into her husband in the kitchen when it came time for me to leave. Brenda was excited, and tripped over her words as she told him about our thrilling afternoon. He said nothing for a long time. Then his eyes hardened and his face set tight with anger.

"How could you do such a daft thing?" he said. "If anything happened to you, I'd be alone to raise the kids! How could you take such a chance?"

Brenda lowered her head and looked at her camera which contained those precious photos. I detected a tiny smile on her lips. She had no regrets.

Warmth of Family

My good friends often came to visit me at Cliffton Court. They seemed to enjoy the casual atmosphere and seeing my portraits-in-progress. Yvonne and her fiancé Normand, her father Maurice, and my friend Mimi came most often. We relished many happy evenings over dinner and wine. My specialty was beef curry. I cooked it like my African friends in Montreal had taught me, with the secret ingredient of ground nuts (peanut butter). I didn't own a television so we only had conversation, jokes and music to entertain us.

Maurice was fifty-six and we hoped to match him up with Mimi who was forty. But she didn't want an older man. Just as well, because I grew to love this charming Frenchman myself, even though I was his daughter's age. He enveloped us with the warmth of his personality and humour.

Yvonne invited me for dinner whenever Maurice came from Durban to visit her. She was an excellent cook and prepared gourmet French food. Her coq-au-vin with steamed rice was divine. Gigi, her blue budgie-bird, flew freely around her apartment. Its favourite perch was on top of Maurice's head. With Gigi on his head, he still managed to win at card games, and gave the bird full credit for his good luck. Maurice and I fell in love in the warmth of this group.

Peeping Tom

We drank a lot of wine in those days. Local red wine was cheap. We could buy a gallon of it for fifty cents. Someone always came to visit me and shared a glass or two. I still worked at the photo studio in John Orr's department store by day, and painted at home in the evenings and on weekends.

Ryan was back in my life, but on *my* terms. I was no longer dependent on him. He wanted more than friendship from me, although he did not want me to limit his freedom. All right... but in that case, the same should hold true for *me*. I should be free to date others, while he held a privileged place in my heart.

Having said goodbye to Ryan on one such privileged evening of sensual bliss, I prepared to take my bath. To my horror, I noticed a man's fat face peering into my bedroom window with his nose pressed against the pane. I panicked and screamed. He'd been watching us in bed the whole time through a crack in the curtains. He had dark hair and bloated features which freaked me out.

"What are you doing, you pervert!" I yelled.

"Is… eh, Johnathan here?" he said stupidly through the glass.

I remembered a tip on the news that if a peeping Tom came around, a girl should scream and make lots of noise to attract attention. I shouted as loud as I could.

"Get the hell out of here, you bloody creep! I'm calling the police right now!"

Suddenly, he was the focus of attention on that quiet night. I'm sure the whole neighbourhood could hear my shrill obscenities. He took off like the wind and I heard his footsteps running down the hill to his car in the parking lot. Then came the screeching sound of tires as he peeled away at lightning speed. I felt vulnerable.

A few days later Ryan came to visit me. We'd been drinking our favourite wine for hours and talking in my living room. Then came a knock on my front door which opened right into the living room. Outside stood a dark-haired man.

"Is… eh, Gregory here?" he said.

When I saw him, all I could think of was that bloated man in my window a few nights ago. Instinct kicked in; he was not getting away with it! I grabbed this man by the collar, lifted him inside and slammed the door.

"Are you the peeping Tom?"

"God, no!" he said, opening his eyes wide with fear.

"Are you *sure* you didn't come to my window last week? You look just like him!"

"N-No, not at all," he said. "Why, do I look like a peeping Tom? I feel very offended."

He was gasping for air and started to shake.

Maybe it wasn't him after all...

Ryan sat calmly in his chair, amused by this whole scene. Suddenly I felt like an idiot and released my grip. My captive opened the door and leaped out to freedom.

"That was pretty funny," Ryan said with a grin, which made me feel even more foolish.

Two days later, I was invited for coffee to my gay

neighbour's apartment right next door.

"What happened when that couple knocked on your door the other night?" he said.

"A couple? Are you sure?"

"Yes," he said. "I thought somebody was knocking on *my* door. But when I opened it, all I could see was you lifting the guy into your apartment as if you had first dibs on him!"

I couldn't believe it! I only saw the dark-haired man and not the poor girl who waited outside my door until I released her companion. We started to laugh over how it must have looked. Thankfully I never saw the peeping Tom at my window again.

Midnight in Johannesburg

I missed Ryan. I still loved that damn man. Why did we ever break up? It was very late as I sat alone painting in my small apartment. Pastels were strewn on the table by the window, and a portrait hung on my easel to work on. This one was important. It was of a beautiful French lady dressed in beige lace and wearing a cameo broach. The woman was the deceased mother of Yvonne, and the cherished wife of Maurice who said she was the great love of his life. Now she was dead. Such a sad story. The red wine beckoned me, and the more I drank, the sadder her story became. First there was one empty bottle, then there were two.

By now, the painting was drenched in tears. My apartment reverberated with the whoosh of the French lady's ghost and her heart-breaking story. I had to get out of there! I missed Ryan desperately and decided that I must see him right away. He was staying with our good friends Peter and Patricia a mile away.

It was after midnight on that dark winter night. Tears of loneliness rolled down my cheeks and the walls started spinning around and round. Where was Ryan when I needed him? I removed my old painting clothes and foisted my naked body into my long black winter coat. It had black fur on the bottom hem and a big black hood also trimmed with fur. To be safe, I thought I'd better bring some weapons in case I got attacked, and stuffed four paint-brushes in my pocket.

God must have been looking after me that night as I stumbled onto the streets of Johannesburg, sozzled and wearing nothing but a black coat. A group of African men were watching me meander down the sidewalk, so I puffed myself up to my most imposing size and marched with exaggerated confidence.

"Don't mess with me or I'll kill you with my brushes," I heard myself mutter.

They whispered among themselves as they stared at me. I must have looked like a witch in my long black coat and hood. The fur covered my face so it looked like I had no face, just a black hole. When I got close to them, the men parted like the Red Sea, clearing a path for me.

I finally stumbled upon the house where our friends lived and groped for the door. It was late and the family was asleep. Ryan slept in their living room, so he answered my knock. Surprised to see me, he helped me off with my coat. Like a true British gentleman, he instantly averted his eyes.

"Here, put this on," he said, handing me a shirt.

I smiled, thinking---how many times has he seen me naked, yet he still reacts with good British manners. We spent the night in each others' arms, and he comforted me with the warmth of his love. It felt good being with him again. Next morning, the family was surprised but not shocked to see me when they got up for breakfast. They knew I was impulsive. The atmosphere was friendly enough with knowing smiles and nudges. I felt my face turning red. Nobody said anything about my showing up in the middle of the night to sleep with their guest; it was awkward. After a strong coffee and small talk, I walked home in my long black coat, embarrassed by my nighttime escapade.

Meeting Rasputin

I was promoted to Manageress of my own photo studio in Braamfontein, and walked to work every day from my place in Cliffton Court; first through Hillbrow, then down the hill past the hospital and lavender jacaranda trees, next past the bronze statue of the three soldiers and into the business center of Braamfontein. It took me an hour and a half. I walked a lot in those days.

At work I took photo sets and passport pictures just like at the other studio. I had no co-workers, but customers always came in so I was seldom lonely. Once, I put my foot in my mouth. Three robust black women came in for passport photos. I took some, but the pictures turned out dark. The next set was lighter.

"These are better, see?" I said cheerfully, "they're not so dark."

"Not at all. Black is beautiful!" they snapped back, and paid for the first set.

Touché, I deserved that.

I always had one of my oil pastel portraits hanging in the store window in case somebody wanted me to paint them. It was my own little side-business. Naturally there were official store photos in the window too. After all, it was my job to take photographs for the company. The big boss came by one day and saw my portrait of a man hanging in the window. If he thought there was a conflict of interest, he never said anything. Nor did I ask his permission. We were both uncomfortable with what remained unsaid. I was thankful that he left without bringing it up, as my artwork in the window earned me extra income. If a customer wanted me to paint a family portrait, I photographed them in the studio and used those pictures as references. That way, the company made money and so did I.

One day as I sat at my desk watching pedestrians walk by my big window, a man stopped and looked at my pastel portrait for a long time. He finally came in to talk. He was from France, but his English was perfect. He had long black straggly hair and dark eyes, almost like Rasputin, the mystic advisor to the Russian Czar's wife.

"That's an impressive portrait in the window. Did you paint it?"

"Yes, I'm allowed to hang it there." *I lied.*

We chatted a bit, then he took out some of his pencil drawings of faces which he carried in a briefcase. I studied them and wanted to say something nice. But they didn't convey the soul of the person, although the proportions seemed correct.

"They look very accurate," was all I could say, and they truly did look accurate.

He said that he wrote articles for a prominent French magazine and drew portraits on the side to make extra money. He told me that he used to live in France and was the esteemed spiritual leader of a group of followers on a mountaintop commune; they were his disciples. He also claimed to be working for Interpol. His dark eyes glistened from under his eyebrows as he spoke. He asked to keep in touch with me, so I gave him the studio number.

I regret ever introducing Rasputin to my good friends. He came by the studio one time and found Ryan there. One conversation led to another, and he soon infiltrated our group and seduced my good friends. He cultivated a Svengali-like hold over Ryan, who by now had found himself a job selling art supplies. Along with the job came a bright green Volkswagen beetle so he could drive around and promote his company's products. He also managed to find his own apartment in Hillbrow, leaving the hospitality of our friends Peter and Patricia.

Ryan revered the "prophet" Rasputin, and drove him wherever he wanted to go, usually to hustle portrait clients. I often saw his green beetle driving around town when he was supposed to be working. Rasputin was always in the passenger seat. I don't know why Ryan permitted himself to be led around by that man. Maybe it was through some kind of hypnotism.

"Here's a present for you," Ryan said one day as he proudly handed me a pencil drawing of myself, complete with shading.

Ryan could never draw anything, yet this drawing was extremely accurate. He said the prophet taught him how to do it. He wanted to show me how it was done, so we drove to Rasputin's lair where the secret was revealed. An apparatus with enhanced numbers and graphs projected a photograph on paper. All the so-called artist had to do was pencil in the image. No wonder the portraits were accurate. But they lacked soul or personality.

So, this is what Rasputin did. He chatted-up people wherever he went and showed them the pencil portraits which he carried with him. Unsuspecting housewives were easily impressed. He talked his way into many homes, enjoying cake and cups of coffee while securing portrait deals, cash only.

Things about this man just didn't add up. He scared me. He soon developed a romantic relationship with Marilyn, enjoying her womanly charms for a couple of months. To my dismay, he had a hypnotic grip on both Ryan and Marilyn. I no longer trusted the man, and was sorry that I'd let him permeate our group.

Ryan eventually got fired from his job. I suspect he spent too much company time chauffeuring Rasputin around and didn't sell enough art supplies. Sadly, the art company took their car back. Both Ryan and Marilyn eventually wised-up to that they were being manipulated. The rascal Rasputin slowly evaporated from our lives.

Thankfully, Ryan soon found a new job at Iberia Airlines and was able to keep paying for his apartment. He was back in the travel industry where he thrived. We saw each other every week as good friends and more, but suddenly contact from him stopped.

Days turned into weeks and I began to worry. We had no home phones, so I walked to his ground floor apartment one evening and knocked on his door. He seemed annoyed and opened the door just a crack. There he was, safe and sound, but covered with many red spots on his face. Ryan had chicken pox! He was angry with himself and embarrassed for catching a childhood disease. He was ashamed that I'd seen him. Reluctantly, he opened the door. I laughed and kissed his spots, relieved that he wasn't hurt. I loved that rascal-man.

A New Car, 1974

I bought a car, my first car ever---a cute little red Austin. Harry found it through his auto shop. He knew I wanted a car. Granted, it was used and not yet certified, but he worked hard to fix it outside my apartment at Cliffton Court. I heard him cursing as he lay on the ground underneath it. After three attempts, it finally passed the inspection.

I felt exhilarated, and planned to leave on a painting adventure to the Transkei homeland along the south coast. During practice runs with my car, I tried my best to drive on the left side of the road according to the law, but instinctively reacted to my right a few times and nearly caused accidents. Drivers swore at me. Yvonne drove with me once and said she was afraid it would be her last day on earth.

Following my plan, I quit my job at the photo studio in mid-December and gave notice on my flat. It was summer in South Africa, so my winter clothes and furniture were put in storage. My place was now empty. I was ready to leave when Ryan invited me to spend Christmas and New Year's Eve with him in his Hillbrow apartment. He gave me a colourful Mediterranean cookbook in which he wrote "Here's hoping." He laughed when I understood that he hoped my cooking might improve. We spent some happy days together.

This was the last time I'd be seeing him for awhile

because he had found himself a new job as Manager of the local airline in neighbouring Swaziland and planned to move there. After working at Iberia in Johannesburg for six months, he wanted a change. He was excited about his future in another country and asked me to drive him to the airport right after New Year's Eve. This I did in my newly-acquired car. I left him at Departures and waved him off with a kiss. He looked smart in his suit and tie. We would always be special friends.

After dropping Ryan off, I spent the weekend with Yvonne since I wouldn't have enough gasoline to get to the south coast. All petrol stations were ordered closed on weekends due to a world-wide oil shortage. These constraints were a real headache. Drivers had to plan their trips carefully. The speed limit was lowered to 25 mph in cities, and 50 mph on highways. Nobody was happy with these new rules, especially truck drivers. In spite of these restrictions, news reports proclaimed that South Africa had good stocks of oil reserves stored in underground tunnels of abandoned gold mines.

Yvonne and I enjoyed a happy weekend, well worth delaying my trip for. Her fiancé was away so there were just the two of us. We went to a scary movie called "Frogs" with Ray Milland in which animals turned against the humans. It gave me nightmares afterwards. I found it strange that such a kind, gentle person like Yvonne would enjoy horror movies. Regardless, it felt good to spend time with her. She was family.

On Monday morning we said our goodbyes. She hugged me fiercely, as if it might be the last time she'd ever see me due to my bad driving. I laughed at her fears, and set off in my fully packed red Austin in the direction of Durban. It would take me eight hours to get there. Her father Maurice lived there, and he would be my first stop.

Luckily, I learned how to drive a standard on my mother's Morris Mini-Minor in Canada many years before. That little Mini was Mom's first car. She was so proud of it that she drove it in circles in our back yard, buzzing through the laundry which hung on the clothesline.

But driving on the left side of the road proved challenging for me. Even worse was trying to keep up to the maximum speed limit of 50 mph on the highway so other vehicles wouldn't plow into me. If I pressed the gas pedal all the way to the floor, I managed to keep pace with the other cars. Drivers honked at me constantly. There was nothing I could do but drive as fast as my car would go.

About three hours south of Johannesburg, the fourth gear started to knock. There was a dreadful noise, and then it ground to a halt. I started to panic. This was not supposed to happen! I was near the tiny town of Warden in the farming province of the Orange Free State where the staunch Dutch Afrikaners lived.

A kind couple stopped and towed my car with rope to the only garage in the place. The sun was blazing hot in this sleepy, dusty little town. The mechanic shook his head as he looked at my car. The front side axle was completely worn out and they didn't have the spare part. The new part would have to come from Durban, and that would take three days. This was bad news.

I fumbled in my purse for Maurice's phone number. Still trembling, I was relieved to hear his voice on the line. Like an angel, he drove five hours north to Warden with the spare part. The garage was closed by the time he arrived. I waited for him in the darkness by myself, worried that he might not spot me. But there in the distance I could see the headlights of his familiar car. It was so damn good to see him! I flew into his arms as he got out of the vehicle. We booked a hotel for the night, grateful to find anywhere to stay. After settling in, we enjoyed a hot meal of schnitzel, mashed potatoes and ice-cold beer at a restaurant up the road, the only one we could find.

Next morning, the mechanic fixed my car as well as he could, shaking his head all the while. At last, Maurice and I set off in our separate cars. He followed behind me at my top speed of fifty miles per hour. Cars honked at him first, then at me. He'd never driven that slow. We drove over the misty Drakensburg mountains in blinding rain and pitch darkness. It was alarming not to see the outline of the highway. I caught myself holding my breath at times, and kept my eyes glued to the luminescent cat's eyes in the middle of the road. We drove five hours straight, stopping only once for a snack. Finally, the welcome city lights of Durban glowed in the distance. We arrived at his apartment, glad to be alive. I felt that I had a true friend in Maurice and loved him dearly. He was a good man.

The spectacular view from his apartment overlooked the yacht club in the harbour. But the sweltering heat and humidity were oppressive; the air felt saturated with moisture. Maurice was a tall man with lots of flesh and folds. Sweat poured from both of us, and we had to shower three times a day. He wore a strong deodorant---Right Guard for men, the scent of which filled up the whole place when he sweated. But that didn't matter, I adored the man.

In his charming French accent, he always told me how beautiful I was (a lie, of course) and that my paintings were masterpieces (another lie) and that I had gold in my fingertips (sheer flattery). He knew how to say wonderful things that a woman longed to hear. It felt good to hear such superlatives, even though he made me laugh each time as I knew they weren't true. It was the French way, and fed our love and our sex.

We enjoyed a few days together in Durban, and took a little trip to Giba Gorge in the mountains where we ordered horses to ride. I sat on my horse and waited while the workers readied Maurice. But something was missing; the whole picture looked comical. The big man sat on his horse, his legs dangling without any stirrups.

"How can you give me such a dusty saddle?" he complained to the workers, gesturing with his hands to the saddle.

I burst out laughing, doubled over on my horse. The attendants immediately set out to dust the saddle. I tried to tell him through peels of laughter that he should ask them to add some stirrups as well. Embarrassed, Maurice realized the true cause of his discomfort. Properly fitted, we trotted along the mountain path to the gorge. I rode up to the edge and looked below. The view was straight down a steep cliff.

"Why do you go so close, ma chérie? Aren't you afraid to fall?"

I wasn't afraid. It felt exhilarating to stand at the edge and look down. The sight filled me with awe.

One evening we went to a restaurant called "Chez Cecile," owned by a woman from Mauritius. She served delicious home-cooked specialties in a small bungalow which she'd bought to accommodate the restaurant. As her reputation for authentic cuisine grew, her quaint restaurant was always full. The large room held about ten tables for guests. She did most of the cooking herself, and personally came to the table to welcome you and tell you the specials. The lighting was warm and romantic, with fresh roses and a candle at each table. You could bring your own bottle of wine. I just loved the taste of spicy Mauritian food.

It seemed that Cecile and Maurice were friends from the old country. When Maurice introduced me, he presented me as a portrait artist. She looked at me, then back at him a few times, probably wondering about the nature of our relationship. They continued to chat. Then she turned to me.

"Please come to my house tomorrow at 3 o'clock and we'll talk. I want to order a portrait from you."

I was surprised to have a new customer so quickly, and began to suspect that she owed Maurice a favour. I didn't mind. Next afternoon, Maurice drove me to her luxurious cliff-side home overlooking the beach at Umhlanga Rocks. She served us ice tea on her patio, where potted palm trees wafted in the ocean breeze and an azure blue sky reflected on the sea below.

I snapped photos of her posing in a lounge chair, and would paint her portrait from those pictures. She paid me a generous deposit. I promised to bring the finished painting to her in a couple of months.

"Her restaurant business must be going well," I said to Maurice as we left her lavish home. He agreed that it certainly must be.

The day after, Maurice's nephew Gilles (who was also Yvonne's cousin) called and wanted to visit. I remembered meeting Gilles when I was living with Ryan in Joburg. Just for fun, before he came to Maurice's place, I put on a black wig and heavier eye makeup to see if he would recognize me. He did. Still laughing, he was amused that I should play such a prank on him. We spent a couple of pleasant hours conversing over lunch. He and Maurice talked a lot, mainly about extended family. Everyone from Mauritius seemed to be related.

On to Port Edward

A few days with Maurice in the sweltering heat of Durban was enough for me. I set off by myself toward the Transkei. The coastline was breathtakingly beautiful. I loved the sound of waves breaking over the rocks and the smell of salty air from the ocean. But it was a two-lane road and I got stuck behind a long truck loaded with bananas driving thirty miles per hour. I didn't dare to pass it without risking a head-on collision. There was no choice but to follow this truck at a snail's pace past many little towns, the last one being Margate. Shortly after Margate came a sign which read Port Edward Holiday Camp.

My car started sputtering and needed gasoline. There just happened to be a gas station near the sign. A jolly little man came out to serve me. He was the owner, and was surprised to see a young woman travelling by herself in this part of the country. It was getting dark. The Bantu homeland lay just down the road.

"Is there a hotel at the holiday camp?" I said, peering into the dense forest around us and getting nervous about driving through the homeland at night.

"Yes miss, it would be the perfect place to stop. You shouldn't be travelling any farther alone, especially not through the Transkei."

The Holiday Camp served as a resort for the South African Police and their families, although they rented to civilians too. This was good news and I drove into the camp.

It must have been by Divine intervention that I landed in this place. My accommodations were humble but perfect for me. The cost was only $2.50 per day. I marvelled at my round white adobe hut with a thatched roof, one small window and a door. There was an electric hotplate, toilet, sink with running water, table and chairs, and one bed.

The walls were bare but I loved the place, especially the view from my open door. Right outside grew wild orange and red gladioli with leaves which radiated brilliant green when the sunlight streamed through them. Daylight glistened off other vegetation too, their leaves shimmering as they swayed in the wind. Songbirds trilled their melodies while other little birds brought trees to life with music as they chirped unseen in the branches.

In the distance, I saw lush sugar cane fields with neat rows for walking between. Banana trees grew on the grounds too, with odd-shaped flowers. The air was fresh and sweet from vegetation. This felt like heaven. I could see the ocean nearby and was grateful to be here. I must have lived in this part of the world many lifetimes ago. How else could I explain why I was so comfortable here?

A lizard scuttled across the floor of my hut, but its tail came off when I accidentally stepped on it. I worried that it must be suffering without its tail, so I killed it. Someone later told me that lizards drop their tails on purpose when wounded. It made me sad that I ended its life for nothing.

Insects seemed to thrive in the thatched ceiling above me. I sat eating dinner at my table when a huge spider appeared right in front of my face, having climbed down the silken thread it was spinning. I screamed! The terrified spider scrambled back up its string. Another time, crickets were screeching somewhere in the hut. I couldn't sleep with that racket and had to find them. They were in my shoes. I scooted them out the door.

African insects were gigantic. Each morning I'd wake up to at least one enormous dead moth the size of a dinner plate lying on the ground outside my hut. I cleaned up the casualties and set up my easel on the flat area in front of my door. It was the perfect place to work. I had Cecile's portrait to paint, and photos of other friends whom I could draw as samples.

As the days passed, I started gathering a crowd of curious onlookers who stood around and watched me work. Gradually word got out that an artist from Canada lived in rondavel number ten. The camp locals were friendly and came by most days to chat with me. Some of them asked me to paint their children or other family members. This allowed me to earn more money and stay longer at the holiday camp.

I really liked it here. My days were gloriously spent painting and swimming in the ocean. The beach was just a short jaunt down the hill. I usually sunbathed in the rock-pools left behind after the tide went out, and splashed refreshing sea water on my face and arms. It was paradise. I could stay here forever.

⌒

Maurice came from Durban to visit me one Saturday. This was a welcome surprise, warm hugs all around. We strolled down the hill from my hut to the beach. I wanted to harvest fresh oysters which are exposed when the tide is low. Maurice set his folding chair on a flat rock formation in the shallows. The sight of him made me smile; he looked like King Neptune sitting on his throne. He'd brought a bottle of white wine and two glasses from home, while I provided live oysters for lunch which I plucked off the rocks. I had no idea those lumpy gross shells were oysters until someone from the camp told me. After that, I went for daily lunches to the beach, bringing my hammer and chisel. Those delicacies were alive and delicious. I opened the shells with my chisel and squeezed some lemon on them. They reacted to the lemon, and into my mouth they went. Truly luscious!

Maurice and I couldn't ask for better than this---fresh oysters, cold white wine, warm sun and each other's company. But Maurice seemed moody and said very little. He muttered to himself as he poured more wine.

"What's wrong, Maurice?" I asked.

"Today is the anniversary of my wife's death," he said. "I lost her two years ago."

So, that's why he came to visit me. He hoped I might take his mind off this sad anniversary. But he couldn't shake his mood that day although we tried to make the best of it. He spent the night with me in my little rondavel, and admired the pastel portrait of himself hanging on the wall. I painted it as a sample, along with Ryan and a few other friends. Fourteen paintings of friends and new clients kept me company in my hut, all neatly taped to the walls around my bed.

Maurice and I made sweet love to the sound of crickets and frogs singing in the night. This burly affectionate man made me feel safe, and I loved him for the wonderful man he was. Next morning a group of black women on their way to work saw him coming out of my place. They laughed and waved at me as I said goodbye to this much-older man getting into his car to leave. They knew. I smiled and waved back. They were teasing me.

⌒੭

The throng of people watching me paint in front of my hut

began to grow. Word spread, and more onlookers placed orders. In the crowd was a young couple whose names were Jeff and Julie. They lived in a large army tent on the resort property and seemed interested in getting to know me. Jeff worked as a foreman for a construction company which built cottages in the area. His wife Julie decorated the interior of those cottages. They made a good team.

To my great pleasure, they often invited me to their place for dinner. We were the same age, and they seemed to like me as much as I did them. They pretty well adopted me and I felt part of a family again. A shortcut through a high cornfield took me to their tent. To scare snakes away, I sang at the top of my voice and stomped my feet loudly while walking. Snakes are supposed to slither away when they feel vibrations, but the poisonous rinkhals is lazy and won't flee so there was always a danger of stepping on one. Numerous pythons in the cornfield kept the rats at bay. It was frightening to walk through there, but well worth it to see my friends.

Julie once took me for a drive to the nearby Transkei homeland where the Xhosa people live. Nature there was raw and breath-taking. We walked along a sandy white beach and admired the adjacent rock wall which had been artistically eroded by weather, thus exposing beautiful layers of coloured sand from ages past.

A young Bantu woman was washing clothes in a grotto where a stream of fresh water fell from the ledge above and collected in a shallow pool. This grotto was almost hidden by lush green ivy growing on the hillside, and moisture clung to the surrounding boulders which were covered with moss.

The woman scrubbed her family's clothes with soap and hung sheets to dry on a stone outcrop. She seemed well-fed and healthy, not bothered by the white intruders staring at her (mostly me). I couldn't help it. Strands of her hair were baked with clay, the weight of which straightened and lengthened it. She wore colourful beads in each strand of hair, and silver bangles on her arms and lower legs. I later learned that beads and bodily decorations denoted her clan and rank within the family, and many more meanings unfamiliar to me. She must have been an important woman because she carried herself with dignity. I admired her smooth brown skin and asked to take her photo.

"One Rand!" she said, exuding confidence.

This payment was well worth it as I later painted a portrait from that photo. Afterwards, she gathered her washing and carried it off in a basket on her head.

I spent many happy evenings with Julie and Jeff, enjoying the warmth of their friendship. Sitting across from Julie in their large tent was a feast for the eyes. Her blond curls framed her pretty face as she looked at me with milky blue eyes, animated as she spoke of her dream to open a little shop with a Spanish theme. Her two large silver rings bore a pattern of Viking ships which twisted in a flash of glitter on her fingers, while her shear flowered blouse fluttered when she moved. She offered much to look at; a person could get lost in her decorations. I didn't have the patience to wear rings and bracelets. They got in my way.

"Why don't you dress more like an artist, Eva?" Julie once said.

Her words surprised me. *I am an artist, why do I need to dress like one?* I never wanted to attract attention and have people turn around to gawk at me and say "she must be an artist, look at the way she dresses!" Except for a pair of small gold earrings from my mother and a gold necklace from Grandma, I was simple and unadorned.

Julie's husband Jeff had dashing good looks and sun-streaked hair. He usually wore no shirt on his tanned chest, and smiled the most glorious smile except when he complained about how his employees kept making off with company building supplies for their own homes. He also grumbled that after he paid them, many of his workers wouldn't return to work until their money ran out.

"Such is life in Africa," he said. "It will never change."

⌒〇

Jeff loved Julie. He fell into the one percentile of men who are attracted to chubby women. He confessed that he was enormously turned on when a heavy woman jumped on a trampoline and he saw a bit of fat jiggling. Julie and I were both a bit plump, although I thought we looked fine. It never occurred to me that I was plump. I felt strong and healthy.

One evening Julie and I were washing our hair and joking around in the camp washroom. We shrieked with laughter at something silly. Almost immediately, Jeff appeared at the door with a rhino whip in his hand, out-of-breath and ready to fight. He thought we were screaming and being attacked. That darling man came to defend us!

Meeting Max

Max burst into my peaceful life at Jeff and Julie's one evening. We were both invited to dinner in their spacious tent. He owned the construction company they worked for, and had flown in from Pretoria to see what progress they'd made on the cottages.

After they talked business, Julie offered us a bowl of tasty beef stew, fresh warm bread and a glass of cold beer. We sat on comfortable garden chairs around a card table covered by a red cloth, while candles on the table gave off a golden glow causing live shadows to bounce around the amber walls of the tent's interior.

Max seemed intrigued by the Canadian artist who had landed in their midst. He went out of his way to pay attention to me. He was middle-aged and bore the portliness which comes with success, a charismatic take-charge kind of guy who makes things happen. I appreciated that quality in a man. My friends noticed his interest in me.

"Ahhh, we've seen that look in his eyes before, Eva," Julie said after he left. "He's interested in you, be careful!"

I wasn't afraid of becoming prey and never gave it another thought. He was married with three young sons, thus not fully available to me. But as time went on, this dynamic man came to Port Edward on business more often than usual. He was lively, with tons of personality and ideas. He wooed me and took me to cozy restaurants in the nearby town of Margate. Against my better judgment, I started falling for him. I enjoyed his strong character and good sense of humour. He made me laugh. I loved his positive outlook on life. He charmed his way to my heart and into my bed.

But Max also enjoyed playing devil's advocate. One evening he invited me to a casual soiree hosted by the camp's Chief of Police and some other officers. He wanted to show them my collection of slides which I'd taken on a bus trip to Soweto, the African shantytown near Johannesburg. Urban black people were obliged to live in those shacks and return there every evening after working all day for white people in the city. It was against the law for them to live within the city limits of Johannesburg, unless the maids had live-in quarters on the white family's property.

Max knew full well the police didn't like people taking photos of their shame or anything that made the country look bad and could be used as propaganda against them. So, I don't know why he wanted me to show those slides. I bet he was daring the police to react. I was nervous for what they'd think of me.

Thankfully they said nothing as they viewed slum after dusty slum on the screen. They gave me a few askew looks however, and may have wondered why I would film their worst living conditions. I can honestly tell you that I'm not a political person, and was simply interested in seeing all aspects of my new country.

To Maurice in Durban

After three months of sun and sea in Port Edward, I had enough. The novelty wore off. Even paradise gets boring after awhile. My car was gone. I abandoned it after yet another breakdown. I was so exasperated with that damn thing that I never wanted to set foot in it again! The jolly owner of the garage agreed to take it off my hands. He fixed it and gave it to an African from the Transkei with instructions to never drive it off the homeland.

Julie offered to give me a lift to Maurice's place in Durban. As I packed my clothes and art supplies, I looked around at my rondavel hut and little piece of heaven for the last time. It had been a great experience. Then we drove off, along that beautiful stretch of coastline. Julie enjoyed going to the big city and hoped to do some shopping later.

When we arrived at Maurice's apartment, I gave my big angel-man a huge hug, thrilled to see him again. I think it was mutual; he smiled and lifted me in his arms. He greeted my friend warmly as well, and seemed delighted to have two young women in his home. Julie was a little reserved at first and may have been surprised at my predilection for older men.

Maurice invited us to sit down for smoked meat sandwiches and salad which the maid prepared for lunch.

But I soon observed there were fewer household items than before---less silverware, less tablecloths, less dishes, less of everything. Maurice hadn't noticed the loss. Then I remembered what Mimi told me from her experience of living in the Belgian Congo, that housewares gradually and imperceptibly disappeared. Poor Maurice, most of his late wife's fine things were gone. I said nothing as it would break his heart. Julie left us after lunch while I stayed a few days longer with Maurice in Durban.

Cecile's portrait was finished and needed to be delivered. When Maurice and I arrived at her palatial home in Umhlanga Rocks, I spotted a woman relaxing on a lounge chair and asked her if I could speak to Cecile.

"It's me!" she laughed.

I looked again. This lady in no way resembled Cecile.

"I just had some work done," she chuckled.

I was dumbfounded by the change in her appearance. All her character lines and smile wrinkles had disappeared. At a loss for words, I showed her the portrait which was painted before surgery.

"Well, it's a good souvenir of my former self," she said and laughed.

I felt guilty that she'd spent money on a painting which was no longer valid, but accepted her payment with thanks nevertheless.

Durban was unbearably hot and humid in the summer. Maurice had no air-conditioner in his apartment. It proved impossible for me to sleep with him in his stifling bedroom located in the apartment's interior. He snored loudly. We bought nose drops for him and earplugs for me, but nothing helped. I asked if he would mind me sleeping on the couch out on the enclosed balcony. It was much cooler, with windows which opened to the ocean breeze. He minded, but I slept there anyway. He seemed offended and took it personally. I regretted that I'd hurt this wonderful man's feelings. He was my guardian angel, older and wiser than me. He never fought with me and only helped me. I truly loved this easy-going, good man.

To Mimi in Melville

Maurice agreed to drive me to Johannesburg where I'd stay with Mimi in the suburb of Melville while he visited his daughter Yvonne in Hillbrow. Having given up my place at Cliffton Court, I no longer had anywhere to live. I was glad when Mimi asked me to house-sit for a couple of weeks while she went to Australia. Her daughter was away in Brussels, so their place would be empty in any case. I intended to go job-hunting in their absence.

After they left, I took buses to Johannesburg to look for work but was having no luck. When Mimi and her daughter returned from overseas, I still had no job. Mimi told me I could stay with them until I got my bearings. I slept on their living room sofa, worried that I might be a bother.

"Where there is love, there is always room," she said.

Such a wonderful, generous woman, I thought. I lived with them off and on for six months and loved them like family.

Their house occupied the corner lot on a hill, small but quaint. Mimi enjoyed tending to her garden in the back yard. There she weeded fragrant white jasmine and purple irises which grew beside clusters of tall elephant grass. The yard was surrounded by a stone wall and overlooked green hills in the valley below. You could see the skyscrapers of Joburg in the distance, alongside a mountain of yellow dirt which was characteristic of a former gold mine.

Sunsets were magnificent. We often ate dinner at the picnic table in the back yard and watched the sun go down. I loved sitting near scarlet bougainvillea which climbed the white stucco walls of the house.

Preparing meals at her home was an event. All three of us had an assigned task. Mine was trimming the green beans, cooking them and making cold bean salad with fresh garlic and olive oil. Mimi cooked in bulk and froze the food so she could easily whip something up on working days. I learned much from her.

Her ensuite bathroom had a large window beside the tub where she could relax in a hot bath and look at the tall fluffy reeds planted right outside. Nobody could see in because she was hidden by the stone wall. She pampered herself by placing lit candles around the tub, treating herself to small luxuries.

⌒◡

I loved to watch Mimi and her daughter get ready for work in the morning. It felt like being in a flower garden, with spritzes of fragrant perfume and many twirls in front of the full-length mirror to decide which necklace or belt to wear. A hundred decorative necklaces hung from hooks beside the mirror. The ladies looked fabulous each morning.

Sometimes they gave me a lift downtown on their way to work. Now, driving with them was another matter. Mimi was passionate and temperamental and drove like she talked, with fervent hand gestures in the air and often letting go of the steering wheel. She cursed at slow drivers in French, made sudden turns and jerky stops. One time she turned her head completely around like an owl to look at me; it was disconcerting! Then she almost hit a lamp post. I was dizzy but fully awake by the time we arrived downtown, and felt as if I just drank twenty super-charged espressos!

Every dateless Saturday night with Mimi was an athletic affair. She had energy to burn and wanted to move furniture around. I helped lift things from one spot to another, then change of plan and back again. From her years of living on the plantation with her husband she learned to do many things, including sewing clothes for their daughters and building furniture. She recently built a bar and bar stools for her living room, and tacked an antelope skin on the bar. I was in awe of her many skills; she could even make mayonnaise and liverwurst from scratch!

Mimi told me that after her husband died, she moved from the plantation to the busy city of Kinshasa, capital of the Congo. There she met and fell in love with Maarten, a South African pilot who lived in Pretoria. He stayed with her whenever he flew through Kinshasa.

She told me amusing stories of their life together whenever he came to visit. My favourite was about her baby chimpanzee which would never leave her side. He even clung to her in the shower. That capricious little monkey was the source of much delight. He would grab Maarten's newspaper from him as he sat reading it, then put the paper over his head and run around shrieking. All they saw was the newspaper running out the door! Then he would swing on the neighbour's clean washing, leaving fingerprints on everything.

One time they got fed up with his antics and banished him to the outdoors for a couple of hours. Their dog came in, walking suspiciously heavy. Wouldn't you know it, that smart little monkey found a way in by hiding himself under the dog's stomach and holding on tight. Once in, he flew screeching around the furniture. And when the sun rose at five in the morning, he would throw his plastic cup at Mimi to wake her up for his breakfast. He screamed and hurled things until she got up to give him his biscuits and milk with sugar; then he let her sleep until 7 am.

But peace in the Congo didn't last. The revolution happened in 1960-65 when the black population rose up against colonial rule by Belgium. One hundred thousand people were killed. Mimi told me she had to flee the country with her three young daughters and abandon all her things. Planes came from Brussels to rescue white nationals. As she stood high on the ramp by the airplane's door, she threw her car keys to the crowd below.

"I hope my car will help one of you!" she called out to them.

Everyone lucky enough to leave did the same thing. Material possessions meant nothing anymore.

Safely settled in Brussels, Mimi got a job as a ground-hostess for an airline company at the airport. Her daughters were educated there in Belgium. Maarten was still in her life and stayed with her whenever he flew through Brussels. This love arrangement lasted for at least a decade, but she was finding his absence between flights unbearable and wanted more of him. She truly loved this man. Eventually she moved with her now-grown daughters to Johannesburg to be closer to him.

However, this was too close for comfort for Maarten. He was a married man and had been leading a double life all these years. Now that Mimi only lived one hour away from him instead of half a continent, she seldom saw him. Maarten's wife knew about their affair and was making his life a living hell, even humiliating him in public. So now he was towing the line and being a loyal husband, the rascal. That's why Mimi and I moved furniture for hours on a dateless Saturday night---all that pent-up energy.

"I've been such a fool to think he would leave his wife for me," she said one evening. "Everything between us was perfect in every way. I cried for weeks and years, missing him." Her voice trembled.

I felt her anguish and ached along with her. She told me that Maarten said he couldn't possibly leave his helpless wife who needed him, and that she was strong enough to survive without him.

"Mimi, a man won't leave his wife and children unless he's truly miserable," I said, "and he's got to be more unhappy than happy. His love affair with you was making his boring marriage more tolerable."

I could see that my words didn't comfort her. She shook her head and tried to hold back the tears. I held her while she cried softly.

⁓

A storm was brewing outside. Electrical storms over Melville were spectacular. Black clouds formed a well-defined wedge, cutting into the red sunset underneath. Then came fierce thunder and lightning, piercing claps and blinding light which shattered the darkness.

We awoke one morning to find Mimi's bird cage open and her favourite white budgie-bird dead and mangled on the floor. Feathers stuck to her little dog's mouth while Matisse wagged his tail joyfully.

"Oh no, Matisse!" She cried, smacking the dog's backside. She was furious.

That female budgie had been the favourite of all the males as they jostled to sit beside her on the swing. We didn't know why she was so popular; I suppose she had budgie sex appeal. Now she was dead. Mimi still had ten brightly coloured budgies left, but didn't want to hold them captive after this.

"Go and be happy and free!" she said, as she carried the cage to the back yard and opened the wire door.

We watched them fly away into the world, like coloured poetry or music notes. Mimi was upset for days. I tried to uplift her spirits, but this passionate woman felt everything deeply. It was not easy to calm her down.

To make matters worse, we returned from the city one evening but Matisse wasn't there to greet us at the door. We searched the house and the yard, but he had vanished.

"My God, now someone has taken Matisse!" she said.

We scoured the neighbourhood, walking up and down each street and desperately calling his name. If he was being held captive in one of the houses, Mimi hoped that Matisse would bark at the sound of his name. But no bark of recognition came. We did this for days with no result. Finally, she had to accept that he was gone.

To Port Edward with Max

I was thrilled to see Max pull into the driveway in Melville. He had invited me to fly with him to Port Edward on business for ten days. I welcomed the change, and looked forward to spending time with him and our good friends Julie and Jeff. My clothes were packed and so was my easel. I hugged Mimi goodbye, then Max and I set off for the airport.

We flew from Johannesburg in a Cessna with six other passengers. I was awestruck by the beautiful coastline of Natal from the air. It was breath-taking, with miles of white beaches and blue ocean. We touched down smoothly and hopped into the rental car waiting for us. The weather was glorious on that happy, sunny day. We'd be staying at one of Max's company cottages near Port Edward.

Arriving at the cabin, I set up my easel and oil pastels in the spacious bright kitchen. The room was open-concept with lots of light from windows which overlooked the forest. All the interior walls were light coloured pine which kept my spirits uplifted. Max worked with Jeff during the daytime at a building site while I painted portraits in the cottage. We had a few good days until the unthinkable happened.

⌁

"Here, take my gun," Max said trembling, "and shoot if you have to."

He showed me how to take the safety off and pull the trigger. Most white men in South Africa during the 70's carried a gun, and some women too; Julie carried a small pearlescent pistol in her purse. But I'd never held one in my life and hated the violence that guns beget.

Max choked back tears from what happened the previous night when we visited our friends for dinner in their tent. All four of us were in a good mood, enjoying an excellent meal of Afrikaans Boerewors (farmer's sausage) washed down with a bottle of local red wine. The delicious smell of fried onions, potatoes and sausages filled the tent. I admired Julie's choice of wild orange lilies to make the table look pretty. We felt happy as we relaxed in our chairs.

Max was especially cheerful that evening. Business was going well and he seemed to be living life to the full. Lately he travelled a lot and was seldom home in Pretoria. He mostly worked on building projects in Port Edward with Jeff and Julie, this wonderful couple I'd grown to love. That evening was spent eating, drinking, and listening to deep-sea fishing stories.

"Don't believe a word he says," Julie said, laughing. "Jeff always adds an extra two feet to every fish he's ever caught!"

In the middle of our laughter, there was a knock on the tent flap door. Two policemen asked to speak to Max alone. They knew where to find him; the police knew everything in those days. Max's tanned face turned pale. He went with them outside in the darkness and we could hear their muffled voices. Then there was silence followed by broken sobs.

They finally came inside. Max told us the awful news that his ten-year-old son in Pretoria had been run over on his bike in their neighbour's driveway. The woman hadn't seen him when she was backing up. The hospital tried desperately to save the boy's life but couldn't. Their son was dead; it was a terrible tragedy. Max's wife tried urgently to phone him to come home right away, and finally located him through the police in Port Edward who were here now.

We heard Max in heated discussion with the police about how to get home to his family but they couldn't help him. There was petrol rationing, so it was impossible for him to drive through the night to Pretoria nine hours away. Nor could he hire a private plane. Nothing could be done until morning.

A bomb had dropped. The police left and we stood there in shock. The void was palpable.

Max and I left our friends in the tent and headed back to our cottage fifteen miles away. We drove in silence. Talk was painful. We knew each other well, but nothing I could say or do would comfort him. It was late when we reached the bungalow and went to bed, hoping that sleep would numb the sorrow. But it didn't. Max couldn't stay in bed and paced around the bedroom. He was trapped there until morning with me, and moved feverishly around the room.

"The worst thing is that I hardly knew the little guy," he said, his eyes downcast.

I was tender and loving and tried to comfort him, but he would have none of it. He burst out of the room and went outside where he sat on a rock for hours, alone with his grief. The spotlight shone on his husky body, head down and cradling it in his big hands. I felt that I didn't belong with him then. He needed much more than me.

In the morning his bag was packed, his eyelids red and swollen from the night. He gave me his loaded gun for protection before he left. We'd heard reports that a white woman in the area was recently murdered by blacks in some barbaric ritualistic ceremony. She was found with her breasts cut off beside a nearby river. As horrifying as that was, I needed to remain in the cottage to finish portraits which I had to deliver in the area before returning to Johannesburg. I already had their deposits and didn't know when I'd be back that way again.

I no longer felt safe. The cottage was isolated and the nearest neighbours lived far away. Max told me to use his pistol to protect myself if an intruder breaks in. It lay beside me on the table with the safety off as I painted. At night I slept with it on my night table, terrified that an attacker might crash through the windows or break down the door. Would I really be able to kill a man in self-defence or just wound him? I didn't think I could kill anyone. I lay there in the dark, waiting fearfully for the dawn.

I spent the next week alone in the cottage day and night. There was food in the fridge so I didn't need to go out. I listened nervously for any little sound of danger, and worked hour after hour, one portrait after another, until they were all finished. But Max's son's death weighed heavily on me. I spent many sad days thinking about what happened.

As a single woman in my twenties, I loved life and being in love. Max's wife and family were his business and I asked nothing of him. But after this catastrophe, I felt an overwhelming guilt. Did that innocent boy five hundred miles away die as a punishment for our sin---Max's and mine?

A sudden knock on the cottage door jolted me out of my reverie. It was Julie! She came to ask if I wanted to stay any longer after what happened. I was relieved she'd come, and couldn't wait to get out of there. I packed my bags and artwork, cleaned up the cottage and loaded my things in her car. She would drive me to Maurice's place in Durban.

I entrusted her with Max's loaded gun as she'd be

seeing him sooner than I would. I didn't know if I could or ever would see Max again. The whole thing had been too sorrowful. I felt so much guilt.

Julie and I were both deep in thought as we drove. The boy's tragedy hit us hard. When we reached Maurice's apartment in Durban, he could sense there was a problem.

"What's wrong, chérie? You don't look happy today."

My angel man listened patiently as I told him what happened. Then he took my hands and wrapped them in his and told us how sorry he was. It was comforting to see him again; he made everything better.

Julie left for home after some coffee and cookies.

It was hard for me to shake the sorrow. Then I thought about my own family in Canada. I missed them...yes, even my volatile father. I longed to see them again, but there was no way I could afford the airfare.

New Beginnings

Maurice's daughter Yvonne worked for a travel company in Johannesburg and often phoned him. When she called him this time, she asked to speak with *me*.

"Guess what?" she said, I could hear the smile in her voice. "My boss is looking for somebody to lead a tour to Canada and I thought of you right away!"

I could hardly believe my ears... *I wanted that job!*

We decided the best strategy would be for me to call her boss from Maurice's place and tell him that I'm from Canada and heard about the job from Yvonne. I should say that I'll be coming to Johannesburg on June 6th and ask him if we could meet then. Getting that job meant so much to me that I was afraid to call him. Then I remembered some good advice a friend gave me long ago, namely to take the bull by the horns. It's been my motto ever since.

I dialed the number and was relieved when the boss sounded almost jovial that his search for a tour guide might be resolved. He agreed to see me when I got to Joburg. I went around smiling for days with my spirits as high as the sky. This was no coincidence. Once again, I attributed my good fortune to Divine intervention. There could be no other explanation. Max's tragedy had been replaced by some degree of hope.

My angel Maurice drove me eight hours north to Mimi's house in Melville while he stayed with Yvonne in Hillbrow. Looking back on my life now, I see how much he and my good friends did for me, all those kindnesses which I took for granted.

My job interview with the boss was coming up and I needed to shop for something beige and business-like to wear. *I never wear beige.* I found the perfect beige skirt, a matching beige vest, and long-sleeved white blouse--- tasteful, appropriate clothes. After I hemmed the skirt, Mimi took one look at me. My hem resembled waves on the ocean.

"My God, I can't let you go to your interview like that!" she said, shaking her head.

She fixed it flawlessly. Next morning, I dressed for work along with Mimi and her daughter, looking in the mirror and twirling. I looked discreet and conservative, with clean long blonde hair which matched my beige outfit.

My heart was beating fast when I got to the boss's office. To my relief, he was a kind-looking older man who put me at ease. He seemed to like my exuberant personality and traditional look. I got the job! *Thank you, God.* He also told me that he expected professionalism, and that the tour-leader must have good morals and not get romantically involved with the passengers or it would be instant dismissal. I could live with that and hastily agreed. My only thought was that of seeing my parents again.

My first tour to Canada would depart in four days and I was rearing to go. They gave me a crash course on how to be a tour guide across Canada. On the day of departure, I was handed airline tickets for twenty-six passengers and myself, plus $200 for tips and miscellaneous expenses. I kept these in my purse at all times. Thankfully, all arrangements had been made in advance. I simply had to accompany the passengers and make sure our itinerary (flights, buses, side-trips, hotels and meals) went smoothly. I felt confident that I could do this, no problem. I'll be seeing my parents in Montreal soon!

Chaos!

Everything that could possibly go wrong on that first trip did. My passengers' many complaints shattered me. I had no idea that passengers complain when things go wrong, or even that anything *could* go wrong, or that all their anger would be directed at *me!* During my training, this was not mentioned.

On that hapless trip, we first boarded an Iberia airline on June 19th and flew from Johannesburg to Madrid. That busy city was a whirlwind of art museums, palaces, Flamenco dancers and traffic. The passengers sensed my inexperience when I left one poor woman stranded at a restaurant. She failed to turn up for the bus. I didn't know that I was supposed to count heads and wait for stragglers. I assumed they would show up on time like they were supposed to. Another passenger's luggage was lost and didn't arrive until our last day in Madrid. They blamed me for everything; stress was mounting. I was a nervous wreck!

Then we flew across the Atlantic and arrived in Montreal. It was a relief to come to a familiar place. We checked in at the Queen Elizabeth Hotel downtown where I called my mother to let her know that I'd arrived and had some free time for a visit. My darling Mom picked me up from the hotel. It was so good to see her. After big hugs and tears of joy, she drove me to our family home in Rosemere.

The place was just as I remembered. The blue spruce

in the front yard had grown after four years, and Mom's pink rose bushes near the front door were in full bloom. They filled the air with their sweet scent. She'd polished my brother's silver sports trophies which were proudly displayed on shelves in the living room, and her ornamental Viking ships adorned the mantle-piece. My father was home too, sober and happy to see me. Both of them were overjoyed that I was alive and hadn't been eaten by lions in Africa.

Time flew by in the warmth of my parents' company. They loved me no matter what I'd done. It almost made me cry to be so loved and missed. The thought crossed my mind to desert my passengers and remain with my parents in Canada, but I knew that would be unethical. Mom drove me back to my hotel for the night.

On our second day in Montreal, we took a four-hour bus ride to historic Quebec City, the charming French town of music and cobble-stoned streets. After lunching on famous French-Canadian onion soup and meat pie in a quaint restaurant, we were scheduled to take a sight-seeing tour of the city. Our driver parked the bus on a side street and left us, because a local driver was supposed to ferry us around the city.

We waited and waited, but no driver appeared. That day was stifling hot. The engine was turned off, so we had no air-conditioning. Nobody came to tell us what was happening; they had all vanished! My passengers' nerves were frazzled by the sweltering heat and expected *me* to solve the problem. We suffered on that hot bus for one and a half hours with no information and no one in sight. My seething passengers looked like swollen red lobsters, their faces moist with sweat. Angry words flew in my direction and I got blamed for this disaster too. At long last we learned that all the bus drivers in Quebec City had just gone on strike, tough luck for us. Word finally came that our original bus driver would return us to Montreal, forgoing sight-seeing in Quebec City. Complaints assailed me all the way back. I hid in my hotel room for the remainder of the evening while my passengers cooled down in theirs.

This tour was turning out to be a nightmare. I was completely stressed-out. My chin erupted in an ugly red rash which became embarrassing. When I approached someone to talk, they backed away for fear of catching something. It was as if we were dancing a comical tango; the farther they backed, the closer I came in order to hear them. They stepped back, I danced forward. Finally, I gave up and saw a doctor in Montreal who prescribed antibiotics. I popped them like candies.

Next day we flew to Toronto and stayed at the classic Royal York Hotel. We were whisked away for an afternoon bus tour of the city. First to Casa Loma---a one hundred-year-old castle in the middle of town, then past luxurious homes with lush manicured gardens. My passengers gazed in awe at all that opulence. Only the best areas of town were shown.

The day after came a bus trip to Niagara Falls, a must-see for tourists. This was the first time I'd seen the falls myself. It was a wet but interesting experience as we donned our rain gear for a walk on the ridge under the tumbling falls. Above the falls the water was peaceful, with little indication of the doom awaiting anyone who fell in. The calm water was inviting; I forced myself to resist.

༄

The following day we boarded a plane to Calgary, the heartland of Alberta's ranching country. Before leaving South Africa, I was told by my boss that some of the elderly spinster ladies would have to share rooms in two hotels in

Alberta due to overbooking. I agonized about *when* I should break the news to them, and figured the best time would be in mid-air. The spinsters were furious with me when I told them.

"Why did you wait until now to tell us?" one of them said. "I would never have gotten on the plane if you told me before!"

All four women were really angry. I hoped they would calm down before we landed. At least they couldn't jump out of the airplane. We settled into our rooms at Jasper Park Lodge, a stately log structure in keeping with the old west. The spinsters were still enraged and didn't look at me. Thankfully time heals, and the women grudgingly accepted their fate.

That afternoon we took a sight-seeing tour through Banff National Park, viewing herds of buffalo with their molting brown coats. Little calves sheltered close to their mothers. How spectacular the sight of those great herds must have been when thousands of them roamed the plains before the white man came.

On the way to our next hotel, we drove through breathtaking snow-capped mountains. At one high lookout, we stopped to take photos of Peyto Lake below with its opaque, milky-blue water. This colour only comes from glacier water. We finally arrived at Chateau Lake Louise, another famous but overbooked resort. Summer was peak season and hotel officials had to be well organized. Each group of tourists was given a designated time to eat. All I saw in the dining room was a sea of white heads---elderly tourists from all over the world, hundreds of them.

Next morning, one of the angry spinsters cornered me.

"Do you know what happened last night?" she said, "I was soaking in the bathtub when Helga came in to use the toilet for a bowel movement. Do you know what she said to me as I lay naked in the bathtub? She said 'Don't worry, I won't look!'"

I tried to stifle a laugh and almost choked. She was definitely not happy.

⌒

The next day was damp and gray. I felt like exploring the grounds, and found a path below the chateau which was built around a pond. There was nobody there but me and a hotel employee dressed in a kilt and playing the bagpipes. He stood on a small pier jutting into the pond, and played my favourite tune---Amazing Grace. He played it soulfully with intense feeling and dignity. The sanctity of the moment gave me goosebumps and brought tears to my eyes. I stood still and respectfully appreciated the music at a distance. Then it started to rain! Could I leave while he was playing, or would that be rude? He kept playing for me and I couldn't leave. We were both getting soaked in the downpour. I stood my ground and listened courteously until the melody finished, then we sprinted our separate ways. That dear, noble man.

⌒

My passengers and I then took a train through the spectacular yet foreboding Rocky Mountains to Vancouver, passing one jagged snowy peak after another. I was surprised by the number of climate zones we saw along the way. There was even one section with deserts and tumble-weeds. When evening came, we were assigned our sleeping compartments. I kept to myself in my private room, still popping anti-biotics and crying. I basically cried my way across Canada. The remarkable beauty of this country was lost on me that first trip.

By the time we reached Vancouver, the embittered spinsters no longer had to share rooms and were on the verge of forgiving me. Our group then took a day trip by ferry across the Georgia Strait to Vancouver Island. There our bus drove us to the magnificent Butchart Gardens.

A more gorgeous place I've never seen! It's what I imagine the biblical Hanging Gardens might look like, with lush green foliage planted in curved rows amid begonia blossoms which grew between Cypress trees, and bushes of every texture and variety. Thousands of flowers presented a profusion of perfume and colour; hollyhocks in blushing peach, yellow honey-suckles, blazing red celosia and luscious pink roses. Blue delphiniums stood tall behind them.

My senses were overcome with ecstasy! I wanted to faint from the beauty of it all, or lay down in a flower bed and succumb. Those gardens were spectacular. The climate was moist like English weather, perfect for roses. Even the spinsters seem to blossom a bit.

Meeting an Old Friend

Near the washrooms in Butchart gardens, I found a phone booth and some privacy. I wanted to call John, an old friend of mine with whom I'd driven across Canada seven years earlier. He was living somewhere on Vancouver Island now. I first met him in Montreal after my third year of university in the spring of 1968. He was about to drive to Vancouver, and offered me a lift when he heard that I'd love to see western Canada and find a summer job there.

John insisted on keeping his convertible roof down for those three thousand miles; it was damn cold. I remember the excitement of negotiating those narrow winding roads around Lake Superior. You had to stay wide awake if you wanted to survive that dangerous road flanked by jagged walls of rock. This in contrast to the boring straight highway through the Prairie provinces, most of which I slept through. Whenever I woke up, there were the same golden fields of wheat on each side of the Trans-Canada highway. That road was dead straight and flat for hundreds of miles. I was told by students who grew up on the Prairies that they cry with joy to see those endless fields of wheat and know they've come home. Not me.

Memories of John came flooding back to me as I rifled for his number in the phone catalog. He had tons of personality, and made me feel alive during those months we spent together. He loved his red MGA convertible which he cleaned and waxed and loved above all else.

"Isn't she beautiful?" he would say, admiring her glossy curves as he polished her. I felt like I was competing with that car for his affection.

It was early May when we drove across Canada. We camped for four nights and stayed in hotels for three. We were the only ones in those wilderness campsites so early in the season. I had nightmares of starving bears coming out of hibernation, but they never did.

When we finally reached Vancouver in his little sports car, John and I parted ways according to plan. I found myself a room for rent in a large house in Shaunessy Heights, a posh area with azaleas and colourful crotons growing in flowerbeds. My landlady also rented rooms to seniors who haunted the corridors in their bathrobes all day. It was terribly depressing. I felt close to death myself just seeing them wandering around like that.

Without John, I never left my room, not knowing what to do or where to go. I was supposed to be looking for a summer job. Feeling afraid and lonely, I called him to come over one evening. But instead of coming through the front door like a normal person, he climbed up a tree to the roof and jumped in though my window. I suppose he thought that was more exciting. He was not quiet.

Next day, the landlady confronted me in the laundry room, her accusing dark eyes piercing me as she spoke.

"And here I thought you were such a *nice* girl. You can't stay here anymore!"

So, John got me kicked out of my room. He had also rented a little room for himself like I did. Going forward, we decided to rent a place together. We found a clean studio apartment near Stanley Park. He'd been hired by an engineering company out of town, and returned to our apartment most weekends.

For my part, I got a job with Holiday Magic cosmetics and tried to sell makeup. I would be earning commission only. It was a pyramid scheme which I discovered during training. The company driver let us salesgirls off in designated areas where we knocked on doors and asked to speak to the lady of the house while handing her a red rose so she wouldn't slam the door in our face.

I tried the job for three days, drinking cups of tea and listening to endless stories of unhappy marriages and family problems. Not one single piece of makeup did I sell. I quit and found another job in a film processing factory. But I caused a riot on the assembly line by actually wanting to *talk* to the lady sitting next to me while we worked. No conversation was allowed; I was warned.

I ate very little when John was out of town, and lost fifteen pounds in two weeks by walking around the seawall in Stanley Park and swimming in the ocean pools built beside the shoreline. I wanted to improve my appearance. That's when I first dyed my hair blonde. It suited me well, better than my natural brown colour. I also bought a new turquoise summer dress and wanted to surprise John when he got home. I was ready for him when he walked through the door.

"Is that really you? What did you do?" he said, and had to look twice at me. A slow smile lit up his face. He definitely liked my new look and was more affectionate to me on that weekend.

On Saturday nights, John and I would go on a date to the harbour and look at the big ships which he was passionate about. As we sat on the concrete wharf, a huge albatross with a massive wingspan glided past. I've never seen such an enormous bird. Another time we drove up to Gross Mountain and rolled back down the steep winding road with the engine turned off, his idea. He was full of life and never short of interesting things to do. Being a Leo, he was definitely in charge. Donavan's song Hurdy Gurdy Man played on his radio, and one night we saw The Graduate with Dustin Hoffman which just came out in the movie theatre. We laughed so much. Life with John was good. I even considered postponing my last year of university to stay with him in Vancouver. But when September drew near, the pull to return to class and finish my Degree grew stronger. I had enough money saved for a train ticket back to Montreal.

Now, seven years later, John was married. We'd kept in touch sporadically and I knew he lived somewhere on Vancouver Island. He had a common surname, so there were many people with that same name in the phone book. I didn't know which John was him by looking in the catalogue. Not having enough coins to waste by calling them all, I asked the operator to question each John if he was born in Tunbridge Wells. The second John was. He was flattered that I remembered his birthplace, and seemed delighted to hear from me. I told him about my new tour-guiding job and short stay in Vancouver. He wanted to meet.

My passengers and I took the ferry back to the mainland, and John arrived next day to say hello to me at my hotel. He had booked himself a room for the night. He said he enjoyed watching me stroll across the lobby floor as he stood on the balcony above. It was good to see him again, with his round spectacles and boyish face with dimples in his cheeks when he smiled. He couldn't resist meeting his old friend who'd come all the way from South Africa.

He invited me for dinner at an intimate little restaurant. We talked non-stop about our past, and about this---my disastrous first trip with twenty-six passengers. I was feeling tense like a wound-up spring. He said something disparaging about South Africa and its repressive Apartheid regime.

"Why would you even be living in such a country?" he said, shaking his head in disbelief.

I was sick and tired of having to defend the country to people who had never been there. My nerves were already shattered, and that comment was the last straw. I snapped! Without thinking, I took my wine glass, cracked it on the table's edge and pointed the broken part at him, twisting it in the air right in front of his face.

"Don't you dare speak of things you don't have a clue about. You believe all the bullshit propaganda you've heard!"

His mouth hung open and his eyes grew wide as he gaped at me. The whole restaurant went quiet. I felt the stares of the other dinner guests and grasped what I'd just done. *Oh God, they're all looking at me!* I quickly got up from the table and went to leave.

"Come back here woman!" he said when I reached the door.

So, I went back to him and sat down. He smiled and seemed pleased with himself that he could make me sit down. That annoyed me even more, so I got up again. He paid quickly and we left, each walking back to the hotel on opposite sides of the street. I was boiling mad, but mainly embarrassed.

"I haven't had such an exciting time in seven years!" he hollered from across the street.

The fresh air and walk did me good. I mellowed somewhat by the time we reached the hotel, and was calm enough to have a quiet drink and chat with him. He left next morning to go back to his life, and me to mine. It was good to see him again. We kept in touch occasionally through the years until he got busy having kids and raising them.

Our tour's last stop was in London for a couple of days. I was exhausted, and preferred to shelter in the solitude of my hotel room. I slept for hours and hours... delicious, welcome sleep. When I finally saw daylight, I heard some of the passengers talking about experiencing the night life in London, but they were vague about where they were going. Someone mentioned a titillating new play called HAIR where the actors got naked. That would be completely forbidden in South Africa. I decided to go. When I got to the theatre, scattered in the audience were half my passengers. They pretended not to notice me, as though embarrassed to be seen at this risqué event.

Once back at the travel office in Johannesburg, I expected to be fired after that chaotic trip across Canada. It surprised me to learn that my boss expected a tour-leader's first trip might be an emotional disaster. He knew in advance I would take my passengers' complaints personally, and told me that I'll be well-seasoned for my next trip out. To my relief, mistakes were forgiven and I was granted another chance. My second trip to Canada would be in ten days time. In between tours, I stayed with Mimi in Melville.

An Intrusion of Thought

Relaxing now at Mimi's house, I reminisced about my first tour across Canada and the pleasant visit with my old friend John in Vancouver. Then my mind started wandering to when I first met him in 1968 and felt that pull to return to university in Montreal instead of staying out west with him. A dark memory surfaced, in spite of my best efforts to be rid of it.

After taking the train to Montreal and reaching home, I connected with friends and fellow students. It was late summer and still party-time. Students and teachers alike were arriving from all corners of the world to find lodgings near the university. Classes would be starting in a couple of weeks. One of my girlfriends told me she'd been invited to a party being held for staff and graduate students on St. Urbain Street, and asked me to accompany her.

The party was in full swing by the time we arrived. Drinks flowed, and sensual Blues music played while students and teachers conversed. One man in particular took an interest in me. He had just arrived from overseas and would be teaching English Literature at the university. He might have been in his early forties and looked pretty good, sturdy with broad shoulders. We danced and talked and drank. I must have drunk too much; the room was spinning.

He kept offering and I didn't refuse. People were leaving and he asked if he could drive me home.

"No, it's okay," I said, "I'm gonna take the last bus. I live far from here."

"That's no problem, I'll take you."

Such a kind man. Rosemere was forty-five minutes away on the autoroute. I gave him directions and slept while he drove. When we arrived, he woke me up. But I didn't recognize this place. This was not my parents' house in Rosemere! He said he needed to use the washroom, and ushered me inside his ground floor apartment and locked the door.

"Come and rest here for a minute," he said, patting the edge of the bed.

This felt weird, but I sat beside him. In a flash his personality changed. He pushed me down on the mattress, pulled off my skirt and panties with strength that surprised me, got on top of me and held my wrists down hard.

"I want to go home! You promised you'd take me home!" I said, starting to panic.

"Not now, not now. Maybe later," he said, pinning my arms hard as I tried to push free.

I screamed and tried to jolt him off my body but he kept me pinned down. He would not let me get up.

"I don't want to hurt you, but..." he said, as he grabbed me and pulled me back.

I was a prisoner! He held my wrists with one hand as he unzipped his trousers. Then he penetrated me over and over again. This went on for a couple of hours. I hated him for it. Then he needed to use the washroom, but hesitated as he glanced at the door in the entrance.

"Stay here and don't you dare move!" he said, pointing his finger at me.

This was my only chance. After he got to the bathroom, I whipped on my skirt and panties and made for the door. The lock was jammed...*damn it!* Then I heard the toilet flush. My heart was pounding. After a few tries the door latch yanked open and I ran out as fast as I could, terrified that he'd come after me. I ran and ran. It was still dark, around four in the morning.

I got winded and started cramping, couldn't run any more. I wandered around the empty streets not knowing where I was, and feeling dirty with his ejaculate dripping down my legs. The sound of a vehicle approached from behind. I was terrified that it might be him, but it was a Gazette delivery truck. Relieved, I waved them down to ask for directions. When they heard what happened, they said they'd drive me home. I was grateful.

They didn't say much as we sat in the truck, but I'm sure they had their thoughts. They drove two hours out of their way to drop me off at my parents' house. Mom and Dad were still asleep. I didn't tell them or anyone else about that awful experience. I tried to forget it, and hoped never to lay eyes on that man again.

꿈

Our courses at university were starting and I felt that same exhilaration which I always did at the beginning of a school year. There was a chill in the autumn air, and leaves were turning brilliant red and orange. I had already attended two classes that first day; my third class was a Literature course. We students were all seated in the room, waiting for the professor to arrive. The doorknob turned and in he walked.

Shit, I couldn't believe it---*it's him!*

I felt faint. He pretended not to recognize me. I didn't know if I should leave the room, scream at him, or melt into the woodwork. He acted calm, and even looked mildly attractive in a light blue shirt which showed off his broad shoulders. He talked a bit about the course and asked us to introduce ourselves, starting from the other side of the room. Surely, he must be worried about what I might say. I think he was squirming on the inside; beads of sweat dripped down his forehead. *Good. Be scared, you bastard!*

When my turn came, I introduced myself just like all the other students. I did not reveal to the class that he had raped me. I'm sure his strategy would be to keep calm and deny everything if I were to have an outburst and accuse him in front of everyone. After class, I went up to him. He did not apologize or give any sign of recognition that he knew me---like it never happened. I asked to see him in his office next day.

I knocked on his door at the appointed time. He sat behind his desk all proper-like, not bothering to look up. I took a chair opposite him. Again, he uttered no words of regret or acknowledgment that he knew me. I wanted to yell at him and call him terrible names while he sat there busying himself with paperwork, pretending that he'd never met me or held me captive while he raped me.

"I need to change out of your class since it conflicts with my schedule," I said, thinking that was the simplest solution.

"Sure, no problem," he said calmly, not even blinking.

He crossed me off his list of students. I thanked him and left his office.

I can't believe I just thanked him for changing my course!

The man showed no emotion. I could have ruined his life! He must have given some thought to all this beforehand. I'm sure his ploy would be to stay composed and deny everything, even having met me. He'd done a good job of acting calm so far. I didn't go to the police or university authorities as it would be his word against mine. Nobody would believe me. Besides, most of the anger had gone out of me. I got my revenge by seeing him squirm in the classroom. That was enough. He knows what he did. Thankfully I never saw him around campus again.

Reflecting back on that experience, I did not let him ruin the attraction I would always feel for men. He was a bad apple, and I'm sure there are others like him. I survived without being physically injured. But who knows what might have happened if I hadn't escaped? In any case, I did not let this incident embitter me, although the memory has stayed with me.

"Would you like some coffee?" Mimi said, breaking my reverie as she sat down beside me at her kitchen table in Melville. "Are you dreaming about your next trip to Canada?"

She smiled and handed me a steaming cup of coffee.

Second Trip to Canada, with Love

My next tour to Canada was a real pleasure. Any complaints went in one ear and out the other, and didn't devastate me like on the first trip. My boss was right, that I would be stronger. I enjoyed the trip, the passengers, and meeting my parents again. The credit for this happiness goes to a big teddy bear of a man called Danny, a gentleman farmer from Swaziland. Yes, I broke the cardinal rule about not getting involved with a passenger. But in my defense, our friendship evolved naturally. He was serene and unflappable, the only bachelor on the tour. Feeling that I had an ally in him gave me confidence to lead the group. It's amazing how life changed for the better when I felt that I had a friend for moral support.

I wasn't the only one who appreciated him. Many of the single ladies in our group sought him out. He told me amusing stories of female passengers throwing themselves at him. One woman turned up to his sleeping compartment on the train wearing only her nightie. He politely turned her away but chuckled as he told me about it. He seemed pleased that he could garner such desire. Danny and I kept our romance a secret from the other passengers. It was comforting to have him with me as we toured Canada... wonderful, in fact.

In Jasper National Park, my passengers and I boarded a large glass-enclosed snowmobile for a tour on the Athabasca Glacier. This patch of ice originated from the ancient Columbia Icefield, hundreds of thousands of years ago. Fingers of its thick ice gradually crept down between the mountain peaks until it reached a certain altitude and melted. We sat high up in this caterpillar-like machine, its engine churning as it crawled up the glacier.

Another group of tourists rode in a similar vehicle about two hundred yards ahead of us. Suddenly it toppled over! Stunned, we watched helplessly as the machine in front of us lay on its side. This could have happened to us! The drivers called for help on their radios. Thankfully one of my passengers was a retired doctor who always carried a medical bag with him, as if he knew accidents could happen anywhere. He put his jacket on, took his bag and walked over to the capsized snowmobile.

We stayed parked for half an hour until our doctor returned with news that four people were seriously hurt---one with a broken pelvis and others with concussions and broken bones. Help was on the way, so we continued our excursion and were secretly grateful that it didn't happen to us.

Further up the icefield we all got out and walked on this ancient snow. This was fun for the passengers. Many of them had never seen snow before and even had a snowball fight. Danny enjoyed talking with the doctor and his well-groomed wife with wavy white hair. She and her husband still held hands after many years of marriage.

"How do you and your husband manage to keep the romance alive for so long?" one of my passengers asked her when we got back to our hotel.

This elegant lady adjusted her pearl necklace, took a

sip of sherry, and looked the person straight in the eye.

"Because he's never seen me sitting on the toilet," she said with a gentle smile.

Good advice. I made a mental note.

On the tour, Danny and I enjoyed each other's company in private. But one evening we had a fight during drinks in his hotel room. I can't remember what it was about, probably something silly. I slammed the door and pretended to go out. But I really went into his closet, this being out of his line of sight. It was a childish prank, but I wanted to play a trick on him. I could see him lying on his bed through the crack in the closet door. He had food sent up, watched TV, burped and farted. Then he ran a bath and got into it.

After ten minutes, I emerged from the closet and opened the bathroom door. He was soaking in his bath with dirty socks floating everywhere. *He was washing his socks in his bath!* He looked up at me with a raised eyebrow, but remained calmly stretched out in his bath. He was so wonderfully unflustered. I just loved that about him.

"So, no hard feelings about the argument?" I said, teasing him.

"Well, no hard feelings, but..." he said with a bashful smile.

Perhaps he was embarrassed that I'd witnessed his private moments and seen him naked in the tub washing socks. I laughed and let him finish his bath alone.

When this tour finally ended in Johannesburg, my passengers parted ways with sweet regret. Everyone had gotten along well. Danny and I also exchanged addresses with a promise to meet. I looked forward to seeing this good man again.

Missing Danny

My third trip across Canada went well enough, but I missed Danny. By now, I had learned to be diplomatic and even defused arguments between passengers sometimes. Getting along smoothly wasn't always easy for a group of strangers thrown together in close quarters for a month. Danny had been a stable, comforting influence on my last tour. He was a solid guy emotionally; nothing could unhinge him. To me, that's a great quality for a man to have.

I often thought about him and remembered that one of his hobbies was collecting match-boxes. So, I saved matches for him from every town and restaurant which my tour visited---hundreds of colourful match-boxes, each one a work of art. By the time our trip was over, I had a small suitcase filled with them.

After the tour, I stayed at Mimi's house in Melville. Danny phoned me there one evening and asked me to meet him in Pretoria. He said he didn't have time to pick me up because his small plane was being repaired and he needed to pick up some Persian carpets from customs which he had bought in Istanbul.

How did he expect me to get to Pretoria, an hour away? I felt offended and said no, because I didn't have a car and wanted him to pick me up. We said goodbye and that was that. In my heart I longed to see him but didn't want him to take me for granted. In the end, my heart won the conflict and I ordered a taxi to his hotel in Pretoria.

Reception rang his room but he wasn't in. My heart sank. I asked the clerk if she could let me wait in his room. No, not possible. So, I paid for an adjoining room. I convinced the front staff that I'd come a long way to see him and he had invited me there. They finally agreed to unlock the door separating our two rooms. I was eager to surprise him when he returned to the hotel. Where was he? What would I do if he brought a woman back to his room? I suddenly felt apprehensive.

Whatever the outcome, I placed the collection of colourful match-boxes on his coffee table. They created a beautiful array of colour, and were laid out in a circular pattern. It would be the first thing he'd see when he came in. The door between our rooms was wide open, and I waited in mine with no lights on.

An hour passed. At last, I heard the doorknob turn and somebody entered. Then came silence while he grasped the situation. Cautiously he entered my darkened room and I popped out of the shadows! I loved surprising him. He seemed happy to see me, although needed time to fathom what just happened.

It felt good to lie beside my big comfortable Danny again. He was warm and held me close. I felt secure. Next morning, we enjoyed a classic breakfast on the hotel's shaded veranda where a breeze wafted through, carrying the sweet scent of nearby roses. Tables were covered by elegant white table cloths and folded cloth napkins. Our waiter brought fresh orange juice in a glass pitcher, bacon and eggs, toast, strawberry jam and fresh coffee. The smell of strong coffee in the morning was good. Danny took my hand and smiled.

"Glad you came," he said.

I really liked this man and gave his hand a squeeze. His business associate joined us for breakfast and grinned when he saw me. I felt embarrassed for what his friend must have thought of me, the woman who came all the way from Johannesburg to spend the night with Danny.

The two of them had business to conduct after breakfast, so Danny called a cab for me and I returned to Mimi's place in Melville. I tried to look on the bright side, and remembered his delight at the match-box collection and me in the adjoining room. Danny and I stayed friends for several years after that. Whenever we met, he spoke about that marvellous surprise visit at the hotel and the way it was done. I sometimes wonder if he ever married. He was a good man.

Trip to Mexico

My next tour would be to Spain, Puerto Rico and Mexico. I looked forward to it, and hoped to visit a high-school friend who now lived in Puerto Rico with her husband. There was no time to write and let her know. Ten years had passed since we last met.

I greeted my group of passengers for the first time at Jan Smuts Airport in Johannesburg, and always made sure to dress a little frumpy for their first impression of me so as not to seem a threat to any of the wives. My long hair was pulled back tight in a bun and I wore a matronly dress which showed my plump belly. That should put the ladies at ease. This was a manageable size of only twenty passengers. They seemed like a good bunch.

We landed first in Madrid, and slept soundly in our hotel rooms that night. Next evening, our group met in the lobby to be chauffeured to a wine cellar for authentic Spanish food and entertainment. I wore a long black dress for the occasion. My blond hair fell over my shoulders, and I put on make-up and eyelashes. My passengers stood waiting for me in a row along the wall. They stared at me, not sure I was the same person or not.

"What a transformation!" one fellow said, his mouth ajar.

I laughed and took it as a compliment. But I felt like I

had just revealed my alter ego---one woman by day and another by night.

The wine cellar was dimly lit and romantic, with low ceilings and arched adobe doorways painted white. The aroma of Spanish food was intoxicating---delicious paella containing shrimps, garlic, chicken, clams and artichokes mixed with spicy rice. Attentive waiters, smartly-dressed in black suits with white shirts and bow-ties, served us bottles of wine with a flourish.

A sexy flamenco dancer made a dramatic entrance in her long cherry-red dress. She snapped the castanets with her fingers and stamped her dancing shoes in time to the music. A swarthy man sitting on a stool behind her played guitar, focussing his attention on her and the sensual rhythm of her movements. They were in sync with each other. The dancer's long black hair swooshed as she twirled to the beat. My passengers and I were mesmerized by the passion of this erotic dance. It was like we always imagined it would be.

∽

A couple of days later, we flew across the Atlantic to Puerto Rico, arriving at the luxurious El San Juan Hotel in the early afternoon. My passengers had a free evening to explore the city on their own, and I was eager to find my old friend Emily whom I hadn't seen since high school. I had her address in Rio Piedras and called a taxi to take me there.

We drove a long way and finally arrived in Rio Piedras. I gazed in disbelief at the run-down apartment building with peeling paint and laundry which hung over the balconies. Children in tattered clothes played in the street. *Poor Emily, what's happened to you?*

The taxi driver scratched his head and stared at the tenement building. This was not the correct Rio Piedras. We continued driving to another area called San Fernando (still in the Rio Piedras region) and arrived at a pretty house in the suburbs with trees and flower gardens. My old friend was doing okay after all.

Emily answered the door and turned white. I was afraid she'd keel over with shock at the sight of me. She was cooking supper when I knocked. She hadn't changed much except that she was grown up now. We chatted a bit and she invited me to stay for dinner. Her husband came home from work shortly after. I'd never met him, but he was a jolly, husky fellow with dark hair who kissed her when he entered. Then another guest came to the door, a good friend of Emily's.

We sat at the dinner table and I vaguely remember Emily and her girlfriend talking about personal issues. My brain was cloudy and I couldn't concentrate on anything that was said. Fuzzy words buzzed in the air above me. Soup was served and I crashed, my head falling hard on the table. I was asleep---jet lag. They put me to bed right away, I needed sleep. Next morning, we talked over breakfast. I felt like a klutz after what happened, but no matter; they seemed to forgive me. Emily dressed and went off to work as a teacher, while her husband drove me to my hotel which was on the way to his office. I'm glad that I met them.

After two days of seeing the sights near San Juan and lazing around the hotel pool which was surrounded by palm trees and flowering hibiscus, we flew to Mexico. Once there, our bus took us past hillsides covered with hundreds of little square houses painted in bright colours of turquoise, orange, red, pink and yellow, on the outskirts of the city where labourers lived.

I was flabbergasted to learn that twenty-five million people inhabited Mexico City. It was not like the sleepy

Mexican towns we've seen in western movies. This was a bustling metropolis with people dressed for the office.

In a town square in one part of the city, lively mariachi bands played folk music in their traditional glitzy outfits and big sombreros. Five different bands stood back-to-back in the square, simultaneously playing a different folk melody for the tourists. This created a humorous cacophony of music. Seeing them, I remembered that my sculptor friend Hennie asked me to bring him back a sombrero.

One of my passengers was an extroverted sixteen-year-old girl who was unleashed on me by her parents. I should not have to bear responsibility for an adventurous minor. She was pleasant enough, and rushed to the hotel's piano to play for an audience any chance she got. I noticed she made friends easily with the Mexican boys who hung around the lounge.

It took me a few days to figure out what she was up to. She'd call me around 9 p.m. to say goodnight and that she was in her room ready for bed. But next morning on the bus tour, she appeared tired and smelling of unwashed sex. My guess is that she was out partying with the boys all night. Perhaps young girls don't know that sex has a smell, and a woman must clean her privates afterwards.

I didn't want to upset the girl by confronting her, but at the end of the tour I told another passenger who was a friend of her parents that the girl was popular with the local boys. I said no more than that. They could figure out the rest if a problem cropped up later.

Nevertheless, we had a fabulous group of fun-loving passengers, and still had romantic Acapulco to enjoy. As usual, our hotel was first class, right on a long white beach. But this beach was bustling with pesky vendors trying to sell souvenirs. And that wasn't all. As I lay sunbathing, young Mexican men came up to me and proposed to offer me a good time for a price. I couldn't believe it! Why would I need a gigolo? It was downright insulting and I shooed them off. But I had a good look in the mirror when I returned to my room... *did I look older than I was?*

An attractive middle-aged brunette in our group who wore bright red lipstick, had found herself one such young stud. She proudly introduced him to us.

"This is Alfonso," she said, stroking his muscular arm as she gave us a wink. "We're having a good time."

Sure, why not? I nodded as if to say it's okay. She's on holiday, after all.

I really liked this group, and threw a party in my hotel room for them on our last night in Mexico. I ordered wine and refreshments, and hired a local band with a singer. My passengers enjoyed this party. They sang and clapped their hands to the music. We'll have good memories from this trip.

From Acapulco, we flew east to Mexico City, changed airplanes, and continued another twelve hours across the Atlantic to Brussels. Exhausted, we arrived in Brussels in the early morning and could rest for three hours at a hotel before our afternoon flight to Johannesburg. My passengers checked into their rooms to freshen up. But my room faced the noisy traffic on the street. It would be impossible for me to sleep. I asked the front desk to switch me to a quieter spot facing the back of the building.

It was heavenly to rest for a few hours. I took a hot bath and soaked long enough to relax my tense muscles. Sleep came easily. I felt completely refreshed after those few hours, got dressed and went down to meet my passengers in the lobby. But when I got there, they seemed terribly upset and talked loudly to me all at the same time.

"Where have you been?" they said reproachfully.

It seems that all hell broke loose as I lay sleeping! In the lobby my oldest passenger, Mrs. Estee, a sweet lady in her late seventies, was stretched out on a bench while another person gave her mouth-to-mouth resuscitation. They tried desperately to reach me, but the front desk forgot to make note of my new room number. In the chaos, I turned for help to Dr. Mayer, one of my passengers. Everyone was pressuring him to save Mrs. Estee.

"No, I don't have my medical bag with me! I can't take responsibility for this!" he said, throwing up his arms in exasperation.

Mrs. Estee opened her eyes and showed more signs of life. My distressed passengers were all assembled and waiting for our bus to the airport. Mrs. Estee wanted to leave with the rest of us, but due to her health she'd need special permission to fly. When we reached the Brussels airport, the authorities asked over the loud-speaker for a doctor to present himself to the health station. A couple of my female passengers offered to remain with me in Brussels in case Mrs. Estee took a turn for the worse. I looked at them, mystified.

"Why would you do that?" I asked.

"In case we can help," one of them said with a shrug. "We've got nothing going on, no need to rush home."

How very kind. They wanted to help me if serious problems arose, which through their maturity they'd be better equipped to handle than me. I thanked them for their offer, should it come to that.

A vacationing doctor at the airport showed up to examine Mrs. Estee, checking her heart and vital signs. He then gave her a mega-dose injection of vitamins. The poor dear was simply exhausted from our long flight. She and I were then given our very own transportation by ambulance to the airplane way out on the tarmac. My other passengers were already on board the aircraft.

My group occupied the back section of the Jumbo jet. Mrs. Estee needed three seats to lie down flat. Everybody was upset with what happened to her at the hotel, and those emotions caused a chain of events. Suddenly, another passenger grabbed her head in agony. She was struck by a fierce migraine which seared through her head with blinding pain and also needed three seats to lie on. She was unable to speak. Her friend covered her eyes with a cold wet cloth.

Then, I heard a commotion in the next isle and saw Mr. Swanepoel bending over his wife as he held her tightly. This couple was in trouble; the woman was convulsing from an epileptic fit. I grabbed Dr. Mayer who was sitting a few rows ahead and told him to come quickly. He asked for a spoon from the flight attendant, and stepped in to hold down Mrs. Swanepoel's tongue to keep her from swallowing it.

"I'll take responsibility for this," he said to the distressed stewardess as he leaned over Mr. Swanepoel to grab the wife. This time he wanted to help. The good doctor redeemed himself in the end.

There was complete mayhem in our section of the plane. Concerned flight attendants rushed back and forth to check on the two passengers who were laid out flat and the one who was convulsing. We delayed the flight for half an hour. At long last we were cleared for take-off for the long thirteen-hour flight to Johannesburg. It had all been too much. For the duration of that flight, my focus was on my passengers, handing them blankets and bringing them water. Other people on the airplane wondered why they didn't get the same attention from me.

A Greek man was seated next to me. He'd been watching me work and was sympathetic to my plight. I mentioned to him that I planned to look for an apartment when I got back to Johannesburg. I loved Mimi, but didn't want to impose on her any longer. The man gave me the address of an apartment building called "Balnagask," and insisted that it would be perfect for me.

"Promise me you'll look into it," he said.

He was so adamant that I had to swear to check it out. Once again, I thought how wondrous it is that God puts the right people in our path at the right time.

Balnagask

I was thrilled with my new ninth floor apartment. It was bright and clean with large windows, glossy hardwood floors and a balcony which faced the sunlight. That Greek man certainly did me a favour by insisting I look. The Balnagask building lay at the corner of Paul Nel and Banket streets in Hillbrow, not too far from the center of Johannesburg. My sunny apartment overlooked green trees and a football field belonging to a school; it was quiet and private. The rent was only eighty-five Rands per month which I could easily afford on my tour leader salary, or even just portrait painting alone.

But I had no table or chairs or living room furniture. Somebody told me about a warehouse downtown filled with sofas. I found the place and eagerly tried all the couches. I was looking for something big that I could melt into, and must have sat on a hundred of them. Nothing was comfy. I began to feel like the girl in the "Princess and the Pea" fairy tale.

I asked the portly salesman if I could try the sofas up in the loft. There were hundreds up there too. He started to huff and puff and look at his watch, his face turning red with agitation. But he didn't say no, so I climbed the stairs to the loft.

After sitting on most of them, I finally found the perfect set---a cream-coloured cloth sofa with two matching arm chairs, wonderful for sinking into and sitting for hours. The furniture was delivered to my place, along with a small pine dining table and four chairs. My life was complete. I looked forward to my next tour which would be to the Far East and Israel, but not for another month. I had to wait. In between tours, I worked in the travel office... so boring. I'd much rather be out exploring the world.

A humorous surprise greeted me each day when I got home from work. My sofa and chairs had moved to a different spot in the living room. The building management hired maids to clean the glossy wooden floors daily, even if they were spotless. The maid must have found my lack of furniture disconcerting, and tried her best to find an inspiring location for my sofa and two chairs. One day they would be grouped by the window, the next day they stood alone in the middle of the room or along the wall. I found it amusing, and welcomed her initiative to make my place look nice.

❧

Ryan dropped in briefly. He was visiting from Swaziland for the weekend and staying with friends. He carried something wrapped in paper which he seemed eager to give me.

"I've brought you something," he said, proudly handing me the gift.

Vibrant orange and red colours spilled out of the parcel---long sun-filter curtains for my windows. I was confused.

"Why?" I asked.

He grappled for an answer, thinking it was obvious.

"Because I think you should have some curtains!"

The thought never crossed my mind. I loved to look out with nothing between me and the view of nature. My reaction seemed to disappoint him.

"They're beautiful, thank you!" I said quickly.

His expression brightened. He spread out the length so that I could fully admire them. It's true, they were gorgeous. We hung them up. The flamboyant colours added zest to my place. We stood back and marvelled how the sun streamed through the red and orange cloth, thus reflecting a warm glow of colours on the walls.

Ryan glanced around my apartment and seemed pleased for his contribution. We sat down to chat. After some coffee and a cigarette, he dashed off. I later bought matching corduroy cushions in red, orange and yellow to dress up my cream sofa and chairs, just the right splash of colour needed.

I loved my place. My collection of African curios looked good on the window sill. There was an elephant sculpture in dark ebony, dry gourds, and unusual bottles which held pretty dried flowers. Looking out my window, I felt content in this cozy apartment facing the afternoon sun. It bathed my home in golden light, warm and friendly.

Meanwhile, I still had portrait commissions to complete. My easel was set up by the patio doors where the light was brightest. During the day I worked at the travel office, and painted when I got home and on weekends. The art exhibition in Joubert Park would take place in a few months and I needed to prepare for it. I painted proud Bantu and Zulu tribesmen dressed in traditional garb from photos I'd taken. I felt a strong desire to express my fascination for the colour variations of their velvet skin, their muscular bodies and timeless laughter. Those beautiful people are living, breathing, works of art.

Waterlogged

Everything was *almost* perfect in my new apartment, but intense summer rains poured every afternoon for half an hour each day. Water dripped from the elevator's ceiling and covered the floor with a big steamy puddle. *Dare I go in?* I took a chance and pressed the button to the ninth floor. The door screeched shut, too late to escape. It jerked and carried me upward. Machinery rumbled above and below me, making a grating roar when the door should have opened but didn't. It passed my floor! When it got to the top, it quivered on its cable and thundered down, gathering speed before reaching the bottom with a loud thud. *I'm going to die!*

A few seconds passed. I pressed all the floor buttons as it soared upwards, but it was no use. It never stopped. I rang the alarm thinking help would come. But then the lights shut off and everything went black. Even the alarm went silent as I jolted downwards at horrifying speed.

"Help!" I screamed, again and again. My heart was racing. Alone in the darkness, my legs wobbled as I clutched the walls. Suddenly the elevator jerked to a stop between floors and the doors opened a bit. *Please let it stop long enough for me to get out.* I managed to push the doors apart with strength I didn't know I had, and hauled myself over the ledge between two floors. I climbed out just in time and collapsed on the floor, lying still for a few minutes. Then I took a paper out of my purse and wrote OUT OF ORDER.

Swaziland with Ryan

Back at work, the boss gave me two weeks off before my scheduled trip to the Far East. I was delighted to get away from the office, and called Ryan in Swaziland with the good news. He came on the weekend to pick me up. I was happy to meet him again, and looked forward to seeing where he lived now.

We drove for four hours to Swaziland, past the capital of Mbabane to his quaint cottage in the countryside. His home was a welcome sight as it appeared on the horizon. Our plan was for me to paint during the day while he was at work in the city. Besides, I had a valuable portrait to deliver in Swaziland.

Ryan's shaded patio was the perfect place to sketch. I loved being there. The cottage was surrounded by green fields, with only the buzz of insects and bird songs to compliment the stillness. It was built on a hill overlooking a dirt road below. Ryan rented the cottage from his German neighbour who lived next door. This neighbour was married to a Swazi woman and they had three children. Ryan told me that especially German men are attracted to exotic black women and their lack of sexual inhibition. There was no Apartheid in Swaziland. Races could mix freely.

I was sketching on Ryan's patio when his maid snuck up behind me, her eyes wide with alarm.

"Mamba!" she whispered, pointing at something in the

overhanging vines in front of my nose. I had no idea what she meant.

"Mamba!" she said again.

I peered deeper into the tree. A bright green snake was dangling from a branch looking straight at me! I stopped breathing. The snake was completely camouflaged in the leaves. I cautiously moved my chair back and got up slowly. We went into the house and shut the door; only then could I release my breath. A highly poisonous green mamba, I later learned.

One reason for my visit to Swaziland was to present a portrait which I'd made of His Majesty King Sobhuza II, long-time ruler of the Kingdom of Swaziland. I painted it in Johannesburg from a photo in a travel brochure. To be truthful, I hoped the King would ask me to paint his many wives and pay me generously for doing so.

His Majesty wasn't able to meet me in person, so I presented the portrait to one of his ministers and waited to hear back from them. Meanwhile, I was revelling in this visit with Ryan, my friend and former partner. We got along well even though we broke up two years before. The love was still there. We were comfortable together.

Waiting for him to come home after work one day, I followed the cloud of dust that was Ryan driving his pickup along the dirt road. I think he was happy to have someone to come home to. When he parked in the driveway, I saw a little red motor scooter in the back of the truck.

"How do you like it?" he said, stroking the lustrous metal as he spoke. "I bought it for short trips around here."

We sat on the porch admiring it, and toasted its purchase with cold beer and shots of whiskey. He named it Rosy. Ryan didn't want me to ride it yet, but showed me how to start it and a few other things I couldn't remember.

I had to ride it! Before he could stop me, I hopped on and raced down the road. It was glorious to speed past the forest with wind blowing through my hair. This was the life! Then I heard a car behind me. It was Ryan; he was following me. I laughed as I looked over my shoulder at him. Suddenly the road in front of me disappeared and I flew into the bushes with the scooter landing on top of me. It happened so fast!

The underbrush was dark and filled with thorns which hurt like hell. Ryan stopped and extricated me from the shrubbery. My arm was badly scraped and so was my face. So that's why he came after me, the darling man. He knew this might happen. He hoisted the scooter into the pickup and we drove back to his cottage. I was sore. My wounds festered and swelled after a couple of days in the African heat. The local doctor put me on antibiotics, but I couldn't show myself in public for a few days until the scars on my face got better.

Ryan cooked us some trout almondine and new potatoes with fresh bread and butter. We drank cold Chardonnay and toasted our special friendship. The candles on the table gave off a warm glow and I couldn't be happier.

Days passed and my face was looking better. I guess Ryan felt that I was no longer an embarrassment, so he suggested we visit the local pub in town. It was part of the Royal Swazi Hotel, the best hotel in Mbabane. At the bar, he introduced me to a few ex-patriots who were in the country on contract work---British engineers and other nationals charged with bringing progress to Swaziland. We drank a lot in the pub that night, and afterwards headed to the hot springs to sober up. Natural sulfur hot-springs were guaranteed to cure all your ailments. But you had to swim there in the nude, that was the unwritten rule.

Only stars and moonlight lit the dark night sky. South African tourists of all races came to Swaziland to get away from the strict Apartheid rule. I doubted that many black men in South Africa had set their eyes on a naked white woman, yet there I was for all to see. A couple of young black guys helped me climb from the main pool into the hottest water-tub---a big metal barrel from where the hot spring originated. I could feel their eyes feasting on my full breasts and lady parts as they lifted me in. We were all too drunk and having fun to make an issue of anything.

That night Ryan embraced me in a dark corner of the hot spring where deep water concealed our love. I'm sure I heard him say "I love you," for the first time ever. Next day there was no hangover, only sweet, outrageous memories.

My heavenly holiday in Swaziland came to an end. We decided that I should fly back to Johannesburg instead of driving there. Ryan was the Manager of the local airline and had easy access to tickets. He drove me to a tiny airport and waited with me while luggage was being transported to the small plane.

I could hardly believe my eyes when I saw that the wooden trolly which held the passengers' bags was being hauled by a strong black woman who pulled it to the airplane by a thick strap tied around her waist. She stooped forward with the weight of her burden. This was so wrong! How could this happen in Swaziland which was a black-ruled country? I felt terrible for her and wanted to speak out to stop it. But nobody else said anything. They just let it happen and stood there in their business suits, ready to board the plane.

While we waited, Ryan pointed out one of the other passengers---a black woman wearing an elegant pant suit and a flowered scarf around her neck. He whispered that this was actually a guy who travelled to Swaziland to be operated on by a prominent surgeon who'd lost his license to practise in South Africa for performing sex changes. Now patients were forced to come to him in Swaziland. He said this scandalous case was famous and had been in all the newspapers. I was curious, and felt that I simply had to sit beside this person. Once on the plane, I maneuvered myself to a seat beside her.

It was a fascinating hour in the air. She called herself Gloria. We talked continuously and I asked her many questions. She answered honestly in her deep male voice. There was dead silence on that plane while the other passengers eavesdropped on our conversation.

She told me that all her life she'd been embarrassed by her male genitals, and finally made the decision to have surgery to become a woman. It happened in several stages. She had just undergone the last step. Her big concern now was the reaction she'd get from her colleagues when she returns to work dressed as a woman. She was a man the last time they saw her. She said that her mother and sisters always loved and supported her, and her face lit up when she spoke of the future. More than anything, she wanted to find a wonderful man and get married. I thought this person was incredibly brave. More people like her should have the courage of their convictions. At some point the steward came and offered us drinks.

"And for you *miss*?" he said facetiously, looking straight at her.

Gloria took it well and didn't flinch.

⁓

When I arrived home, there was an official looking letter stamped from Swaziland in my mailbox. I was thrilled when

I saw that it came from The King's Office. He received the portrait I painted of him! I tore open the envelope and read the words:

> "Dear Madam, Thank you for your letter. I am commanded to extend great appreciation from His Majesty for the wonderful portrait you have presented to His Majesty. He wishes to know, however, if it will not be possible that you put one or two red feathers on it because that will complete the wonderful work you have done. Yours faithfully, M.B. Mdiniso, Private Secretary to His Majesty."

I was over-the-moon to receive this acknowledgment from the King of Swaziland, and rang his Office long-distance from a payphone. They wanted to transport the portrait to my apartment by limousine the next day. It would take them four hours to drive from Mbabane. It seems that I had demoted the King by painting only ONE red feather in his hair instead of three. Well, it's because I felt that feathers in a man's hair were a bit... frivolous.

Next day the limousine and portrait arrived with much fanfare. A well-dressed driver in a dark suit and tie came with his security escort. He carefully unwrapped the parcel and gently laid it on my table. It took me forty minutes to add the additional feathers while they waited dutifully. I still smile to think that my artwork was accompanied by a security guard and driver. I'd like to believe that my portrait of King Sobhusa II still hangs in his palace to this day. Such an honour, I thought. But no mention was made of painting the King's many wives.

Some days later around nine in the evening, there was an unexpected knock on my door. I recognized the manager of the pub at the Royal Swazi Hotel. Ryan must have given him my address. He asked if I could do him a big favour and let his black female companion stay at my place for the night, because it was against the law for her to stay at any of the hotels in Johannesburg. She was the lead singer at his bar in Swaziland. His eyes pleaded with me.

"Of course she can stay," I said, hardly able to say otherwise.

He breathed a sigh of relief and thanked me warmly. Then he left his charge with me.

She was dressed like an entertainer and wore a fluffy white fur jacket, black slacks and big gold loop earrings. I offered her some tea and cheese sandwiches, and we talked about her family in Swaziland. I didn't ask what she was doing in Joburg.

That night she slept on the couch in my small studio apartment. I felt humbled and embarrassed that a talented star who worked at a first-class hotel in Swaziland was sleeping on my sofa because she wasn't allowed to stay at a hotel in South Africa. And the law was such that if someone saw her coming out of my apartment, there would be questions asked. It was a sorry state of affairs.

Unlucky Far East Trip, 1975

At long last, time came for my highly anticipated trip to the Far East and Israel. Sadly, this tour would be my undoing. I had a big group of thirty-two passengers, led by a tightly-knit clique of ten friends who insisted on being seated together for all flights, and everything else too. This wasn't always possible to arrange.

"Have you ever been to the Far East?" one of those men asked me shortly after take-off.

"No, sorry I haven't."

"How the hell can you be our tour guide if you haven't been there?"

I was so taken aback by his question that I had no answer and just stood there looking at him. I should have known his attitude was a prelude of things to come. He and his friends lacked confidence in me, which in turn made me feel incompetent. What I *should* have said is that we'll be picking up local tour guides everywhere we go. It's all been arranged from head office. His comment made me sad.

We flew a very long way to Japan with no rest. First, we flew thirteen hours from Johannesburg to Brussels, arriving there early in the morning. Most of my passengers waited in the airport to change planes, while that group of close-knit friends headed into town for a few hours. They went to the diamond dealers which Brussels is famous for.

There, the ladies sold their valuable diamond rings which earned them enough money to pay for their Far East trip. *Clever.*

At midday, we boarded an aircraft and flew another eighteen hours, touching down in Anchorage, Alaska to refuel. The word Alaska inspired fears of freezing to death for my South African passengers. One of our men, a heavy man to begin with, wore his big raccoon coat to stroll inside the Anchorage airport. He looked comical, like a big bear. I'm sure he overheated as he waddled around for an hour in the warm airport fully dressed in fur.

We continued flying from Anchorage directly over the North Pole. It was breathtaking and terrifying at the same time. The sun shone over endless snow-covered mountains as far as the eye could see. Life stood still. My passengers hadn't slept for two days, and were now sitting up fast asleep in the daylight. It was eerie. Everything seemed in slow motion. I looked out the window and prayed we wouldn't crash. There was nothing below us but frigid snow mountains in never-ending sunlight, silent and motionless.

After the fifteen-hour flight from Anchorage, we landed in Tokyo on my birthday. Nobody knew it was my birthday but me, and I secretly wished myself a happy day. Having flown forty-seven hours from Johannesburg without stopping at a hotel, we were exhausted. I think the company could have planned a rest stop or a shorter route from South Africa. Maybe this was the cheapest way to do it.

In bustling Tokyo, I strove to enjoy the trip in spite of those ten passengers who seemed determined to undermine me. They griped about almost everything, and blamed me for not being able to cater to all their demands or pay special attention to them. Their attitude sowed discord in our group and created an undercurrent of rebellion. It was troubling for me and the others.

⌒

Winter had come to Japan. Tokyo was very clean, although in my mind the city overflowed with people. Thousands of people everywhere. It seemed like slender Japanese women all wore the same style coat---long and dark. I didn't see one fat person. They were all slim. I felt larger than most of them.

People were polite and greeted each other by bowing rather than shaking hands. Our group stood out as tourists but were treated with respect and kindness. I felt there was a sense of honour amongst the Japanese. Even the humblest of shops kept their floor swept and tidy.

In restaurant windows, plastic replicas of the food served inside were put on display to show availability. Before being served our meals, the waiters brought us a tray of hot, wet cloths. We didn't know what they were for, so my passengers washed their faces and necks. I learned they were to clean our hands before eating, very hygienic.

We took many interesting side excursions. I enjoyed walking inside Nijo Castle in Kyoto which was hundreds of years old. The ruler had installed musical notes under every floorboard so he could hear if intruders came to attack him. The sound of our group walking on this floor created an interesting melody.

I remember ornately carved pagoda roofs and magical green gardens, with trees pruned into round clusters like a stairway to heaven. Curved bridges connected one side of fairyland to the other, and stepping stones allowed visitors to cross ponds filled with red and white koi. In some parks, concrete prayer lanterns were built on each side of walkways. Local Japanese people wrote greetings to their dearly departed, folded them and put them in these lanterns.

Our visit to Mikimoto Pearl Island was fascinating. There we learned how cultured pearls are created. First, a grain of sand is injected into the gonad of the oyster. Then they're put back into the sea bed and left alone from two to five years. During this time, a white pearly substance accumulates around the sand grain and a pearl is born.

Female divers called Amahs wearing white clothing dive into the oyster beds to collect those that are ready to harvest. It's a matter of chance what colour the pearls become---whether yellow, beige, pink, blue or white. Women workers dressed in black with white scarves on their heads, sat at large tables under a bright light and sorted the pearls by colour and shape. It's hoped that visitors would buy a necklace or two. I bought a pretty beige pearl necklace for my mother in Canada. She'd have to wear it often to retain the luster.

Our local guides Cherry and Tsuyoshi were wonderful. They remained with us for the duration of our tour in Japan. At one of our hotels, my room faced a golden sunset over the ocean where floating racks of seaweed beds swayed on the surface. The Japanese cultivate seaweed and eat it as commonly as North Americans eat chips. Everybody munches on it, even at the movies. And instead of chocolate boxes, you can buy ornate gift-boxes of seaweed and beautifully wrapped parcels of dried squid with their heads still on, *I'm not kidding!*

At Hakone, we stayed at a mountain resort nestled in a pine forest near Mount Fuji. At this resort we enjoyed soaking naked in large sulfur hot-springs in the forest, men in one pool and women in another. Locals used the resort as well. Most of my passengers ordered a massage in their rooms, and so did I. We were given the choice of a male or female masseuse. I asked for a male, I don't know why... perhaps because it felt more natural to be touched by a man than a woman. Later that evening, a delicate man dressed in white came to my door. He stood in the entrance shaking. Perhaps he didn't have too much professional experience, or maybe he was anxious about what else might be expected of him.

Once in my room, he asked me to undress and lie face down on the bed. He took out scented oils from his case and started to work. First, he released the tension knots in my neck, back, arms, legs and buttocks. Very relaxing. Then he turned me over for the same treatment on my front. But the experience of massaging my naked female body proved too much for him, and I permitted an indiscretion. It would not be the last. That trip to the Far East harboured secrets.

A couple of husbands hit on me. They seemed happily married so I don't know why they would. Maybe they got a kick out of trying to seduce the tour guide. That aside, weeks of dining in restaurants, trying to keep difficult passengers happy, and drinking whiskey in my private time took its toll on me. I felt friendless and alone.

Our Japanese guide Cherry came to see me one evening and found me sobbing inconsolably in my room. All the frustrations of that trip and its passengers poured forth in my tears. I asked her to lie down beside me and hold my hand. Her motherly instinct knew that I needed someone to comfort me while I cried. She was wonderful and didn't ask why I was unhappy. My sorrow was so intense that I couldn't even talk. I just cried and cried. I cried for my indiscretions and the hollowness of meaningless sex, and for the constant craving of what I yearned for most---to fall deeply in love with a man who would love me in return.

When Cherry felt I'd cried myself out, she tucked me in and said goodnight. I wondered what she thought of me.

Next day, my group and I were scheduled to fly to Taiwan. We arrived in Taipei on December 25th. The mainly Buddhist population doesn't celebrate Christmas there, so my group of passengers raised a glass in our hotel restaurant to wish each other a Merry Christmas. We were booked to tour around the Taiwanese countryside for a few days. My most vivid memory from that place was of seeing farmers plowing their flooded rice paddies using water buffalo.

Those five defiant couples didn't tour with us in Taiwan. They flew ahead to Macau to shop for deals. I didn't try to stop them. Macau is located right across the Pearl River Estuary from Hong Kong. You could see Hong Kong in the distance. I don't know how they managed to change their flights or get into their hotel early. Perhaps Cherry arranged it.

When we arrived in Macau, we joined that wayward group of friends at our hotel. They were all excited about the great deals they'd found in the shops. That vibrant city was pulsating. People spilled over into the streets, more people than I'd ever seen in my life! Brightly coloured neon signs stuck out from shops, each competing for attention. The place buzzed with activity. The scene in front of my eyes was in perpetual motion. Some locals cooked in the alleys behind the main streets. For me, the stench was nauseating.

Shoppers love Macau, with its dizzying array of merchandise screaming to be bought. I didn't feel like shopping and felt better when we got away from the crowds for a boat ride in the harbour where we saw people living on houseboats. I was struck by the overwhelming dark green and brown colours of the scene. Brown covered sampans were tied to each other and housed families. The water smelled dank. Green or black tarpaulins were fastened over other ships where more families lived, their inhabitants dressed in dreary browns. Women cooked meals and washed clothes for their families on those boats. How all those vessels managed to maneuver in that congested harbour was beyond me.

⌒〜

After a few days in Macau and Hong Kong, we flew to neighbouring Bangkok. I'm told it's a magical place where all things happen. Men especially love it, because "man is king," in Thailand. Local women treat them well. I've heard that anything goes in Bangkok.

Thankfully, our tour was organized to hide the seedier side of life there. We visited magnificent temples with walls covered by mosaic which twinkled like shining stars, and golden rooftops glistened in the sunshine. We saw how silkworms produce their silk, and enjoyed lunch while watching graceful Thai dancers in ornamental head dresses and extended metal fingertips. Those smiling women performed outdoors for us. They danced on the lawn while we ate lunch at tables set in the garden.

For me, the most interesting part of our visit to Thailand was our trip to the Floating Market in Bangkok. Waves from countless tourist boats threatened to overwhelm the flimsy shacks built on stilts belonging to people who lived on that brown river. Thai farmers plied their colourful fruits and vegetables in boats up and down this busy canal, while we tourists were ferried in covered barges to view this lifestyle very foreign to us.

I think the locals must have iron-strong immune systems to live on that waterway. We saw one man crouch on a platform by the river's edge outside his wooden shack. He washed himself, brushed his teeth, and probably emptied his potty---all in the same water. We westerners would surely die.

Israel

The last stop on our tour was Israel. Armed guards met my passengers at customs in Ben Gurion Airport and promptly singled out two dark-skinned young men of Indian descent. With no explanation, they led those frightened boys to a separate room. They didn't ask to speak to the tour leader (me) but just took them away! I tried to intervene, but the officials had no interest in talking to me. I felt helpless and at a loss for what I should do.

One of my elderly passengers was a retired Member of Parliament who tried to present himself on behalf of the boys. He rejoined us ten minutes later but didn't know if he benefited the situation or not. We were detained for over an hour while officials grilled the teenagers about their backgrounds and possible terrorist links. I can't blame them for being careful, but those boys came from affluent South African families who could afford to send their sons abroad to expand their view of the world.

When the officials were satisfied that the young men posed no threat, we were permitted to leave. Our Israeli tour guide met us in his army uniform right outside the airport. After he put us on our bus to the hotel, he threw his rifle in the trunk of his car and drove back to the army. I liked him; he was no-nonsense.

Jerusalem was especially pretty. Buildings were constructed from light-coloured Jerusalem stone. We visited all the places mentioned in the Bible---the Old Jewish Quarter, the Wailing Wall, and the grotto where it's said that Jesus was born. I stayed in that small grotto with earthen walls for a long time and prayed to be forgiven for my sins on that tour. Then we followed Jesus's last walk where he bore the cross along Via Dolorosa. We continued by coach to the Garden of Gethsemane, and eventually ascended to The Mount of Olives. It was awesome to see those holy places.

While in Jerusalem, I looked up a former classmate from the London Film School---Rachel, who lived in Kiriyat Menachem, a suburb of East Jerusalem. She had married a fellow Israeli student and they both found jobs in the country's film industry. She made cookies for me and served tea in her small kitchen. To my delight, their four-year-old son Aaron joined us. He was a beautiful boy with dark hair and expressive brown eyes. I hugged him fervently, and longed for a child like him of my own.

Rachel told me they worried about the safety of their son due to political upheaval and terrorists on Israel's borders.

"Why don't you send Aaron to me in South Africa?" I said. "I can keep him safe until things settle down in Israel."

She stared at me with big blue eyes, stunned that I could even suggest it. She didn't answer. I kept repeating that I'd love to care for him until she sent for him. I may have said it too many times.

"Okay, okay Eva!" she said to shut me up, then turned her back on me to wash the dishes.

I should have realized that no mother would give her precious child to someone else for safe-keeping unless disaster was imminent. She would want to protect her own child. Aaron was a captivating, bright little boy. I yearned for a husband and children to love. Would it ever happen?

"You're very lucky," I said, hugging Rachel goodbye.

Hopefully she understood my heart's desire, but I fear she may have thought that I wanted to take her child from her.

No trip to Israel would be complete without a swim in the Dead Sea. This was my happiest memory from that ill-fated tour. The passengers and I had fun. We could sit in the water, stick our feet up very high and stay like that without sinking. My group laughed as they floated near the top of the water; it was such an amusing sensation. The salt and mineral content in the Dead Sea is very high at 50-55 %. It stung a little and left my hair oily and tasting of licorice.

On our last night in Jerusalem, I was walking towards my hotel room and saw Charlie, a husband from that difficult clique, standing in the corridor watching people pass by. He smiled and seemed relaxed as he surveyed the scene. He said his wife had a terrible cold and he'd rented another room so he wouldn't catch it from her. He asked me casually if I'd like to come in for coffee since he had a coffee-maker.

I had nothing to do but pack my bags, and took it as an innocent invitation. We chatted about how much he had enjoyed the tour. He produced some biscuits which he offered me, along with freshly brewed coffee. He asked if he could add a shot of brandy to the coffee. Yes, please. It was pleasant to have a friendly conversation and laugh again, as I'd felt lonely and confronted on this trip so far. One thing led to another, and to my surprise he caressed my leg in a way that set me on fire. Then he kissed my neck which drove me mad with desire. This was unexpected and I should have left right away, but I didn't. He brought my body to life and I hungered for more. The nerves in my body were alight and I responded to his every touch. He seduced me with his sexual prowess, and seemed pleased with himself to have given me pleasure and aroused such passion in me. Hopefully he would keep this indiscretion to himself. This was not supposed to happen.

Next morning our group assembled in the foyer for our departure to the airport. Charlie was there too but he wasn't seated with his wife. He was still smiling, lost in dreamland with a goofy look on his face. I paid no special attention to him and treated him like any of my other passengers.

Aside from Maurice who was twice my age, no man since Ryan had truly captured my heart. I used the men who were attracted to me to satisfy my own hunger, but longed to find one that I could love again. My recent liaisons gave me momentary pleasure with no strings attached. I didn't expect or ask for anything. Although I still treasured Ryan in spite of everything, he had hardened my heart and spoiled me for other men. I no longer dared to say that I loved a man in case it scared him off. Nor could I trust any man. Ryan's infidelities taught me that most men are unable to commit to one woman. Only a happily married fellow or one scared of getting caught might be able to resist temptation. I longed to develop feelings for someone and get ensnared by love. If the magic happens, there's the possibility of a happy ending. If there's no magic, the affair ends and the cycle begins again---searching and hoping.

As these thoughts coursed through my mind, I was grateful that this unhappy month-long tour to the Far East had come to an end. I wanted to forget it ever happened. Our arrival in Johannesburg was only hours away.

Office Fight

After returning to the travel office, I had a big argument with my boss and a girl in the office. First came the argument with the girl. I hadn't heard the rumour that she was sleeping with the boss's nephew. Perhaps their affair made her more privileged than the rest of us. She was a beautiful married woman, and I was placed at the desk right beside her. I heard what she said to customers on the telephone; nothing but negativity came out of her mouth. She didn't try to sell tours or be helpful to clients, no enthusiasm. None of my colleagues could see past her beauty or hear what she was saying but me.

After a few days of listening to her rubbish, I couldn't stand it any longer. I picked up my small desk and moved it across the floor to the other end of the office. I sat there and did what little filing they asked me to do, and wrote letters to my parents. This protest did not bode well for me. The boss asked to see me in his office, his face red with anger.

"What the hell is the matter with you?" he said.

"Well, I'd much rather be out on tour than sitting in the office."

"You'll do what you're told, or you can bloody well piss off!" He pounded his fist on the desk.

I heard he'd said the same thing to other employees when he wanted them gone. But those girls got so upset that they took their things and left on the spot. I wondered if he had heard about my indiscretions on the last tour? More harsh words were said by both of us. I left his office and slammed the door on my way out.

I did piss off, but not before attending a birthday party that afternoon which he hosted in the office for one of his employees. Not wanting to give him the satisfaction of seeing me leave upset, I drank a glass of red wine with the rest of the staff, ate the birthday cake and socialized. I think the boss was uncomfortable by my presence; he didn't look at me. I was crying on the inside but stayed until the last hour and took the bus home with Yvonne. That's when I told her I won't be returning to work.

"What? Oh no!" She was surprised, especially that I'd been composed enough to stay for the party.

It was just as well that I'd be leaving. Even though all my expenses were paid for, living in hotels and eating rich food, drinking alcohol and managing difficult passengers was a stressful, lonely life. I had to be satisfied that I'd seen so much of the world. Those luxury tours would have been impossible for me to afford on my own. But now, I had to think about what to do next.

A Strict Diet

Thankfully, I had enough money saved to live on for the next two months. Another art exhibition at Joubert Park would soon take place and I started preparing for it. My paintings usually sold well there. Meanwhile, I'd heard about a great diet doctor who came highly recommended. I weighed 164 pounds and felt terrific, but it's possible that I should weigh less for my 5'2" height. Mimi and I were the same height, and she was very slender. I visualized myself as slim as her.

The diet doctor was charismatic, with laughing brown eyes. We were a group of twenty fat people who'd come to him for a miracle. First, he lectured us with instructions for two days, after which we followed a diet based on the findings of Dr. Simeons. This included periodic injections of Human Gonotrophic Hormone derived from the urine of pregnant women. We were given sterile needles and vials containing the serum to take home. I injected myself, usually in the upper buttock. It was creepy. I had to make sure to squirt a little liquid into the air before sticking the needle in me. It had to be a different spot every time.

The doctor also stressed the importance of drinking at least ten to fifteen glasses of water per day to flush out fat and toxins. We had to measure every ounce of food, and fear for our lives if we ever broke that diet. He said if we ate even one grain of sugar the diet would work in reverse and we'd gain weight. He had us hypnotized. I hung on his every word. I weighed my meat or fish in advance and froze the portions. The diet was working. After two months I weighed 132 pounds. Our caloric intake was extremely low (about 600 calories) although the food was nutritious. I lost weight, but lacked my former energy. It was all I could do to drag myself out for a walk every day to the grocery store.

On one such trip to buy food, I carried my handbag on its strap over my shoulder. I picked out a piece of filet mignon, fresh cod fish, some fruit and green vegetables. As I walked in the produce isle, I felt a feather-like touch on my side but thought nothing of it. When I got to the checkout to pay, the cash in the upper compartment of my purse was gone! I looked around incredulously. Whoever got into my purse and delicately plucked the cash without my noticing, he surely deserved it. He was very good at what he did. I couldn't be angry. I was truly flabbergasted, and admired his dexterity.

Next day on my walk, a jolly black man greeted me with a gigantic smile. He bowed, tipped his hat and said, "Good morning, Madam." I smiled back and wondered if it was him. If so, at least he was grateful. His cheerful greeting may have been his way of saying thank you.

At night I was freezing cold, just as the doctor predicted I would be. There was much less fat on our bodies to keep us warm. I slept fully-clothed with pantyhose, jeans, big socks, under-vest, sweater and a hat. Warm blankets covered me, and my portable heater was turned on beside me. It would take another month of strict dieting to reach my goal of 116 pounds. After reaching my target weight, the doctor would teach me how to gradually introduce more foods and stabilize my weight.

That diet was a turning point and taught me discipline for the first time in my life. I hadn't touched a drop of alcohol for two months. When friends came to visit, we sat on my comfortable furniture and enjoyed each other's company. Everyone was welcome. Some of my acquaintances didn't know one another, so I introduced them and we discussed all sorts of interesting topics. I could easily serve them wine and cheese while I drank only water. In the daytime I painted portraits, while guests came to see me in the evenings. Having no telephone, it was always a surprise who would show up.

When my friends invited me to *their* place for dinner, I went for the pleasure of their company. I was content to sniff the buttered garlic prawns or whatever they were eating without being tempted to indulge. It wasn't difficult because I completely believed the good doctor about the fate awaiting me should I ever break the diet. I was the perfect patient.

He Came with Angels

A well-dressed man and woman knocked on my apartment door. They came to save my soul. They were Jehovah Witnesses spreading the word of God. I recognized the man, Carl, a good-looking blond fellow from Czechoslovakia. He remembered me from the ill-fated casting company in downtown Johannesburg where he brought us a set of glossy photos in high hopes of getting a modeling job. He was tall and muscular, and escaped his country when Russian tanks rolled through Czechoslovakia in 1968.

Standing before me now, he was a changed man. He was just an ordinary guy back then, but now he was quite extraordinary, beautiful and spiritual. He had found meaning and purpose in his life. It almost seemed like there was a halo above his golden hair and that he was filled with the holy spirit. I definitely needed saving, but didn't want to commit to regular visits and politely declined their offer for a second appointment.

Two days later there was a knock on my door. It was Carl. He came alone this time and said he wanted to teach me about the Bible.

"I think you would be receptive of the Lord," he said, as he gestured to the Bible in his hand.

Still being on a strict diet, I couldn't have much of a social life in any case. This restrictive diet was transforming me physically, so perhaps it was fate that I should become a better person spiritually as well. I agreed to weekly visits from this lovely man who was so keen to save me. He brought his Bible which we read and discussed each time he came.

One evening as I stood at my easel working on a portrait, I felt a slight brush against my back as if a feather touched me. I looked around to see what it could be, but there was nothing there. A second later, Carl knocked on the door. It's as though his spiritual angels came before him to announce his coming. I was impressed, and he took on an even brighter glow.

As time went on, he became truly beautiful in my eyes. We sat respectfully across from one another to discuss the Bible, or rather---the Jehovah Witness's version of the New Testament which was foreign to me. I had a hard time accepting some of their beliefs, especially that only 144,000 souls will get into heaven on the inevitable day of Armageddon. What about the millions of other good people who surely deserved to be there? But all of that didn't matter. The important thing was that *he* believed it. His faith made him sublime, holy and untouchable.

He tried earnestly to convert me. Once weekly visits became twice a week, and soon three times per week. In my view, he came accompanied by a host of angels in their divine light.

His church advocated there must be no sex before marriage. This doctrine was supposed to increase the desire between a man and woman, thus making their union special and blessed. He spoke to me about his church's rules of expected behaviour, that women should be modest and not look directly at men, but rather cast their eyes down when speaking to a man... *really?* Also, men and women were segregated at church. I listened to his every word, although I didn't always agree.

As weeks passed, I became captivated by this lovely man who did not make a pass at me or try to have sex because we were not married. I think he was falling for me too. Did I really have to marry this fellow for him to make love to me? I was considering it.

Over a period of two months, I grew dizzy with unfulfilled desire for this golden man with high principals. He told me all kinds of wondrous things about Jesus and the Almighty. I looked forward to each visit. My heart swelled with anticipation and he was all I could think about. He was unavailable, hence my yearning for him grew to fever pitch. How do you make love to an angel?

Suddenly the visits stopped. There was nothing!

Then after two weeks he showed up at my door. But no spiritual beings announced his arrival; something was missing. He was an ordinary man again. It seemed like he had stopped believing. How tragic. The beauty of his person and the magic web his spirituality had woven around him was gone. He no longer talked about getting into heaven through good deeds. I was disappointed by the lack of holiness which usually surrounded him; he was like a deflated balloon.

Now a regular guy once more, he picked me up and carried me to my bed. He wasted no time on foreplay. Both of us had repressed our desire for two months in favour of heavenly ordinance, but now his religious principles had flown out the window. Our consummation was enjoyable, but the magic of his person was gone. He was no longer special and untouchable. My angel had fallen from grace.

I asked what happened to make him leave the church. He said that he'd become disillusioned by their strict doctrine. He confessed that it was against their rules that he, as a man, should preach to me without a second person being present. Also, his girlfriend returned to live with him and she didn't agree with his church.

I didn't know he had a girlfriend. It seems they broke up before he joined the church. Without her, he became a lost person searching for direction. When he encountered some Jehovah Witnesses out canvassing, it was just what he needed. He soaked it up. Their religion gave purpose to his life and he found comfort in belonging to a "church family." Now he was empty and adrift again, a different person from the man I'd become fascinated by. Sadly, I lost interest in him without his beliefs which had made him so beautiful.

Getting Slimmer

ABBA's song SOS blasted through my walls every time my neighbour had a party. It drove me crazy! I lay in bed fully dressed in my hat and sweaters, trying to sleep and keep warm while being forced to endure that song over and over again. One evening I reached my limit and pounded on his door. He and his roommates invited me in, happy that an additional female had dropped in from the heavens.

About twenty guests were sprawled on sofas and easy chairs, or dancing to that infernal song. My neighbour introduced himself as Frank. He was so friendly that my resolve to show outrage at the noise soon melted away. After spending half an hour in the warmth of their hospitality, I went home. They turned their music down.

Still following the strict diet, I eventually reached 110 pounds. My friends told me that I looked like a bag of bones, so the doctor coached me how to get up to 116 pounds. This turned out to be my perfect weight. I felt good. Needing new clothes, I bought some white Capris and colourful batik T-shirts which suited me well.

During the night, I ate cream puffs and chocolate éclairs, savouring delicious fresh cream on my tongue and enjoying it immensely. My heart sank when I realized that I'd broken my diet and would gain back all my weight. This was followed by a huge sigh of relief when I woke up and realized it was just a dream. It felt so real. All that good taste and satisfaction without the calories.

After those fifty pounds came off, I could fly like a bird up nine flights of stairs to my apartment. Before this, my friends had to push me up hills. Now my upper thighs didn't rub together in the heat. My only complaint was that my tail bone hurt to sit in my bath or on other hard surfaces. This was a new experience.

To my surprise and delight, the slimmer I got, the more men turned around to look at me. Some even asked for directions. *When do men ever ask for directions?* Amused, I would smile back and answer their pretend questions.

One afternoon, I spotted a former passenger from my Far East tour sitting alone in a coffee shop. He was an older gent who'd taken the trip with his young wife. His wife was insanely jealous which I learned on tour when I walked beside her husband in the narrow hotel corridor, thus forcing her to walk a few steps behind us.

"He is *my* husband!" she screamed at me.

Shocked by her outburst, it took me a second to grasp her problem.

"Of course," I said, and fell in behind them, letting her walk beside her man.

Poor fellow to have such an insecure, jealous wife.

Seeing him now, I wanted to say hello and sat myself down at his table. He looked around nervously, afraid somebody would see us.

"Sorry, but I can't be seen with you. You've lost so much weight that you're not the same person. One of my wife's girlfriends might drive by and see me with a woman and then I'll be in big trouble!"

With that he jumped up and ran away. As I watched him rush out, it dawned on me that I must look very different now. I was half flattered and half offended by his sudden departure

There was a knock on my door one day. To my surprise, it was the diet doctor himself. My jaw must have dropped to see him standing there.

Not knowing what else to do, I invited him in. He sat on one of my easy chairs which by now had migrated to the window thanks to the maid's sense of decor. I offered him carrot sticks and water. He didn't drink coffee, and I had no alcohol in my cupboards. He asked me to sit next to him on the armrest of his chair. Weighing only 116 pounds, that was no longer an issue. He seemed at ease and started to chuckle.

What's so funny?" I said.

"I can't believe I'm sitting in this place with you and munching on carrots!"

He looked around my sparsely-furnished studio apartment with a wooden crate for a coffee table. Perhaps he thought he was slumming it, being here. I was a bit confused as to why he'd come. Maybe he considered me his weight-loss success star and felt entitled to drop in, but I was starting to feel uncomfortable. I didn't want to get involved with him and suggested we go for a walk.

He put his arm around me as we strolled round the block and talked about the diet. He looked down and mumbled something as we walked.

"Pardon?" I asked.

"No, you must never think about it as bullshit," he said, still looking down.

What? I stopped and stared at him. At that very moment, I realized that all of it *must* have been bullshit, or why would he mention that word? Suddenly I understood that I'd lost the weight by following a low-calorie nutritious diet and sticking to it with no exceptions. It was as simple as that. I'd lost fifty pounds in three months and received instructions on how to maintain the weight. The doctor had done his job well and kept me true to that diet. But the spell was broken now. I felt disillusioned to guess the simple truth, yet it had worked. That diet would change my life forever. And the good doctor soon understood that any future maintenance appointments would be strictly professional.

A Surprise Visit

Max came to my door. I almost fainted from shock. It had been months since we last met. The sight of him brought back sad memories of being with him when his son was killed. We'd never been intimate after that. I couldn't. Now here he was ....

"Do you ever wonder if God was punishing you for cheating on your wife?" I said thoughtlessly, ignoring that I bore part of the blame.

He lowered his eyes, not expecting this cool reception. An awkward silence followed.

"I've come because I'd like you to paint portraits of my three boys," he said, shrugging off my heartless words.

He wanted me to go to Pretoria with him and choose some photos from his family albums to paint from. He seemed sincere and genuinely wanted me to do this. We chatted a bit, and I got over my initial discomfort at seeing him. I could certainly use the income.

We drove to Pretoria in his Jaguar, or should I say we *floated*. I've never driven in a smoother car. It felt like gliding on heavenly wings. His home in Pretoria was in a state of flux with renovations everywhere. A pretty woman in white slacks greeted us---Max's wife. I felt a pang of apprehension. I tried hard to pretend Max and I were casual acquaintances and that I was there as an artist to paint their three sons, including the one who was killed.

Guilt must have shown on my face. I felt like a hypocrite and was sure my shame was in the aura all around me. It was hard to look his wife in the eye. I continued to feign nonchalance, but when I saw this lovely woman it was difficult for me to understand why Max strayed. She was friendly and pretty, with long brown hair and a sweet smile.

We sat beside each other on the sofa and leafed through their family albums. Our bare arms accidentally touched. She felt warm and soft. I wanted to put my arm around this woman and embrace her---this grieving mother and wronged wife, and tell her how sorry I was for everything. But I refrained. Eventually we decided on three happy photos of the boys.

Max showed me the wall where the portraits would hang. Then he and his wife took me outside to their back yard where they buried the ashes of their son. There was a marble gravestone with an angel on top, and a red rose bush planted in the ground just below it. I remember the words "Loved and Gone too Soon." It seemed evident that his wife didn't know about me and her husband. It was a somber drive back to Johannesburg with Max.

I painted the three portraits well and tried not to be sad while doing them. Max came to collect them two weeks later and thought they were splendid. His eyes welled up with tears as he studied them pinned to my wall, and tenderly touched the one of his dead son. I felt a kinship with him over this shared tragedy and reached for his hand as he stood there. He pulled me towards him and hugged me tightly for a long moment. Then we sat quietly in my living room while he composed himself. A deep feeling of friendship and understanding passed between us. We both knew this was goodbye.

To Swaziland with Mimi

Ryan invited me and Mimi to visit him in Swaziland for the weekend. He and his buddy Michael would meet us in a pub just across the Swazi border. We looked forward to some fun and drove off on Friday evening after Mimi finished work. We knew it was a four-hour drive and the border would close at 10 p.m. sharp. She did the driving while I was supposed to navigate.

Nightfall came as we drove. I searched desperately on the map for names of towns or routes, but nothing matched the road we were on. I forgot to tell Mimi that I had no sense of direction.

"It's okay, we must be on the right track," I said, trying to sound reassuring.

But we were miserably lost. We were almost out of gas and nowhere near the border. Gasoline rationing was still in effect, so no petrol could be bought after 6 p.m. on Friday. We saw the welcoming lights of a convenience store in the distance. A sympathetic customer gave us a container of gas when he heard we were lost and out of petrol. Then he pointed us in the direction of Swaziland.

Mimi drove like mad to recuperate all that wasted time, but the wooden border-post slammed down just as we reached it. That border was firmly closed until morning.

Nothing I could say convinced those stubborn guards to let us through, and we were forced to spend the night in her car.

I thought about Ryan and his friend waiting impatiently for us at the bar, getting more drunk as the night wore on. It was impossible to call and let them know what was happening. We tried to make ourselves comfortable for sleep but we were freezing. I was afraid Mimi would catch a cold, so I kept covering her face with a sweater while she slept but she kept throwing it off. Eventually morning came and we got through. We cruised around downtown Mbabane and spotted Ryan having brunch at a patio restaurant.

"Ah, you decided to turn up after all," he said, half angry but pleased.

He and his friend Michael had waited for hours at the bar for us. They were convinced we'd stood them up. I explained that we got lost and were stuck at the border all night.

"I was navigating," I said, mumbling into my blouse.

"Ah, that explains it," he chuckled, and shook his head knowingly.

We followed Ryan's car as he led the way, turning left on Pine Valley Drive to his cottage. We drove past fields lit by golden sunlight and arrived at his white stucco cottage on the hill. There we unpacked our bags and relaxed with an ice-cold beer on his shaded veranda. It was heavenly to be surrounded by nature.

We talked about what to do when evening came. Ryan suggested we go to the casino for their special Saturday night entertainment. Later, he cooked us a great dinner of steak and salad accompanied by a bottle of Merlot. Then Mimi and I got dressed in our best, me in a hot-pink décolleté gown and she in a sequined black cocktail dress. We were ready! Ryan's pickup truck was too small for three people, so Mimi handed her car keys to Ryan and let "the Man" drive.

Ryan was in his element, lively and happy as he showed us the different gambling stations in this large casino attached to the Royal Swazi Hotel. The room looked like a cross between a busy arcade and a fancy chamber at the Palace of Versailles. There were mirrors on the ceiling, gold lights reflected on walls, and neon lights flashing on the zinging slot machines; noise and bustle everywhere.

I noticed lots of South African visitors at the blackjack tables and spinning roulette wheels. Gambling was illegal in South Africa, so they came here. Some gamblers were deeply engrossed in their games. They took it so seriously, with worried looks on their faces. Clinking sounds came from hundreds of coins as they spewed from the one-arm-bandits. A few players worked on two of those noisy machines at the same time, turning rhythmically to play from one to the other without stopping, then cursing when they lost. It was all so silly. Looking around, I found it ridiculous and started to laugh at the foolishness of it all. Soon, I was doubled over with laughter. I couldn't stop!

"What is the matter with you?" Mimi said. "You *must* stop laughing or somebody will get angry and smack you!"

Trying to compose myself, I stepped into a corridor where the frenzied players were out of my sight. Once calm, I returned to the party zone where Ryan found me. He came with a Perrier water for me and a beer for himself. We talked for a bit, then he suddenly handed me his drink.

"Hold this for a minute while I go to the loo," he said, then he dashed off.

I stood holding his beer for ten minutes, thirty minutes, and then for one hour. I felt like a fool. Ryan had vanished!

While I waited with beer in hand, Charlie, the sexy

passenger from my Far East tour spotted me. I was surprised to see him and felt a flutter of excitement. *Should I turn and leave?* Too late. I stayed put as he approached me. He'd come to the casino for the weekend with his South African friends and stood facing me now, shuffling his feet nervously like a schoolboy.

"Can I see you again?" he said, after some small talk.

Almost immediately, his two best friends who were also on that Far East tour, came up alongside him, one man on each side. They ferried him back to his wife like a stray sheep.

Charlie must have told them our secret. I had to smile as I watched them whisk him away to safety. Then that whole group who had caused me so much grief on the tour marched over to me, including Charlie and his wife. Each woman held onto her man tightly by the arm. *Silly women, I don't want your men.* They kept staring at my new figure. We chatted mindlessly about nothing in particular and then they left. The ladies seemed satisfied to learn that I was waiting for my boyfriend.

Like an idiot, I held Ryan's beer for two hours. Mimi and I assumed that Ryan must have spotted a lady friend and gone to her room with her. By now, the casino was about to close. Most of the patrons had left except for Mimi, myself, and Ryan's friend Michael who grasped the dilemma we were in. Mimi had given Ryan her car keys so we couldn't even drive ourselves to his cottage. We waited until 2 a.m. then Security asked us to vacate the premises. Michael drove us to his own apartment where we melted into his living room chairs and waited for morning.

Ryan must have figured that his buddy would take care of us. He finally showed up at Michael's door at nine in the morning and asked him what happened to us. Michael said that his two guests were safe and waiting for him. Mimi was adamant that I should not reprimand Ryan for abandoning us on the casino floor, so I said nothing. The ride back to his cottage was depressing. My mood had sunk real low by then. Neither Mimi nor I said a word.

❧

That Sunday morning was warm and sunny. Mimi and I decided to forget about Ryan's bad behaviour and go for a swim at a nearby waterfall. We took Ryan's young dog with us, a golden Lab named Prince. I love dogs and became very fond of him. When he snuggled to my chest, I stroked his silky fur and could smell his special puppy scent. We suntanned on the rocks, lulled by the relaxing sound of the falls. This waterfall formed a wide pool which flowed downstream at a good pace. We knew it was important to swim in moving water because stagnant water bred the dreaded bilharzia parasite.

I felt like a swim and ventured in. The water was cool and refreshing. But the farther out I got, the more concerned the dog became. He paced up and down on the shore barking at me, wanting to rescue me but afraid to do so. He'd never been swimming before. When I was far enough out that only my head showed above water, Prince was in full panic mode and didn't stop howling until I got back to shore, that darling dog.

When we returned to the cottage, Mimi rested while I took Prince for a walk along the dirt road below the house. He was full of joy and bounded in the bushes alongside me. I couldn't see him, but heard him cracking branches as he ran. In the distance, two men walked toward me from the opposite direction. Suddenly there was Prince, right beside me and ready to protect. I loved that dog.

After saying goodbye to Ryan (forgiven but not

forgotten), Mimi and I drove back to Johannesburg by daylight when it easier to find our way. We never did chastise Ryan for what happened at the casino the night before.

Vacation to Paradise

Those months of dieting had been grueling. I'd lost the weight and longed for sun and sea. When Yvonne suggested that we take a two-week holiday to Mauritius, I was thrilled. Exotic, tropical Mauritius! I'd seen photographs of that island paradise with its white beaches and turquoise ocean. This was something to look forward to! We'd be staying with her French-speaking relatives scattered all over the island.

I bought some clothes for the trip from my favourite thrift store---sundresses, long skirts and shorts. It felt surreal to shop for such a tiny size. I didn't have an once of fat on me.

The big day came. We flew to Mauritius and arrived in the city of Curepipe. Our taxi let us off at Tante Lise's home. She was Yvonne's maiden aunt who lived in an older house which Maurice bought for her long ago. Lise was Maurice's late wife's sister. She was overjoyed to have her niece visit and made such a fuss. Yvonne loved being spoiled by doting aunties.

Antoinette, Lise's faithful housemaid, cooked our first meal of roast duck with vegetables and rice. This was awkward. My maintenance diet forbade such food. Duck is a fatty bird, and rice with gravy were a no-no. I just cut up the food and moved it around on my plate, pretending to eat.

The diet doctor's lessons were ingrained in my brain. But I loved a certain squash called calabash which grew in the garden. Lise steamed it for me and I ate the whole thing.

Next, we stayed with Tante Claudette, another of Yvonne's many aunts. Claudette was one of Maurice's twelve siblings. A family photograph on the mantelpiece caught my eye. Maurice's parents were seated in the middle, surrounded by their thirteen children. Such a huge family. I found it hard to imagine a woman's body going through thirteen pregnancies. Perhaps I would have fared the same back then.

A mouse scurried across the room as we sat watching television one evening. Nobody reacted; they simply stayed focused on the screen. A few minutes later it ran back again and that was enough for me! I screamed and ran into the bedroom and slammed the door. They all laughed at me. It was common in Mauritius to share one's house with a few mice, no big deal.

Tante Claudette and her husband ferried us by motorboat to an exquisite beach on an island called Iles aux Cerfs. It was like paradise, with fine white sand and clear turquoise water which drifted in between sandbars. We didn't have to venture far out to enjoy the sea. I ran in the shallow water which joined two islands, the second being Belle Mer. The sun was strong and we cooled off in the calm water. It was glorious.

Yvonne rented a car and showed me the secrets of the island. Waterlily pads grew as big as dinner plates in Le Jardin des Pamplemousses. Their white flowers grew to be colossal. Along the way, we passed East Indian women carrying large bundles of tea branches on their heads. Further on, shaved cinnamon bark was laid to dry on large woven mats outside a shack in the forest. Then we drove past a small pink Hindu chapel decorated with brightly-coloured paintings of gods on each side of the building. Sweet-smelling flowers were planted along the path leading to this tiny temple. Next, Yvonne showed me bayous trees whose enormous twisted roots grew down into the soil. This was a lot to take in. She grew up on this island and knew it well. I felt like Alice in Wonderland marvelling at all this beauty.

We had the most fun staying with another of Yvonne's aunts---Tante Jeanette and her husband, at their beach house in Grand Baie, the riviera of Mauritius. Yvonne's four male cousins from that family arrived to greet us. They lived elsewhere with their wives or girlfriends.

Those handsome young men were Maurice's nephews, related by blood. I could feel their sensuality and was immediately attracted to one in particular. He was dark-haired with brown eyes and full lips. The magnetic pull between us was so strong that in my repressed state of desire, I saw spots and almost fainted. His girlfriend must have sensed the appeal and didn't let him out of her sight.

∽

When Yvonne came to town, it was a happy event. We were invited to a flurry of parties. Her relatives threw a big celebration for the extended family at one of their elegant homes where her male cousins entertained us with their lively rock and roll music. I'd gotten used to my quiet life in Johannesburg, and grew giddy with all this activity around me. Guests laughed, danced, talked, drank wine and ate tasty appetizers.

I looked around at everyone. The women wore long skirts or dresses which showed off their lovely tanned skin. Most of the guys wore white yacht pants and short-sleeved shirts. French people were the elites of the island, the civilized colonialists who owned property and boats. I would never have met any of them if it weren't for Yvonne.

I learned that here like everywhere else in the world, social snobbism existed. There was no official Apartheid like in South Africa, yet there was economic and unspoken racial segregation. Yvonne once mentioned derisively that one of her cousins married a woman of mixed blood and it caused a scandal. Everybody knew who's who on the island. When her elderly relatives heard news of an upcoming marriage, they would say something like "a Montpelier is marrying a Desormeaux," the surnames of old established families.

I was standing at the hors d'oeuvres table and noticed how much the musicians enjoyed playing together. They joked and laughed between songs. One fellow stood out from the rest and played as if he was really having a good time. After the song ended, he approached me to chat. His name was Jerome. He was a distant cousin of Yvonne's by marriage. He asked me where I was from and a few other questions.

There was something intriguing about this man. He seemed funny and intelligent and wore glasses. *I just love men in glasses!* He was fairly short and not especially good-looking, but that didn't matter because he was bursting with personality. We had lots to talk about. The set was about to start and the band called for him. He put down his plate of food and turned to me, gently touching my arm.

"Please wait here and don't leave until I come back. Wait for me, let's talk some more."

I watched as he and the other performers entertained us. He radiated good humour. I felt an excitement which I hadn't experienced in a long time. He told me later that he knew we would get to know each other better.

Our last week in Mauritius was a whirlwind of social events. Jerome was on vacation in Grand Baie and spent every day with me and Yvonne. I learned that he was well-educated and worked as an executive for a large insurance company. He made me feel alive and I cherished every moment with him. Could this be the man fate had in store for me?

The three of us spent our days sight-seeing and swimming. Jerome rented his own holiday lodgings nearby and met us daily. One time his friends asked us to join them for a spin in their boat, but I was fully dressed and couldn't wade out in the water. Jerome was wearing his swim suit, picked me up and carried me to the boat. I felt so petite. If I were fifty pounds heavier like I used to be, I'm sure he wouldn't have noticed me or picked me up to carry me. It was my new secret pleasure---to be lifted in the arms of a man without causing him to rupture a hernia.

Our holiday on this paradise island came to an end. Jerome drove us back to Tante Lise's place in Curepipe so we'd be closer to the airport for our departure. It turns out that he rented the annexed apartment belonging to Tante Lise---she was his landlady! He lived at her place when he wasn't on holiday in Grand Baie.

When Yvonne and I first arrived in Mauritius, Lise told us that she had a boarder. She even showed us his quaint apartment and pointed to his collection of primitive musical instruments which hung on the wall. At the time, I wondered what kind of person lived in this interesting apartment. I had no idea it belonged to the man I'd fall in love with. Our friendship seemed destined-to-be.

After we all ate supper in Lise's kitchen on the eve of our departure, I spent a couple of hours alone with Jerome in his apartment next door. His conversation stimulated my mind. I could see myself with this exceptional man. He was full of life and zest. He proudly showed me each of the musical instruments in his collection, many of them antique guitars. There was also a goat-skin tambourine which he bought when travelling through villages in the countryside. He bubbled with enthusiasm, and spoke of returning to those hamlets one day to collect fascinating folk stories from the inhabitants and preserve them for future generations. His excitement was contagious!

This was our last night on the island. I gave him something loving to remember me by, but didn't want to spoil the possibility of a future with him by letting things move too fast. This was one man I could surrender my freedom to. I loved his exuberant personality, and was unable to see any limits to his intelligence. I really liked that.

Next day, Jerome drove Yvonne and me to the airport. I drank in my last visual memory of him as he stood there in a cotton sports jacket, his wavy brown hair blowing in the breeze. He looked terrific as he flashed me a warm smile. I wanted to memorize the moment. The air was damp from morning dew, while high jagged mountains rose behind him in the background. I took a last photo of him to keep with me always.

As we embraced goodbye, I didn't want to let go. I finally met the man I could imagine settling down with. Then Yvonne and I boarded our airplane. I turned to see him wave at me.

Looking down at Mauritius from the air, Yvonne said that Jerome was enormously popular as a guitar performer and singer. On weekends he entertained in bars, and from what she's heard, he left many broken hearts in his wake. It seems that he was also looking for "the right one."

Our long-distance love affair started through letters, and I learned more about this brilliant man from what he wrote. His intellect and humour shone through in his eloquent writing. We corresponded as fast as the mail could deliver, and formed a spiritual connection. It's well-known that the most powerful sex organ is the mind. I adored him and didn't want to date anyone else. His photo stood beside me on my night table. I could look over at him from my bed and dream about love and happiness forever. On paper, we were meant for each other, and fell deeper in love with each letter. I floated with joy on gossamer wings like the character in Chagall's paintings, intoxicated by thoughts of a happy life together. This man was perfect---intelligent, honest and humorous. I wanted my future to be with him.

In one letter he proposed that I return to Mauritius and spend a couple of months with him to learn if we'd be suitable for marriage. My spirit soared with bliss, uplifted by the thrill of finding the man who could be my soul mate.

"We need new blood in Mauritius," he wrote jokingly, "and you would be contributing to a fresh gene pool."

We set a date in early December for my visit. I eagerly counted the weeks.

Meanwhile, Joubert Park

During the month before joining Jerome in Mauritius, I exhibited paintings in Joubert Park and hoped to earn enough money to pay the rent for my apartment while I'd be away. My faithful friend Hennie the sculptor picked me up each day of the exhibition and helped me set up my display.

The more I got to know Hennie, the more I realized how wonderful he was. Ten years earlier, he married his best friend's fiancée after that friend was tragically killed in a car accident. Hennie picked up the pieces of what was left of his buddy on the highway, a gruesome shock he never forgot. He and his friend's fiancée comforted each other in their mutual grief. Hennie would have done anything for his best mate, even assuming responsibility for his buddy's betrothed. He felt it was the right thing to do.

Hennie proudly wore the big sombrero that I gave him from Mexico. He waved to me from his metal art display as I sat in front of my exhibit. A father and son came by and admired the wooden sculpture which I created in Cape Town---the abstract city containing different stained wood pieces in a long row, with painted canvas blocks representing buildings. It was a stunning piece, heavy and for sale. Hennie was fond of it too, and transported it to each art show for me. The father and son stood admiring it for a long time. But they had no money, and asked if they could pay for it in monthly installments. *Oh dear, not this again.* I took it off my display wall and gave it to them.

Hennie always liked that piece and noticed it was gone. I told him that I sold it, but he was suspicious. So, I listed it as "sold" on paper, and paid the commission to the organizers for what would have been their fee from the sale. They would not approve of artists giving away their work. I regret not giving the sculpture to Hennie.

My weight-loss diet had been draining. I still followed the doctor's maintenance instructions. Not one drop of fat had passed my lips for over four months until one Saturday during that art show when Hennie went to a nearby donut shop and returned with some big greasy donuts for us. I couldn't help myself and hungrily devoured one, and then another. My body was craving fat. Hennie stared at me, his mouth ajar.

"Do you want more?" he said.

A resounding "yes" sent him back to the donut shop. He stared as I wolfed down another two. I'd been deprived; it was beyond my control.

My African portraits were selling well. The older man from my Far East tour who'd run away from me at the coffee shop last month because I lost so much weight, now strolled by with his young wife clinging to him. She glared at my new figure while her husband studied my artwork. He picked a painting of a proud Zulu warrior and wrote me a cheque.

"Why did you choose that one?" I said, curious.

"Because we know the artist," he smiled.

After exhibiting for four weekends, I earned enough money to pay my rent while I'd be away, and some left over.

Day and night my photos of Jerome kept me company. His smiling face on my night table was only one foot away, so close I could feel the warmth of his body and kiss his lips. Our passion grew with each page of our correspondence, so intense it sizzled. The hottest sex I ever had was with Jerome in my empty bed. The mind plays powerful tricks. His photo spoke to me as he caressed my body and made passionate love to me in absentia, orgasm after sweet orgasm. On paper, we were the perfect match. *I will be seeing you soon, my darling.*

I kept my weight down and wanted to look even better for him. So, I bought a series of tensor treatments which made my stomach muscles contract and seem like I'd been exercising. It was terribly uncomfortable, especially when they increased the current. This was shock treatment but it worked. I developed a nice six-pack.

At my favourite thrift store, I searched through the array of pretty outfits. I wanted to look good for my life with Jerome. It was exciting to shop in the "small" section, as I'd always been extra large before going on my diet. I found a red skirt and a black blouse dotted with tiny red roses. Then some bell-bottom slacks, jean shorts and sun tops. I was ready!

I even went to the dentist to be in perfect condition for Jerome. The dentist filled a cavity and was almost finished when he paused, seeming doubtful.

"What's wrong?" I said.

He stroked his chin and peered into my mouth.

"Nothing," he said pensively. "I thought I might have seen an exposed nerve, but I'm sure it's nothing."

Good, then. My teeth were fixed and polished. I was a gift-wrapped package soon to arrive in Mauritius. I longed to see Jerome again, the man who stimulated my intellect with each turn of phrase. A man of honour whom I could respect and admire.

After months of abstaining from sex (except in my mind) I yearned to make love with him. I wanted only Jerome, and raced downstairs to my mailbox each morning hoping to find him there. At last, a thick letter with familiar handwriting arrived---an airline ticket to Mauritius! The day had finally come. I was deliriously happy!

Jerome

Yvonne drove me to the airport, filled with excitement for me. My whole future was riding on this visit. Both Jerome and I were willing to take the risk. The stakes were high for him too, as all his friends and relatives knew that he'd met somebody special (me) and was flying her over. Everyone was hoping for a happy outcome.

My flight arrived in Mauritius mid-morning on a sunny day. Jerome and some of his relatives were on the roof of the airport waving at me. My heart was pounding. I wore my red skirt and black blouse with the roses, hoping he would find me pleasing.

It was great to see him again. He greeted me warmly with open arms and kisses on my cheeks. Everybody kissed me on both cheeks, it was the French way. Then we were driven to a cousin's house where I could freshen up and change after the trip. Jerome helped me to the guest room with my luggage, then he closed the door and we were alone.

I flashed him an eager smile and removed my skirt and blouse, wearing only my pink lace bra and panties. I was dying for sex with him and had waited so long. We had an hour before lunch and I wanted him, assuming he wanted me too. But Jerome's face turned white as he unravelled my arms from around his neck, putting a respectable distance between us.

"Eva, this is not the time or place," he stammered, his eyes wide with alarm. "I didn't know you were like *that!*"

Then he left the room and let me dress.

My heart sank and I felt ashamed. After putting on fresh clothes, I joined the family in the dining room. His elderly maiden aunts were there, as well as numerous cousins. Seeing the chamber filled with relatives who had come to greet Jerome's potential bride, I understood why he didn't want to make love in the next room. We were called to lunch and took our seats.

After lunch, we drove to Grand Baie where he'd rented a little cottage on the beach for us. We didn't talk about what happened in the guest room. I hoped we could start over.

The cottage was small but big enough for two. It had a thatched roof and two large patio doors which opened onto a deck in the back yard where a table and two wicker chairs stood. We would enjoy eating breakfast out there and sometimes dinner by candlelight. A high brick wall covered by green ivy separated us from the neighbours, and lots of trees grew in the yard for privacy.

Inside the cottage there was a bright little kitchen, a living room with a big double bed, sofa, and a large brown wooden wardrobe to hang clothes in. He also found me a bicycle which I'd asked for in my letters, in case I felt like cycling to the market while he was at work. He had done well with all these material preparations to make me happy.

We were like children in the Garden of Eden, teasing each other and playing pranks sometimes. He sparkled with fun, and came home once with an antique horn which he tooted all over the back yard because it made an amusing sound. We were both in love with the idea of being in love. Days passed and we played house. He'd go to work while I kept myself busy until he came home for dinner.

There was a shortage of fresh water in Mauritius, so officials turned it off for a certain number of hours each day. I filled all our pots with water every morning before the shutoff and boiled them for fifteen minutes. Yvonne once told me that water in Mauritius contains amoebas, a kind of parasite which people lived with. I was taking no chances.

Jerome noticed that some of my clothes were still neatly folded in my suitcase. I told him I'd bought some new outfits for our holiday.

"Try them on please," he said.

"Why?"

"Just for me. I want to see you in them."

His request surprised me. *What does he take me for?* I understood then, that being slender and looking good came with conditions unfamiliar to me. I slowly dressed in each of my new outfits and paraded leisurely in front of him, nearly tripping on the carpet. Then I tried to turn around gracefully so he could see the back. I felt like a silly piece of baby-doll fluff modeling clothes for him. This is not who I was.

"OK, very nice. That's enough," he said, and returned to his newspaper with a slight smile forming on his lips. Perhaps he sensed how awkward I felt, or maybe it was that my performance didn't turn him on.

One day as I was preparing supper for Jerome and his best buddy, I noticed a big white mouse with a long, pointed nose sitting on the pipes between the fridge and the stove. To my horror, his whiskers kept moving as he stared straight at me with beady black eyes. I was trying to cook a meal only three feet away. It was disconcerting! I've never cooked with a mouse staring at me, and there was nothing I could do but try to ignore him. This dinner had to go well. I was eager to make a favourable impression with my homemaking skills. The roast beef in the oven smelled good so far, and the table was set just right with wine glasses, silverware and fresh buns. I even picked some daisies from the garden and put them in a vase.

When Jerome and his friend finally arrived, I pointed to the mouse sitting on the pipes. My brave knights came to the rescue. They chased the rodent to the bathroom and closed the door. There was lots of shouting, laughter, noise and scuffles---then silence. They finally emerged breathless from the bathroom. It had taken two men ten minutes to kill a mouse, but its death was anticlimactic. Jerome said he felt guilty about murdering the mouse.

Another time, Jerome and I woke up to missing bananas. The kitchen window frames had built-in steel bars, so we were able to keep the windows open at night for fresh air. A robber used a long pole to lift the bananas from the kitchen counter eight feet away. He must have been hungry. Thank goodness I didn't leave my purse there or that would be gone too.

One afternoon, I returned to the cottage after a swim and found a large German Shepherd shivering in our shower stall. He seemed terrified. I'm not sure how he got in. I was afraid to touch the shaking dog, and there was no way he would be coaxed out. I left him there and waited outside for Jerome to return from work.

Poor Jerome, having to deal with all these domestic emergencies. When he arrived, I told him there was a big dog in the shower. He didn't believe it and went in to see for himself. That dog wasn't going anywhere! He just sat there panting and shivering. Jerome left to speak with neighbours and eventually located the owner. It seems that people who don't want stray dogs in their yards light firecrackers to scare them off. This is distressing for dogs. The owner came over, apologized, and took his dog. We could relax again, but not for too long ...

All these unusual situations happened while Jerome was at work. I couldn't believe my eyes when I opened the wardrobe to get a sweater. A gigantic, hairy tarantula the size of a soup bowl, was climbing on my clothing! I shut the closet door immediately and ran out of the cottage. Once again Jerome was greeted with news of an intruder in the house. Poor guy, he had to show a brave face in all these situations. He fetched a pot from the kitchen, trapped the spider and carried it outside. There would be no more killing of wildlife.

⁓

After a couple of weeks in Mauritius, my back tooth started to ache. It was the tooth my dentist in Johannesburg recently repaired. Soon it became a piercing pain that never left. I felt like yanking it out with a pair of pliers to relieve the agony. After hearing me complain for days, Jerome took me to his dentist. It turned out that I needed a root canal. My former dentist had good reason to doubt his handiwork. He had indeed seen an exposed nerve and placed a filling on top of it. Now it was infected and needed surgery.

The waiting room was filled with farm labourers. The dentist said they don't normally perform such complicated procedures in Mauritius, but he would try. I was grateful for any relief. He removed the inflamed pulp and filled the roots. But he didn't leave me with much of a tooth. A crown would have to come much later. I don't know how much my root canal cost, but Jerome covered it. I was already costing as much as a wife!

Then after three weeks, my dark hair roots started to show. I needed to go to the hairdresser, an expense which I hadn't planned for in all the excitement.

"No problem," said Jerome, and dropped me off at a salon in town.

The ladies were friendly and professional. They did a marvellous job, and achieved the loveliest beige-blond shade I've ever had. But their running water was turned off due to the water shortage. To rinse my hair between procedures, they had to climb down two flights of rickety back stairs to fetch heavy buckets of water stored in large barrels in the yard. I felt sorry they had to work so hard for me, but still found this charming and wonderfully primitive.

⌒

After Jerome left for work one day, I felt like cycling to the market for groceries. I was proud that I could still ride a bike, and flew past local workers digging ditches by the side of the road. To my dismay, I received unusual stares and derisive remarks from them as I sped by. I smiled at them, but they didn't smile back and just shook their heads.

I asked Jerome why people seemed angry with me. He said they were probably offended to see a white woman riding a bicycle. This was *their* mode of transportation. A white woman should be seen driving a *car*. I wasn't prepared for their reaction and didn't ride my bike again.

Trouble in Paradise

Jerome was a celebrity wherever we went. It took us double the time to get anywhere because people stopped him to talk. His popularity as a musician was obvious. I didn't mind, and stood beside him as he chatted to his fans. He loved talking to people. On cooler evenings, Jerome and I sat on the beach where he played guitar and sang for me. Sometimes we'd sing in harmony. Those were happy moments when I had him to myself.

One Saturday morning as we strolled barefoot on the beach, some fishermen pulled their boat up on shore and displayed their catch right there. They laid their colourful tropical fish on a blue tarpaulin in the sand---red fish, orange striped ones, mauve, turquoise, pink and silver. Customers crowded around, haggled a bit, and then paid them for fresh seafood. Somebody even bought an octopus.

But Jerome got antsy when we spent too much time on our own. He wanted us to go out and meet friends.

"Why can't you enjoy just being with *me*?" I said.

He looked at me, searching for the right words.

"Well, you must admit that we've been on our own an awful lot lately," he said, as if I should feel the same way.

He seemed to need the stimulation of more people. Was I not enough for him?

I decided to surprise Jerome for lunch at his work one day. I got nicely dressed in powder blue bell-bottoms with a matching blouse, and waited for a bus to take me to town. Rain drops started falling as I stood there. *Darn!* I looked around for something to shield me, and saw a large piece of cardboard lying on the ground near the bus stop. I reached for it but almost fell over backwards when a mother duck squawked ferociously at me. She owned that cardboard and used it to protect her brood from the rain. She shrieked at me to back off. I admired her fierce motherly instinct, and wouldn't dream of removing her shelter.

Jerome seemed a bit unhinged to have me surprise him at work. This was unexpected; he liked to plan. He appeared irritated and looked around to see if anyone had noticed me. It seemed like he wanted to keep his private life private, and not have to introduce me to his colleagues. He steered me to his office and closed the door. I glanced around the tidy room where everything was neatly placed. He was meticulous. Thick corporate law books were stacked neatly on his desk. He said he was too busy to go for lunch with me, so I walked around town and waited until he finished work. I shouldn't have come. We drove home together.

Help, I can't breathe! I was being strangled and it woke me up. I choked and struggled, elbowing Jerome to make him stop. He loosened his grip when he realized he was dreaming of running with a football---my head! His friends warned him this might happen to his poor wife if he ever married. He suffered from night-time roaming, and did things in his sleep that he had no clue about.

Then he told me what happened some years before when he rented an upstairs room in a house. He woke up early in the morning exhausted but didn't know why. His traumatized landlord knocked on his door and told Jerome that he couldn't live there anymore because of all the thumping, banging and grating of furniture all night long.

"It's not me, Jerome," the owner apologized. "It's my wife, you understand. She didn't sleep a wink last night!"

It seems Jerome had moved the heavy dresser, bed, chairs and everything else in the room, all night long. This was a side of him I did not expect.

⌒⌒

I kept myself clean with daily feminine douches and showers, fresh clothing and washed hair. I did everything I could to appeal to him, but we didn't seem to have the same sexual appetite. Sometimes I wondered if he preferred to play with dirty girls while his future bride should be a pillar of virtue. I felt unloved. Here he had a woman in his bed who cherished and desired him, but he seldom took advantage. We talked about this as we rested one evening.

"Why don't you want to touch me or make love more often?" I said.

Genuinely surprised by my question, he looked at me with wide eyes.

"Can't you see how much I've done to show you my love?" he said, as he motioned with his hand to the cottage. "I've rented this place, I buy our food and come home to you every day. What more can I do?"

My heart was heavy. We had a problem. Then he told me about something he'd read which I didn't think was realistic. He said that every time a man ejaculates, some of his life force is lost and this shortens his life span. Perhaps that belief might explain his lack of interest in having sex with me. Or maybe....

"Are you gay or bisexual?" I said.

"No, absolutely not!"

"Why do you make love to me at all?" I asked.

"Because I know it gives you pleasure."

That answer was not comforting. I thought---*not because it gives YOU pleasure too?*

In spite of the widening gulf between us, we still had social engagements to fulfill. His whole crew of cousins and their wives were invited to our cottage for dinner one evening. They arrived jubilant, looking like they were harbouring a collective secret. I cooked a big chicken curry and made it spicy the Mauritian way. We served steamed rice, white wine, fresh bread and Caesar salad with the hot curry. Our cheerful guests lounged inside and on the deck chairs outside.

The hours passed pleasantly enough and time came for everyone to leave. It seems they hung on for as long as they could. I had the impression their joyful mood had fallen flat, as if they were going away empty-handed. Jerome and I wondered what went wrong. It finally dawned on us that his relatives were expecting our engagement announcement which never came. So, *that's* why they were excited when they first arrived. They all knew the purpose of my visit---to find out if the popular island playboy had finally found a bride. Jerome's intentions were honourable and they all knew about it. But those expectations put too much pressure on us. I felt as though this visit was a test for me to pass or fail.

After one month in Mauritius, Christmas Eve rolled around. We celebrated with a big feast at Jerome's aunt's house in Curepipe, and afterwards attended Midnight Mass. It was a lively church service with Christmas music and singing. Jerome told me later that his elderly relatives wished we were engaged or married already, and not "living in sin." He said they judged me harshly on that point, namely that I could sleep with him without being engaged at least.

Jerome was officially on holidays after Christmas. He had gone all out to made vacation plans for us ahead of time and said we'd be going to Madagascar for the whole month of January. First, we would visit his parents in the family home where he grew up. After one week with them in the capital city of Antananarivo, the plan was to vacation on the primitive island of Saint Marie situated just off the mainland. I appreciated that Jerome was so organized. He had put his whole heart into planning for my visit. But I felt a twinge of sadness. We weren't as happy as we should be.

Before we left Mauritius, Jerome received a letter from his father in Madagascar. He revered his father, and looked at me apologetically as he unfolded the letter in his hands. Then he read it to me. It said that because we were not engaged, they regrettably could not permit me to stay in their house. They would put me up at a hotel instead. That really stung.

Off to Madagascar, 1976

Jerome's older brother picked us up from the airport in Antananarivo. He was tall and elegant, and greeted us warmly with hugs for Jerome and kisses on my cheeks for me. First, he drove us to the hotel to deposit my luggage, then he brought us to the stately family home. This brick mansion was a hundred years old and built high on a hilltop with a breath-taking view of the city below. The outside walls of all three stories were covered by green ivy, and a high protective stone fence surrounded the property.

Inside, I was introduced to his parents who greeted me politely in the foyer. I guess they were curious to meet the woman who had cast a spell on their son. When I saw the dark walnut furniture in the dimly-lit living room, I found the gloomy colours foreboding. Even the staircase leading to the second floor was dark brown.

Jerome's younger brother Pierre and his wife were there too. They'd arrived from Mauritius the day before and would be holidaying with us. They all got along well.

Each day for one week, somebody was appointed to pick me up from my hotel and drive me to their house. I took part in formal lunches and dinners with the family where they discussed politics, world affairs, the economy and religion. These were educated, intellectual people. I couldn't have asked for more cultivated in-laws. When they discussed the Bible one day, I was able to contribute a bit of my newly-acquired knowledge taught to me by Carl the Jehovah Witness and hoped they'd be impressed.

But Jerome wasn't the same towards me after our time in Mauritius. He closed himself off and didn't confide in me anymore. I longed for him to open up and talk to me, and tell me of his hopes and dreams. We had one promising moment just the two of us, as we sat on a small balcony on the third floor. We were chatting when his mother came. She saw we were enjoying our talk and retreated, but the mood was gone.

He adored his mother and put her on a pedestal. She was petite, intelligent, always well dressed and lady-like. He treated her with love and respect. No wonder his requisites were high with her as a role model of what the ideal woman should be. I worried that in Jerome's eyes, I could never measure up to his mother's perfection.

"Did you know that it's Maurice's birthday today and he turns sixty?" she said to me.

She mentioned it casually but looked at me closely. They were cousins by marriage. *Was she gauging my reaction? Had she heard that I'd been in love with him?* I tried not to react at the sound of Maurice's name, but I may have winced when she said he was sixty. Surely this intuitive woman must have sensed my discomfort. Maurice was Jerome's uncle by marriage.

Then I remembered Yvonne's cousin Gilles who was also related to Jerome and his parents. Gilles knew that I'd lived with Ryan. And when he visited Maurice in Durban last year, he found me there too---that time when I wore my black wig to see if he'd recognize me. Word about my past romances must have trickled through to these fine people and jeopardized my chances of becoming part of this respectable family. I had a sinking feeling that I might not be virtuous enough in their eyes.

One morning Jerome took his mother and me to the busy market in the town square. It was teeming with vendors selling their wares under large umbrellas which shielded them from the hot sun. There was lots of activity and bartering. Two women sat in the shade surrounded by clucking brown chickens tied to a pole. The customer could choose one, and the women would wring its neck right there; fresh chicken for dinner! Colourful bargain clothing hung on racks, while red gladioli for sale stood in buckets of water. Some merchants displayed African carvings and skin-covered ottomans.

Jerome asked me which ottoman I preferred. I chose one with a lively primitive design. Next, he asked his mother. She preferred a simpler one, saying that somber is always best. He gave me a little shrug and bought the one his mother liked. I shrugged back and knew that's how it would always be.

New Year's Eve was special. We went to a concert where the host learned that Jerome was in the audience. It seems he was well known in Madagascar too. In front of a full-house, they announced his name on the loudspeaker and asked him to please come down to the stage and perform a song. He hesitated but the audience cheered loudly, forcing him to descend to the platform. He coordinated with the band for two minutes and then played a real showstopper. The crowd went wild and clamoured for an encore. I was so proud to know him, and looked over at his brother Pierre who was beaming too.

Our week in the city with his parents was over. Jerome must have told them that he was disillusioned with our relationship. Perhaps they were too. He seemed downcast. A lingering sadness hung over me too, but I wanted to stay with him for the remainder of this holiday which he had done so much to prepare for. I also entertained a glimmer of hope that our love might still take flight, as we had another three weeks to spend on the remote island of Sainte Marie.

Jerome's brother Pierre and his wife accompanied us to the island. First, we drove overland to the north, passing small villages where indigenous people lived in square huts made of orange clay. Each small courtyard was surrounded by a clay fence. We stayed overnight at a hotel so we could catch a small plane to Sainte Marie first thing in the morning.

When Jerome and I got ready for bed, a group of singers gathered below our window and serenaded us with folk songs. I found it charming. Jerome tossed them some coins and waved. We left a wake-up call for 6 a.m., but that call came every hour starting at 2 a.m. Each time they asked us if we were ready for breakfast. We laughed about that, happy for some comic relief.

The short plane ride to the island was bumpy and we bounced on landing at the airstrip. The hotel's antiquated transportation was waiting to pick us up. I was amused to climb into the back of an old pick-up truck adapted to seat passengers. A canvas tarpaulin hung on a metal frame above us and provided shade from the blazing sun. The ride along that rocky dirt road was invigorating, tossing us from side to side with each deep pothole. We laughed and braced ourselves as best we could, arriving at the hotel in high spirits.

I admired the simplicity of our accommodations. The outside and inside walls were made of reeds, and the roof was thatched with straw. This sprawling ground-level hotel consisted of a long row of bedrooms, each with a private entrance. We were assigned our own little room. There was no electricity, but we had a kerosene lamp on the night table. Mosquito netting hung above our double bed to protect us from malaria-carrying mosquitos at night. I looked for a toilet, but they were in another building along with wash basins made of cut-off metal barrels with water which flowed through a rubber hose. This was really back to basics and I loved it. The grounds were lush green, surrounded by palms trees and coconut groves.

We ate in the main building which doubled as a dining and living room. Dinners were glorious---lobsters, shrimps, and fresh fish caught in the ocean that day, served with vegetables grown in their garden. The owners apologized for not having any meat to offer us. If they only realized what luxury food they were providing. After dinner, we played cards or other games by kerosene lamp in this same building. There was no television or modern conveniences.

I think that Jerome finally decided to make the best of his annual holiday and benefit from the time that remained. At this point, I doubt that he regarded me as his future wife. I was having my doubts too. But I still adored him, especially when he was enjoying himself and took the trouble to talk to me. I missed him.

One day, we took a trail which led to a real pirate's grave. A slab of stone was engraved with the words (translated from the French) ---"Joseph-Pierre born in 1788, died in 1834, buried by his friend Hulin. In passing, pray for him." Hulin had even etched the skull and crossbones insignia of pirates. It was painstakingly carved, and you could feel the love Hulin had for his friend. There was a long history of pirates taking refuge in the bays of Madagascar and of French ships sent to capture them.

Then Jerome showed me a frightful sight hidden near the water's edge---a collection of sun-bleached human skulls and bones, the remains of drowning victims who'd washed up on shore many years ago. They lay openly upon black earth. Several fearsome stone carvings of heads stood guard for these skeletal remains. Spirits and superstition abound in wild Madagascar.

When we got thirsty on our hikes, Jerome asked one of the young boys who followed us everywhere to climb a tree and fetch fresh coconuts so we could drink the sweet water. He paid them each time they did so. One time, we came to a shallow river where our entourage of five boys carried each of us across the water so we wouldn't get our shoes wet. Jerome looked like royalty as the boys made a seat with their arms and carried him. That was fun. But they kept touching my skin and I didn't understand why.

"Don't be offended," Jerome said. "They hardly ever see women with white skin, and they want to know how it feels."

On one of our walks, we arrived at a snack bar. I had to pee and asked to use the wash-room. The woman took me to the back of the store and pointed to a room. *Oh, dear me!* In that room was an earthen floor, a bucket of water, and a hole in the wall. I was to pee on the ground and use the water to flush it out the hole. I had no choice!

There was a Frenchman staying at our hotel who'd been a sailor. He now owned a yacht for hire with him as captain and agreed to transport us around the coves and untamed shores for the day. The weather was perfect with sunny skies and a calm ocean.

For lunch, we pulled into a bay where the captain knew a local woman who could cook an authentic Malagasy meal for us. The inhabitants of that little settlement ran to greet us on the beach. A hefty black woman carrying a baby tied to her back, spoke to our captain. He knew their language and asked her to cook a traditional lunch of chicken and rice for us. She had her choice of pretty brown hens which ran around freely, and prepared it on an open fire in the courtyard. It turned out excellent, as did the rice with added spices and a hint of tomato grown in their garden.

I noticed that their reed huts were built on stilts, something I hadn't seen before in Madagascar. Jerome said it was in case they got flooded by the ocean. After more sight-seeing, we returned to our hotel accompanied by a glorious red sunset. It had been a good day.

Next morning, Pierre spotted a Malagasy fisherman with a rowboat. He paid the man to ferry us around the harbour, and all four of us hopped in. These were shark-infested waters. I wasn't worried and neither were Pierre and his wife. Jerome kept peering into the water looking for danger. I could sense his fear. His nature was lively and highly strung. I knew in that very moment that any one of his calm brothers, cousins or friends, suited my temperament better than he did. I had fallen hard for this man's brilliant mind and exuberant personality. But right then, he felt more like a beloved brother than a lover. Our dispositions were too similar. But I still adored him and wished that we could cultivate the complete love we both longed for. He was a good man. An honorable man.

Once back at our hotel, Jerome sat on the terrace trying to read the book Papillon. Palm trees and greenery filled the background behind him. I looked at him as he gazed into nowhere, lost in thought. His expression was melancholy. My heart ached to make him happy, but he had withdrawn from me. I'd lost him. We hadn't made love in weeks and hardly did so for the two months we were together. I had hoped we could be happy and spend the rest of our lives together, and I know that he originally had the same dream. Everything was different now. We were from two different worlds. He came from a large Catholic family on an island where everybody knew each other, while I was a big-city girl who'd been in love before. This public failure must have been humiliating for Jerome since everyone knew of his good intentions.

Our holiday on Sainte Marie Island was over. Time came for us to return to Antananarivo where I'd catch my flight back to Johannesburg. On my last evening at the hotel, Jerome left me on my own so he could have a bachelor's night out on the town with his buddies. Sadly, this spoke volumes about his feelings for me. I wandered around the empty halls looking for a shop to buy a box of chocolates for his parents as thanks for their hospitality, but all the shops were closed. The Hotel Manager was a friend of the family and came across me while doing his rounds.

"What are you doing by yourself on your last night here?" he asked.

"Jerome wanted a bachelor's night out," I said, trying not to cry.

He shook his head and opened up the confectionery store for me. Next day, somebody picked me up from my hotel and brought me to the family home. I said goodbye to Jerome's parents and gave his mother the big box of Belgian chocolates. Jerome and his oldest brother drove me to the airport. His brother had the good manners to stay with me and wave me off. He kept looking around for Jerome who was nowhere to be seen. Jerome must have rushed off to talk to someone he knew. I felt devastated.

I flew to Johannesburg in low spirits. There was a lump in my throat the whole time as I hid my tears from the other passengers. The problem is---what do you do with the love you still feel in your heart? I loved this man fiercely for months while we corresponded, and in person too. But it seemed like we just weren't suitable to be more than friends. Our love was more cerebral than sensual. He withheld sex from me, or maybe he just wasn't that into me. Without the expression of physical attraction, I think there can only be friendship. It was difficult for me to accept that we might not be compatible. I loved him still, but now that love had nowhere to go.

Once I got back to South Africa, Jerome and I exchanged letters. He wanted to give "us" more time to know each other before committing to a permanent union. He wanted to remain good friends for now, saying that getting to know each other should be time spent apart. I didn't think that was possible. In any case, I had enough heartache and feeling that I wasn't good enough for him and his fine family. But this still felt like unfinished business.

Yvonne heard from her relatives in Mauritius that Jerome was still conquering the ladies and breaking hearts all over the island. This meant that he was still searching for "the one."

Better Times

Thankfully I still had good friends in Johannesburg who lifted my spirits. The best news was that Mimi would be moving to Balnagask. She rented a two-ton truck and bravely drove it herself from Melville. I sat beside her with my eyes closed most of the way, praying for our safety.

She moved into a ground-level apartment and decorated her large balcony with potted palm trees and garden furniture. Mimi loved the sun. From my balcony on the ninth floor, I could see her suntanning on her deck. "Yoo-hoo!" I called and waved, running downstairs to visit her perhaps too often. I felt like she was family.

My friend Amy who used to work with me at the photo studio, also moved to Balnagask one floor below me. By now, she'd found herself a good job as an Office Manager in a large company where her talents shone. I was overjoyed that my wonderful friends lived close to me.

Someone knocked on the door as I sat painting in my apartment. To my surprise, it was Stuart, Ryan's youngest brother. I heard that he separated from his girlfriend and their young child, and was living with another woman. But he and this new woman just had a big fight and she asked him to leave. Now he had nowhere to live and looked like a lost puppy. Ryan must have told him where to find me.

"Mind if I stay here till I find another place?" he said.

I couldn't refuse, and told him he could sleep on the sofa. I felt that I owed it to Ryan to look after his brother for awhile. For the next few days Stuart sat in a chair immersed in a book, escaping the reality of his predicament. He read his book while I painted. We didn't have much to talk about. Then I remembered my friend Amy and wondered if they'd get along. She didn't have a boyfriend at the moment.

"How would you like to meet a friend of mine?" I said. "She's a great girl, and if she likes you, maybe she'll let you stay at her place."

I felt a bit guilty about trying to foist him on Amy, but invited her over for coffee to meet Stuart. They hit it off right away. I could feel the attraction as he poured on the charm. He asked her to the movies and it snowballed from there. The good news was that he no longer needed to stay with me. But he left his book at my place, so I paid him and Amy a little visit.

They seemed completely happy as they reclined on her sofa after she got home from work. He'd forgotten all about the other woman and his sorrow. I marvelled at men's behaviour and how easily they get over a broken heart by simply finding another girlfriend. I've seen it happen time and again, it's like an instant fix. As soon as they find a new woman, they don't grieve at all. I think women take much longer to get over love affairs.

I looked around Amy's place and started panicking when I couldn't see out her windows. She had all kinds of gauze curtains covering the view. She called them "sheer," but I couldn't handle it. I charged over to the windows and pulled open the curtains to look outside. Once the trees and sky came into view, I could breathe again. Closed curtains in the daytime made me claustrophobic. I suppose it was rude of me to do that, but she didn't get angry and guessed correctly that I had my phobias.

Her bosses obviously treasured her. She had a knack for solving difficulties and turning everything into gold. Stuart pointed out the new television her boss gave her as a token of appreciation for her hard work.

"Eva, if you don't notice something soon, I'm going to scream!" Amy said.

I looked around and saw Stuart's red motorcycle leaning against the wall.

"No, that's not it!" she said, and pointed to a black and white kitten flitting around the room. It's true, I hadn't spotted it. I only noticed her gauze curtains blocking my view of nature.

A couple of weeks later, Amy and Stuart invited me for a motorcycle ride by moonlight to Pretoria. I would ride on the back of their friend Tommy's motorbike. I never rode a big bike before, my only experience being that of riding Ryan's red scooter in Swaziland where I ended up in the bushes. Nor had I met their friend Tommy. Perhaps they were trying to set me up with him since Amy knew about my heartache in Mauritius.

They waited for a full moon to introduce me to him for the trip to Pretoria. He and Stuart both had Harley-Davidsons. I hopped on the back of his bike and we drove behind Amy and Stuart late at night when there was no traffic. A bright white moon lit our way. I had full confidence in Tommy's ability. It felt terrific to lean into the curves and sway with his body on the bike. It was like being at one with him and the machine. I got the hang of it, and it felt wonderful. We reached Pretoria in one hour and headed for the Potato Shack. They served all kinds of potatoes---fried, baked, or mashed with sausage. I hankered for a baked potato with melted butter. It tasted delicious, warm and comforting.

Tommy was one of those silent, unkempt types. I felt no chemistry between us and we didn't meet again. Although riding a motorcycle by moonlight with him on deserted roads was an amazing experience.

Joubert Park

I was grateful that another art exhibition would take place from March to April on four consecutive weekends. This would give me a chance to earn some money and build up my savings. But business was slow and we heard there was a recession underway.

I still had no telephone. Potential customers who heard about my artwork had to come to my apartment, unless they met me at the exhibition. I found a note under my door for three days in a row to call Mrs. Vanderhaven. I'd never heard of her and ignored the messages, but she was so persistent that I finally phoned her. She wanted me to paint a portrait of herself and her two boys for her husband's birthday. Her neighbour told her that she should only get it painted by me and no one else. I felt honoured.

We arranged for her and the children to come to my place to be photographed and I would use the best pictures of them to paint from. They all wore white clothing because she wanted the painting to look Victorian and classic. Okay, I could create whatever effect she wanted. With commissions, that was the challenge; customers knew what they envisaged, and I had to translate that onto paper. But it was always my own interpretation of the person's character and their unique look. I tried to capture their personality and get into their thoughts as I painted from the photos.

Her artwork took one week to complete. I used colours of sepia, ivory, brown, rose and beige, just like an old-fashioned photograph. She was excited and happy with the finished product, and paid me well.

⁓

Having no car, I hitchhiked to deliver portraits to customers who lived outside of Johannesburg. My first trip was to a married couple who seemed to hate each other. They had ordered portraits of their two children. The atmosphere in their home was tense as they harped at each other the whole time. The boy sided with the father, and the girl with the mother. Poor children to live in such animosity. My stomach was in knots and I couldn't wait to leave.

The woman drove me to a bus stop where she thought I could catch a bus back to Johannesburg. She parked on the side of the road to make sure I got on it all right. I didn't want her to see me hitch-hiking, so like a good girl I waited for the bus. A "Nie Blanke" bus drove past which was forbidden to pick up whites. Another Nie Blanke bus drove by ten minutes later, and a third one after that. I waited for half an hour. Being white did not always have its advantages. At long last a "Blanke Only" bus came by and stopped for me.

My next trip was to a couple who also lived outside of Johannesburg. There I delivered an elegant painting of a nude woman reclining on light blue satin sheets and pillows. I used one of my picture books on the human figure for reference. This painting was the man's gift to his wife.

When they opened their door to let me in, I was overwhelmed by the expensive knickknacks and ornaments in their home---unusual mosaic vases, bronze sculptures, and original oil paintings in ornate frames.

"Such gorgeous things you have," I said, gazing round

the room.

The husband and wife exchanged chuckles.

"These things are all the result of my husband's guilty conscience," she said with a laugh.

I understood, and still remember her words. The lesson I gleaned was, "beware of gifts from your man which come for no apparent reason. He's been naughty."

Change in the Air

On April 16[th,] came news on the radio of unrest in Soweto township near Johannesburg. Black students were protesting because they were being forced to learn lessons in the Afrikaans language instead of English. This led to demonstrations throughout the country against the Apartheid regime, and those protests were met with police brutality.

For years I heard that whites worried themselves sick about future retaliation by the black majority for having suppressed them for so many years, forcing them to live in poverty and taking away their rights. My white neighbours in the building were starting to panic. Where could they take refuge if the worst came to pass? Fear was contagious. The news broadcasts scared me too. I looked around my apartment. Where could I hide, the closet?

No wonder people were frightened. There were daily reports of increased problems with guerrillas on our border with Angola. Terrorists backed by Communists wanted in. Much of the world hated South Africa during this time of Apartheid. The country's defense depended on the military, but how long could they subdue protests within and terrorists on the borders? My neighbour Frank hadn't been called to serve yet, and now he was really afraid. He received a letter from the government which said that at any time within thirty days of receipt of that letter, the army could draft him to fight. Poor Frank. He was in his forties, out-of-shape and ill-equipped for the rigours of jungle warfare. He started jogging and lifting weights, hoping that might help. You could see the fear in his face, his forehead was wrinkled with concern.

During this time of unrest, I remember crossing a street in Johannesburg where a long line of black people waited for a bus on the sidewalk. They all glared at me. I could feel the undercurrent of resentment; perhaps they thought I was privileged because I was white, although I certainly didn't feel privileged. I didn't know how I should react as they stared at me, so I stopped in front of them to think. Should I curtsy or wave, or blow kisses? I wanted to embrace them all and tell them that the political situation wasn't *my* fault. But they might take it wrong, so I kept on walking.

I remembered Ryan telling me that he lived through the Mau-Mau rebellion in Kenya which ended in 1960. He saw some horrific sights. Kenya was ruled by Britain at the time, when white settlers took land away from black farmers. The blacks wanted their land black, and who could blame them? But it caused great bloodshed on both sides. I tried not to think about Ryan's stories.

The Psychic

By this time, I was receiving dried soup packages through the slot in my mailbox from a lunatic called Gerhart. He approached me at the last art exhibition saying he was an astrologist and wanted to do my Astrological Chart. He also claimed to be a psychic, using his energy to heal people through his hands. His business card read: "Astrologist, Psychic, and Healing Hands." I unwisely let him into my life and introduced him to my friends.

He was a gigantic blond hulk of a man from South West Africa, overweight too. He earnestly believed that he had a gift for healing, and perhaps he did. That's how he earned his living. But he was also a gambler. He came to my apartment once carrying a newspaper which listed all the horses racing next day. He asked me to tell him which names I intuitively liked. I had no clue about horse-racing, but told him which names I thought sounded energetic. He was going to bet on those horses, *silly man!*

Getting a residential telephone installed in Joburg was almost impossible. It took forever. Mimi told me that she'd given Gerhart one hundred Rands because he claimed to have connections at the telephone department and could bribe them for a faster installation.

"What, you gave him a hundred Rands?" I said to her.

She must have sensed from my expression that she'd

been a fool to waste her money. Gerhart had gone straight to the races.

One day he came to my place and asked me to design new business cards for him. But he was a little too friendly and got too close to me. He was starting to scare me. Then he began to caress my leg. I flinched and moved away. There was a strange look in his eyes when he touched me; his pupils were fully dilated as he came closer. He was aroused and decided that he wanted me.

"NO, you're a friend!" I said, smacking his hand away.

"But how can it hurt you?" he asked, wearing a dumb smile.

I definitely didn't want this.

"Stop it! Leave now, please!" I yelled.

He just laughed. Then he picked me up and carried me to my balcony.

"Put me down!" I screamed, pounding his chest with my fist.

"I don't want to hurt you, but..." he said, as he held me above the railing of my ninth-floor balcony. I could see the pavement below.

"Please, no!" I screamed again.

But there was no point in yelling or fighting any more; he was *intent*. I had no choice if I wanted to survive. I gave up resisting, but hated him after that. And I feared him. He was an unpredictable lunatic. And now these stupid packages of health soup and love notes from him every day in my mailbox! I threw them out and ignored him when I saw him on the street. But seeing him at a distance, I felt sad. He had been an unusual friend and somewhat interesting. He wasn't evil, just misguided and mental.

I told Mimi what happened and she wanted me to have him charged. But I didn't go to the police because I figured that an animal becomes more dangerous when he's cornered. I stayed clear of him instead. He knows what he did. It was dumb of me to have opened the door and let him into my life and endorsed him to my friends. I should have been more careful. None of us had anything more to do with him after that.

A Big Surprise

A friend of Mimi's daughter heard about the soup packages in my mailbox and thought it was hilarious. She started putting pebbles and rocks in my mailbox every day on her way to work. I thought it was Gerhart's doing but later learned who the real culprit was. Miraculously, amidst the soup packages and pebbles, there appeared an application to work at the 1976 Olympics in Montreal. My jaw dropped as I read this letter from heaven. This must be God's doing! There was no accompanying correspondence to explain. This had to be a sign that it was time for me to leave South Africa.

As it happened, the explanation was simpler. My father was involved with sports in Canada, and through his connections he managed to secure a job for me as a Hostess in the Olympics. All I had to do was fill in the application and fly home. I was guaranteed a thousand dollars for one month's work. When this explanatory letter from him eventually arrived, he expressed excitement about finding me the job and getting me back to Canada for good. My parents had heard about the Soweto riots and general unrest in South Africa. They wanted me home.

Things were going nowhere with Jerome in any case. He'd moved on with his life and never wrote. I reasoned that if I remained longer in South Africa, I'd likely settle down and have a family, and my sons would be fighting a political battle that was not of my doing. It was time for a change.

Excited letters flew back and forth between me and my parents. I'd scrimped and saved, but didn't have enough money for the flight to Montreal. My original return ticket from six years ago was almost worthless. So, my parents and brother paid for my ticket through Thomas Cook Travel Agency in Montreal, and I picked it up from their office in Johannesburg. My flight was booked for July 1st. On that airfare, I'd also be able to visit my relatives in Scandinavia before the start of the Olympics on July 17th. I was ecstatic and wasted no time giving notice on my apartment.

I sold or gave away my possessions, and packed boxes of things that I wanted shipped to Canada---things like my trusty wooden easel that Hennie made, my art supplies and clothes. There must have been at least ten cardboard boxes. Mimi would bring them to the post office after my departure. Little did I know when I weighed them at home, that they were just a few ounces off. She had to repack them all in order to keep the cost within the funds I gave her. She was so good to me. Looking back decades later, I realize that I took her many kindnesses for granted, and the immense kindness of my other friends too.

Farewell

Before I left the country, Mimi threw a fabulous going-away party for me. She brought out platters of delicious hors d'oeuvres---hot sausage rolls, stuffed chicken pies and my favourite spicy samosas made by a local woman. Bottles of wine flowed freely and guests clinked their glasses to wish me good luck. Lit candles and music created a warm, romantic ambiance.

My best friends and darling Maurice were there to see me off and wish me well in my new life. Ryan was in Swaziland, but Mimi didn't invite him because he abandoned us at the casino and was not to be trusted. Besides, he had his own life and we had no contact at that time. But all my other good friends were there... talking, dancing, laughing and drinking wine.

Guests spilled onto the balcony that splendid June night, and music played on the turntable. My favourite record was "Pata Pata," by South African singer Miriam Makeba. Her voice and that primitive beat gave my feet a life of their own. I couldn't stop dancing and got lost in the music. Both Maurice and Mimi were looking at me. I fluttered close to them and gave them each a kiss on the cheek. It felt good to be with these wonderful people.

For the past two months I'd been dating a British fellow called Edward, a Prince Charles look-alike according to Mimi. Perhaps it was his nose or regal demeanor. In our courtship, I learned that he would only eat or stay at the best establishments, and this he determined by the kind of cars parked outside. I couldn't believe it! I hardly knew any snobs and didn't think that I wanted to meet any more of them.

Edward had brought a good-looking office buddy with him to the party who asked me to dance. It was a slow dance. I felt his body heating up against mine. He started to kiss me, and I got that familiar tingling sensation in my spine which set the nerves in my body on fire. My Englishman saw this and came to intercept. He picked me up, slung me over his shoulder and carried me towards the door. This took me by surprise and I wasn't quite sure how I should react.

"Goodbye everybody, thanks for coming!" I called out and waved.

From my upside-down position, I saw my friends staring at us, uncertain of what to do. But since I didn't yell for help, they did not intervene. This was an unceremonious departure for their guest of honour, draped over Prince Charles's shoulder.

⚬

My departing flight was booked for July 1st. Mimi asked me why I wanted to arrive in Europe at the height of summer when everyone would be away on vacation. That thought never occurred to me, because weather in South Africa is always good and nobody has a special time to go on holiday. I dismissed the thought.

My own apartment was now empty, so Mimi invited me to stay with her until my departure. On my last evening at her place, she asked me to look at something in her closet.

"Come Eva, I have something to give you," she said, as she stroked a light green dress. "Now we are the same size. I want you to remember me when you wear this."

I knew how much she loved that dress and didn't know if I should accept it or not. She saw my hesitation and insisted I try it on. She smiled when she saw me in it; the fit was perfect. It transformed me into a woman who looked classy and svelte, just like her. I already knew how much I would miss Mimi, and didn't need her pretty dress to remind me. She had done so much to help me grow as a person. She was part of my life.

Next morning, she drove me to the airport. Yvonne and her fiancé followed behind but we lost them in traffic. Mimi parked her car and accompanied me to Departures. One last heartfelt embrace, then she looked at me and caressed my cheek.

"We'll miss you more than you'll ever know," she said.

I felt tears coming and started to sob. I knew how deep our friendship had grown over the years. Now I was leaving her and everyone else that I loved.

She waved me off and at last I was in the air. But my good friends were still on the ground, far away. On that airplane I felt sad and alone. Had I done the right thing to leave them? Little did I know they would always be with me.... day after day, year after year, for as long as I live. Remembered, loved, and always part of me.

Scandinavia

My first stop-over was in Copenhagen. At my hotel, I called relatives in Norway but nobody was home. I never told them I was coming. So instead, I flew to Gothenburg in Sweden where my other cousins lived; they were always home.

Once there, I remembered the streetcar number to get to their pretty suburb, and walked up the slope to that familiar house in the curve of the road surrounded by green trees and flowers.

Nobody was home! The door to the house was unlocked and lights were turned on in almost every room. Surely someone will return soon, I thought, as I waited for my aunt and uncle and four cousins. I had a key to the house which they gave me years ago, but didn't need to use it since the door wasn't locked.

That day turned into night. No one came. Where was everybody? I finally fell asleep on their sofa. One lonely day turned into the next. There was a cherry tree in their yard laden with fruit and I set out to eat my fill. I climbed that tree every day, and also found some oatmeal in their pantry. Then I remembered a little shop down the street where I could buy eggs and fresh vegetables.

I waited and waited for someone to return. Needing something to do, I noticed their house could use a cleaning. I scrubbed the floors, washed windows, vacuumed and dusted. I started in the living room, then on to the kitchen, bedrooms and bathrooms. Still, nobody came. So, I cleaned the attic and the basement. Two weeks passed. Maybe Mimi was right that everyone in Europe disappeared on holidays during the summer months.

An ardent admirer whistled loudly at me when I went for my daily walks down the street. I wished he would show himself, although this mystery gave me secret pleasure. One day my fan cried repeatedly, "we have no money, we have no money!" I laughed when I realized my admirer was a parrot. Too bad.

I soon discovered my cousins' record collection and enjoyed listening to the album "South Pacific," especially the rousing voice of the singer as he yearns to find his true love in the romantic song "Some Enchanted Evening." It brought back memories of Jerome and our love affair on the south sea island of Mauritius, and the great hopes we had for happiness. My heart ached when I thought of him.

More days passed and I needed to find out where my relatives were. After making some phone calls, I learned that my aunt and uncle were visiting their daughter Sonya in Paris and would be home in another two weeks. Sonya's sisters, Ingrid and Anita, were working as chefs in the south of France for the summer. I wanted very much to stay and meet them all. Too bad for my job at the Olympics; sorry Dad, but regretfully it wasn't going to happen.

I knocked on a neighbour's door across the street to ask if they knew where my cousin Erik was. An old man answered the door along with a younger man who was his son. The son said that Erik was out sailing and should be back in another week. Then he asked if he could invite me out for a coffee in half an hour. I accepted. It would be nice to talk to somebody.

I returned half an hour later. His elderly father had changed into a suit and tie to greet me. I took it as a compliment, and gave the dear old gent a hug for his show of respect. He was so moved that he reached for my hand and kissed it.

His son then took me to a nearby café. He told me that he just returned from Kenya. I wasn't quite clear on what he did in Kenya, maybe just lived. It was nice to have a conversation, although I wasn't interested in seeing him again.

Gustav

While waiting for my cousins to return, I looked for things to do. Rummaging through my address book, I found the phone number of my older half-brother Gustav who also lived in Gothenburg. He was my father's doing. I first learned about him back in Canada when I was sixteen years old. Dad had been drinking and my parents were arguing. Mom already knew about Gustav, and now he wanted to confess to us kids. This revelation came as a shock to me, although not unpleasant.

Dad told us that Gustav was doing his military service in the air-force in Gothenburg. He wanted me to meet him since I'd be flying to Sweden as soon as high school finished.

"Tell me if you think he really is my son or not," Dad slurred, entrusting me with this enormous judgement call.

Memories of that first meeting with my half-brother years ago came flooding back to me. I was staying with my relatives in that very same house which I just finished cleaning. I found out which squadron Gustav was with, and wrote him a letter saying that I was his sister and asked him if he would like to meet.

Gustav called me on the phone number I'd given to him. He was stunned to learn he had a half-sister and was eager to meet me. He knew nothing about me or my family's existence except from what his mother told him---that his father deserted them. Dad had told me he never even knew his fiancée was pregnant, and that they lost contact during the war. By the time he found out, he was already married to my mother. He sent money and presents to his son, but the boy was never told that Dad sent anything. What a shame.

Gustav and I arranged to meet at the train station next evening; he would be wearing his blue air-force uniform. I felt thrilled to be meeting my older brother for the first time. When I arrived at the train station, there were six young air-force men standing around talking to civilians. I approached the first one and asked if his name was Gustav. No. Then, the next and the next. By now I was feeling foolish. Two more fellows denied they were Gustav. The last one stood there grinning at me, looking amused that I'd been wrong five times. I pretended to smack him for laughing at me, the rascal. That broke the ice and we got off to a good start. He had a sense of humour and enjoyed teasing.

He invited me for coffee and cake at a café not far from the station. We talked and talked. He had gone AWOL in order to meet me, and crawled on the ground under the fence which surrounded their barracks so he could avoid the German Shepherd guard dogs. He seemed to enjoy the risk. As we sat drinking our coffee, he spotted one of his buddies and leaped out of his chair to talk to him.

"Back in a flash!" he said as he bolted.

He was so spontaneous and unpredictable, just like my father. There could be no doubt he was my father's son. He was so darn handsome in his dark blue uniform with flight wings and gold buttons, neatly cut hair and Dad's brown eyes. I was proud to have unearthed such a brother.

He later requested some time off so that we could drive to Oslo four hours away. I wanted Gustav to meet our father's family in Norway. When I introduced him to Dad's brother, it was as if they were looking in the mirror. They were almost identical except for age and height. When they shook hands, I saw the look of pleasant disbelief in their eyes. They had the same shaped face and hairstyle, same brown eyes and capricious smile. It was uncanny. My uncle was speechless for a few minutes, shook his head in amazement and smiled big. When my grandmother met Gustav she was thrilled, and openly showed her delight as she gave him a warm hug. This was *her* good-looking grandson. She couldn't care less who the mother was.

On the phone with Gustav now, he seemed happy to hear from me. I heard the surprise in his voice.

"You're back!" he said, "but what on earth were you doing in South Africa?"

I was prepared for criticism, as Swedes fervently disagreed with Apartheid. I had to defend myself a few times for having spent six years there. I didn't answer his question.

"Well, come meet my family and tell us all about it."

He was married to a lovely woman now, a nurse. They had four healthy, blond children. I wished those kids were mine, and envied him that he was settled with a wife and little ones. They lived in a big white house near the seaside on the outskirts of Gothenburg. Raspberries and gooseberry bushes grew in their yard, while green ivy climbed up the walls of the house and pink roses bloomed in flowerbeds. Their place emanated love and harmony.

The children took my hand and led me to their playhouse which Gustav had built under an apple tree. It was filled with toys and other playthings. I felt myself choking up and wondered if I would ever find a mate and have kids of my own. I yearned for it.

Then Gustav, the children and I, took a walk along a

rocky path to the nearby ocean for a swim. On the way, the youngest boy stopped dead in his tracks and screamed that he changed his mind and wanted his toys. He stamped his little feet and refused to walk another step.

"I don't understand where he gets his temper from!" Gustav said, shaking his head.

I laughed and certainly knew where he got it from--- our dear old Dad!

After a refreshing swim in the cool sea, we returned to the house and sat at a table in their garden. Red and yellow balloons bobbed above the chairs in celebration of their eldest son's seventh birthday party. They served pizza and home-made birthday cake with whipped cream and fresh strawberries. I enjoyed seeing those happy children having fun.

Gustav's mother was also there. She was a pretty woman in her late fifties with soft gray hair and nice skin. I could see why our father had been attracted to her. But she couldn't look at me, being my father's daughter. Hours passed, but not once did she lay eyes on me. I suppose she must have hated Dad all these years for moving on and leaving her with a child to raise while he married another woman and sired a new family. I knew my father loved the ladies. He just couldn't help himself with the opposite sex. I have his blood running through my veins. I am my father's daughter.

Cousins Return

At long last my cousins trickled home---first Erik, then Anita and Ingrid. The girls noticed immediately that the house was sparkling clean. Well, I had to do *something* for the month they were gone. I learned that my cousin Erik had been the last to exit the house. He was the culprit who'd left the doors unlocked and lights turned on, although he denied any memory of it. He was a brilliant doctor, but absent-minded with a busy social life which took him in all directions. In any case, no harm was done. They seemed glad to see me and had lots of stories to tell from their summer.

Erik owned a small sailboat and invited me for a trip to the rocky islands off Sjärgården where he kept the boat moored. The day was sunny with a good wind for sailing. I loved to feel the ocean breeze on my face as we whipped in and out of the island shoals.

Suddenly a jolt shot me forward and I landed hard with my butt on the floorboards. There was a grinding noise as our vessel stopped dead in the middle of the flow. We were stuck! Our boat had collided with a large rock hidden underwater and we were resting on top of it. Erik apologized profusely that he hadn't seen it. He jumped in the water to swing us free by rocking it. After fifteen minutes of panic and hard work, we broke loose and were sailing again.

We cruised into a quiet bay to calm our nerves and eat lunch---ham and cheese sandwiches on rye, with hot tea to drink from a thermos. By the time we were ready to set sail again, the wind had died down and we couldn't go anywhere. A young girl in a rubber dingy passed us and waved. Somewhat embarrassed, Erik asked the child to tow us out to the main water. She did so cheerfully, pleased that she could rescue two adults in distress.

I didn't know how to sail, and thought how marvellous it would be to manipulate the wind. Evening came, and Erik lit a lantern and hung it on the mast. We finished the tea and ate more sandwiches. The night was peaceful and warm with just enough wind to keep us moving. Moonlight danced on the waves, shimmering and alive. Erik brought out his guitar and strummed some folk songs as we glided on the water in the still of night.

My cousin Ingrid drove me to the little village where our mothers grew up. The red and white two-story house was just as I remembered, with a tall flagpole in the front yard proudly flying the blue and yellow Swedish flag.

Inside the home, photos of our mothers and uncle, their parents and grandparents, were reverently displayed on top of the old piano which had stood there for generations. Our grandfather, long since deceased, was a forest inspector. His dark wooden desk by the window held all his notes and letters from one hundred years ago, archived and neatly shelved. Ingrid and I sat on the antique settee below the cuckoo clock and read some of our grandfather's correspondence. From his letters, I gathered that he was well-loved and respected in the town. I was proud to come from such genteel stock, at least on my mother's side.

We climbed the stairs to the attic where I conjured up ghosts of our ancestors and remembered things that had terrified me as a child, such as the sound of rats chewing between the walls. Granny killed a few of them with her broomstick, crying out as she bludgeoned them. Then I saw Mom's ancient nursing coat from fifty years ago hanging there on a clothes rack. It was long and black, still in good shape. I took it with me since it fit perfectly and was back in fashion.

Ingrid and I remained in that house the whole day admiring everything---the family silverware, hundred-year-old crystal decanters with matching glasses, and copper pots which hung on the kitchen walls. All these things were respectfully left exactly as they had always been. This fine old home was now owned by my aunts and uncle, and would eventually be passed down to my cousins. My mother moved to Canada long ago and sold her share of the homestead to her brother. I no longer had a stake in it.

Ingrid percolated some coffee and we drank it outside in the breakfast nook behind the house where lush green ferns and wild roses grew. Our mothers used to make rose hip tea from them in the autumn. Then we picked fresh peas from the garden and ate them just like that. We strolled over to the deserted barn which still had the sweet smell of hay inside. Between the house and the barn, there stood a cold storage cellar which was carved out of a grassy hill with a door leading in. It looked like a troll's home, and was fortified inside by crude wooden walls and a ceiling. Our ancestors stored their produce there to keep it fresh.

Our jaunt around the grounds was rudely interrupted by a couple of trespassers strolling on the property. They completely ignored us.

"What are they doing here?" I asked Ingrid, annoyed at the nerve of them.

"Oh, that's okay," she said. "In Sweden anybody can tent on your land for one night as long as it's not too close to your house."

How bizarre, I thought. Such a liberal country.

My fun-loving cousins had lots of events planned for the rest of the summer. Now here we were aboard the Mina, a tall ship built in 1876. She was Sweden's oldest sailing galley, twenty-five meters long. We were taking part in a regatta from Sweden to Copenhagen. Erik knew the couple who bought the derelict old ship in 1964. They learned how to renovate it by reading library books on how to make it seaworthy. It was a colossal job. New wooden planks needed to be bent with heat to form curves. They bought new sails, new floor boards, and lots of rocks to fill the hull. They were brilliant and spared no expense. Sailing was their hobby, as it is with many Swedes living so close to the ocean. This ancient tall ship was something special. The owners rented it to friends for excursions such as this one.

Sunlight glistened on the waves, and there was that wonderful smell of salt in the air. You could hear the clap of sails as they snapped in the wind. We saw six other tall ships in the distance competing in the race. Those puffy white sails were a magnificent sight. The whole scene reminded me of Turner's masterpieces---his beautiful paintings of ancient sailing vessels gliding on the water which shimmered golden from the sun. Far off, I saw one ship painted black with dark brown sails like a pirate ship. It drifted like a harbinger of evil. I was glad not to be on that boat.

All the guys and gals onboard the Mina knew how to sail except me. They scampered up the sails' rigging, called to each other and followed captain's orders to let down this rope or that. Hours passed, and I became more and more frustrated that I couldn't help them. Then the wind died and we were stuck in one spot, unable to move.

A sudden impulse struck me.

"Any dangerous fish in these waters?" I asked, remembering the sharks in South Africa.

They assured me there were none. Hearing this, I dove from the high deck into the ocean.

"Man overboard!" someone yelled.

There was lots of panic and shouting until they realized I wanted to swim. Some of them followed me into the water, a few them peeling off their clothes for the plunge. One fellow's big dick bounced freely in the air as he jumped in. People in Sweden are very natural and believe that nudity is part of being human.

Our swim provided welcome relief from the boredom when the wind died. The cold Baltic Sea was refreshing as we splashed and laughed. It never occurred to me how I would climb back to the ship again; that deck was a long way up. Thankfully those still onboard tossed down a rope ladder. It was easy for me to clamber up, but not so for my cousin Ingrid who was heavier. She couldn't lift herself from the first rung to the second and was afraid she'd never get back up. I heard the panic in her voice as she called for help. Another swimmer pushed on her backside from the water so she could hoist herself up. It was a battle, but we were soon all accounted for. The wind picked up and we made headway.

Ingrid, Anita and I slept overnight in sleeping bags in the hull of the ship. It was unpleasant, dark and dingy. We were surrounded by rocks which filled the bottom of the boat to keep it balanced. Hard to imagine how a boat could float with so many rocks in it. We heard the sound of mice scampering around.

A cheerful captain and his girlfriend bantered as they cooked breakfast for us next morning in the kitchen below deck. We sat on benches built around a long wooden table bolted to the floor. I remember drinking strong coffee and eating eggs with toast, and cups of buttermilk. Swedes love their buttermilk. Fresh air and light came in through round port holes. Two ancient sepia photos of the ship's original owners hung on the wall in oval frames. The Mina was named after the man's wife, Mrs. Mina Paul.

Once back on land, Anita took me to a "student-fest" for graduates who just finished their university year. This particular celebration was held on a rocky island where two long tables were joined together near some red summer cottages. Boisterous college guys were already seated by the time we arrived, and singing drinking songs at the top of their lungs.

"Skål!" they cheered, clinking their beer glasses.

Anita found a seat while I stood waiting for a gentleman to find a chair for me. South Africa had left its mark on me; men took care of their women. I stood there waiting, and waiting.

"Why are you standing there? Go find yourself a chair!" one fellow hollered.

So much for chivalry. I felt offended, but set off to look for a chair. I found one propped against the cottage wall and squeezed myself in at the table. Then I waited for somebody to offer me a drink. Needless to say, nobody did. I was not used to ordering myself a drink and didn't do so. I sat there dry for the evening and felt out of place.

On our way home, I asked Anita why none of the guys offered me a seat or a drink. She stopped and stared wide-eyed at me, disbelieving what she heard.

"If you don't get your own chair," she said, "that would imply you're not strong enough to lift it!"

As for the drink, she laughed it off and said, "this is Sweden, women can get their own drinks. We are fully capable of lifting chairs and ordering drinks."

Okay, I thought, this is a modern society where men and women are totally equal. But I rather missed being treated as precious. I'd gotten used to it.

Off to Paris

My aunt and uncle finally returned from Paris. It felt good to meet them again. My aunt was my mother's sister, now in her sixties. She was the only sibling who was still madly in love with her spouse. I caught them necking on the sofa once, so cute. We spent a few pleasant days catching up, after which I flew to Paris to visit their daughter---my beautiful raven-haired cousin Sonya. She was working as a translator for an international company there.

When we were younger we always thought French boys were more exciting than boring Swedish boys, so it didn't surprise me that she moved to Paris as an adult. Paris, that exciting city of romance and culture. I remember thinking that she always seemed more French than Swedish with her long dark hair and tanned complexion. She dressed in a coquette way like French girls do, and spoke the language perfectly.

Sonya picked me up from Paris's Orly airport in her sporty red Volkswagen convertible. She didn't look any different from the last time I saw her seven years ago, and still had that warm smile with dazzling white teeth.

We drove to her charming apartment on rue Blainville in the famous Latin Quarter, and climbed three creaky flights of stairs to reach her place. Once inside, I looked around and saw that the wall next to her bed was covered by a shaggy brown carpet, the latest trend.

Her window offered a view of cobblestoned streets and outdoor cafés on several corners just like Vincent Van Gogh's famous painting "Café Terrasse at Night." Small grocers displayed their produce on sidewalk stands where I saw colourful fruits and vegetables, fresh fish on ice, meat, and buckets of vibrant flowers. You could buy wine in every shop. Guitarists played their music long into the night on the street below her apartment. The area was alive!

Strolling through her neighbourhood, we passed delicious cooking aromas from quaint restaurants. The tantalizing smell of escargots with garlic butter drove me crazy, as did many of the other dishes the French are famous for. But I had to be careful not to gain weight again.

I loved the bohemian atmosphere of that area. Paris was surprisingly clean and not that busy. I later learned that most Parisians were away on holiday for the month of August, hence my favourable impression.

While Sonya was at work, I was free to explore the city. I walked all over Paris. My favourite Impressionist artist Claude Monet had paintings hanging in The Orangerie Museum. I especially wanted to see his famous canvas of waterlilies in his garden at Giverny. It was a dream-come-true to see it in person and drink in the beauty of those brushstrokes. He transported me to a scene with lush green vegetation growing around a pond filled with exquisite mauve and white waterlilies. I felt that I was right there, and could smell the sweet scent of flowers growing.

But it cost me ten francs per day to pee in Paris! An elderly woman was always present in the public washrooms with her hand out to take money and give toilet paper. We have such a different outlook on washrooms in Canada. There's no one there to supervise, plenty of free toilet paper, and no one counts the squares.

An idea came to me to draw tourists in the famed Montmartre. This should be fun, although I felt nervous to do it. My paints and pastels were on their way to Canada, but I still had my sketch pad which contained a few of my charcoal portraits. One afternoon I made my way to this celebrated tourist attraction. It was a busy place where artists sat at their easels with paper and pastels, painting the customer sitting in front of them. Lots of tourist dollars to be made here.

I spoke with three elderly French artists who were squeezed into one section. The rest of the artists were foreigners. They said my drawings were good, but there was no room for me to sit and paint in Montmartre. Okay, I thought, then I'll stand and sketch tourists like I saw one woman doing. She was aggressive. She drew the person first and then approached them, showing them her sketch and demanding money for the work done. A charming bully. Being tourists, they bought it. I could do the same thing, why not?

I was trying to work up my nerve, but first decided to have a coffee at the outdoor café in the square and survey the scene. There were at least twenty artists painting portraits of willing tourists who wanted a souvenir from Paris. I spoke to my waiter and showed him my sketches. He thought they were good, but that I didn't stand a chance. He said the art plaza was now "owned" by the belligerent Yugoslavs who had cornered the market. They would muscle me out in a flash, just like they'd gotten rid of most of their French competition except for those three older artists who sat huddled together in the tiny zone designated to them. Times had changed. How sad.

Okay, so painting portraits in Montmartre wasn't going to work. I'd be a tourist instead. I walked past a crowd gathered around one man who suddenly threw a black rat on my neck. I screamed and ran for my life, thinking it was real. The crowd roared with laughter and threw coins into the man's hat for getting a good reaction. How entertaining for them! I was mad.

⁓

One afternoon, I wandered into an area filled with prostitutes standing on the sidewalk waiting for customers. Curious, I kept walking and tried not to stare too noticeably. Some painted ladies wore only fancy bras and see-through panties which revealed their pubic hair, and a sheer negligee over their shoulders. They glared at me as I walked by. Maybe they thought I was gay and wanted to choose one of them. Then I saw a prostitute who looked like the girl-next-door in regular clothes and natural short brown hair, the type of girl you'd want to take aside and ask "why on earth are you doing this? You can do better than this."

I got out of the area. Fortunately, nobody threw anything at me for gawking at them, not like in the red-light district in Amsterdam many years ago when some girls from the youth hostel and I wanted to explore the city. I was seventeen years old, a bit plump with long brown hair and wearing a blue sundress. Lagging behind the other girls, I was astonished at what I saw. Nearly-nude women were fully displayed in their windows and lying seductively on their sofas, their naked limbs illuminated by red lighting. As I walked past two hookers standing on the sidewalk, they grabbed me and pushed me hard into the recess of a building.

"Kom je uit Reeperbahn?" they demanded in Dutch, asking if I came from the famous red-light district in Hamburg. They thought I was from Germany, hustling in their territory. I didn't know if I should be offended, flattered or scared.

"Pardon?" I said, trying to untangle myself from their grip. They were hurting my arms.

"Oh! English, go away, go away!" they said, and shooed me off with their hands.

I caught up to my friends quickly and didn't lag behind again.

❧

Sonya and I had a blast together in Paris when she wasn't working. One Saturday night we got nicely dressed to go for supper somewhere on the elegant Champs Elysees. Along the way, something struck us as being so funny that we couldn't stop laughing. I was doubled over with laughter when suddenly my dress felt warm and wet. I had peed my pants! My long blue velvet dress was soaked. This made us laugh even more. Thankfully there was a café nearby where I rinsed my dress and panties in the washroom and dried them under the electric hand-dryer. We had supper in that café, exhilarated by our laughter and the ensuing mishap.

On a more serious note, we went to a fine restaurant another time and were seated next to some handsome black men. Sonya was friendly and chatted to them while I was more reserved. I couldn't help it. They asked me if I was South African because I was cool to them. I felt sad that my stay in that country had left its mark on my behaviour. I hoped it would wear off.

❧

Sonya made many friends during her five years in Paris. We were invited to one party where she argued with her then-boyfriend, a psycho who wanted to take her away from the celebration because of some perceived jealousy. She was naïve and couldn't recognize a psycho when she met one. I was acutely aware of volatile, unstable men, and convinced her not to leave the party with him even though he was trying to force her. Their argument made the atmosphere tense. I noticed a young man sitting in a corner playing his guitar and approached him to listen.

"Music soothes the nerves," he said in French, and continued to play.

"Whose nerves?" I asked, thinking it was for the benefit of the party-goers.

"Mine," he said, focusing on his strumming.

Then he turned to me and introduced himself as Lucien. We talked some more and I liked what I heard. He had a deep, masculine voice like Jerome. A warm rush came over me. This man embodied Jerome, my lost love!

Lucien was French, played the guitar beautifully and even sang. He was an actor and entertainer, short like Jerome with glasses and a sense of humour. I felt a sudden surge of adoration for him. The love I had bottled up for Jerome had nowhere to go, so it quickly got transferred to Lucien. Maybe we could renew our love in this city of romance. We dated a few times and I felt myself falling in love all over again. When we danced, I felt so comfortable wrapped in his arms that I could stay there forever. It was heavenly. His touch drew me to him like a magnet.

"What on earth do you see in him?" said Sonya, "he's short and ugly!"

I saw Jerome in him... his music, his humour, his deep voice and intelligence, the man I loved and lost. I hoped this time it could work out between us.

Lucien told me he had an acting engagement outside of Paris. I knew which day he'd be returning by train and went to the station to surprise him. My heart double-skipped when I caught a glimpse of him coming off the train. But as he drew closer, I saw him walking slowly with his arm around a little woman, deep in discussion with her. He saw me, nodded, and introduced us. Then he excused himself and continued to walk away with the girl.

I felt sick. I had to sit down on the nearest bench. Jerome had let me down again. I watched them disappear in the distance and the world collapsed around me. I sat on that bench for half an hour, trying to collect my thoughts. Sadly, I realized my affection had been misplaced. It was over, my fantasy ruptured. He was not Jerome.

Old Friends Arrive

Before I left South Africa, Maurice told me that he and Yvonne planned to visit Paris sometime in August. Mimi's daughter in Johannesburg knew of their plans, so I phoned her to ask when they'd be arriving. She said they'll be staying at the Pax Hotel but didn't know when. I pestered that hotel every day until Maurice and Yvonne finally came. They weren't expecting me to still be in Paris, and were surprised when Sonya and I showed up at their hotel with some of Sonya's young acting friends in tow. These fellows were ten years younger than us, *too* young really, but they were fun.

Yvonne kept looking at my cousin Sonya.

"What is it?' I said, wondering why she was staring.

"Oh, sorry. I just find it strange to meet one of your relatives. You never had any in South Africa."

Such an odd thought. She was right however. I had no relatives in that country. That's why I always felt better having good friends who became like family. I needed the warmth of family.

We abducted Yvonne from her hotel and took her to a party for the evening. Maurice was fine with that. He preferred to rest after the long flight from Johannesburg. However, he did comment on how young our companions were, as they could have been his grandsons.

The next day, Maurice called me at Sonya's place to invite me for lunch and a movie while Yvonne was away visiting a friend. This was almost like old times, seeing my beloved Maurice again. But it felt strange to meet him in a cosmopolitan European country. I was used to seeing him in South Africa where he was my strong guardian angel. Now here we were in Paris, having lunch at one of the city's fabulous restaurants.

He ordered salad for us to start with, then an entrée of chicken in wine sauce with mini potatoes, and Camembert with fruit for dessert. Nobody can serve food like the French, one small course after another. This gave Maurice and me time for leisurely conversation and many glasses of wine. I truly enjoyed the familiarity and warmth of his company.

But the movie he took me to after lunch was porn! In South Africa such movies were illegal, so tourists did abroad what they couldn't do in their own country. I felt offended that he'd taken me to a porn movie. I found it boring. The plot never changed and I kept falling asleep on his shoulder in the dark theatre. Each time I woke up, it was the same scenario---glistening vaginas and enormous shlongs in full erection being thrust into moaning women. I didn't complain because he was on holiday and I suspect he did this each time he visited Paris. It was his secret pleasure. My angel Maurice was human after all.

We finished our date with espresso coffee at an outdoor café and watched people walk by. It felt good to be with him again. We made sweet love back at his hotel room. I was sad to say goodbye to him and wondered if we'd ever meet again in person. We never did, although we kept in touch by letter and telephone. I cried after each time we spoke and felt my heart tear apart. I loved that good man, but sadly he was thousands of miles away.

Sonya and My Brother

After Maurice and Yvonne left the city to continue their travels through Europe, Sonya asked me to spend the rest of August with her in Paris so that so that she could take her holidays in September and fly with me to Canada. She wanted very much to meet my brother Viggo again. They fell madly in love seven years before when Viggo was twenty and she was twenty-three. They were both hot-blooded Aries signs. I knew my brother had strong feelings for her, but he ended it because they were first cousins.

Her sister Ingrid told me when I was in Gothenborg, that Sonya never got over him. In Sweden first cousins can marry, but my brother and I were brought up in Canada where intimacy between cousins is frowned upon. Sonya needed to know if love was still possible between them, and if time might have softened the "cousin taboo" which Viggo adhered to.

"I've never met a more passionate man," she said to me, "yet so kind and caring."

Their love affair first started when Sonya and Ingrid visited my family in Canada during the summer of 1969. Before coming to us, they flew from Sweden to New York City to look around. They told us they went for a stroll in Harlem where black people were really nice to them. This was contrary to anything I'd ever heard about Harlem, that it was a dangerous place for whites to enter. Then they went to Cony Island for a swim. Like any normal Swedish girls would do, they changed into their bathing suits on the beach. First, they stripped naked in full view of everyone, then they put their bathing suits on. Everybody gawked at them.

"What was wrong with those Americans?" Ingrid asked me. "Why did they all stare at us on the beach?"

I laughed when I heard her story. Of course most North Americans would stare.

My brother Viggo was an Olympic athlete back then, handsome and masculine. He and Sonya became inseparable that summer of 1969. They talked for hours. I've never seen my brother open-up like that to anyone. She brought out the best in him. I felt their attraction, but didn't learn to what extent until later.

Viggo, our two cousins and I, drove to the seaside in Cape Cod for a couple of weeks. Sonya drove with my brother in his green MGM sports car and I drove Mom's Rambler with Ingrid. Viggo loved to drive at night with no traffic, so we set off when it got dark. I found it hard to see in the darkness and followed his taillights, sticking to him like glue. It took us seven hours to drive from Montreal to Cape Cod---through Vermont, New Hampshire, Boston, and finally into the Cape. We could smell the salt in the air and knew we'd arrived at the ocean.

We drove along the curve of the Cape to the very tip in Provincetown. There my brother's friend Larry let the four of us sleep on mattresses on the floor of his rented cottage. Larry was Viggo's college teacher who was more like a friend. He had accompanied my brother to the Olympics in Grenoble that past winter. During the summers, Larry played in a jazz band at a pub near the wharf. Hordes of vacationers came to Cape Cod for their holidays. I still remember the taste of those delicious fried clams sold in all the snack bars.

It was in Provincetown where I first learned that my brother and Sonya were in love. It made me angry. How could they? Their intimacy was taboo, I thought, in keeping with my Canadian upbringing. After they broke the news to me, I took a long evening walk by myself, sulking and thinking how wrong it was.

I must have walked for a couple of hours, along Fisherman's wharf past noisy party-goers in the pubs. You could smell the fish. The damp night air was cold and I felt alone. Strangers didn't care about me. I realized the only people who cared was my family, they were the only ones who mattered. Heartache gripped me and I missed them terribly.

I hurried back in the darkness to Larry's house. I wanted to embrace them and tell them how sorry I was for behaving in such a way, that their love was beautiful and they were lucky to have found it.

But nobody was home at Larry's cottage! I needed to show my affection in any way I could, so I put sheets and blankets on their mattresses to be ready for when they came back. In those few hours alone, I'd accepted the love between Sonya and Viggo. It was powerful and special. But I couldn't tell my mother that her son and her sister's daughter had fallen in love. She would find out eventually.

Montreal

Mom's had seven years to get over the shock of Viggo and Sonya's love affair before we landed in Montreal. Sonya was nervous to see my brother, but wanted it more than anything.

We landed at Mirabel airport and saw Mom waving at us from the rafters as we walked through customs. Sonya came as a Swedish tourist, and I was a returning Landed Immigrant. I'd been studying and living abroad for seven years and didn't think that would pose a problem, but it did.

An Immigration Officer ordered us into a small interrogation room and closed the door. He kept us there for one long scary hour, asking probing questions about what I did in South Africa, what was Sonya's occupation, and what we intended to do in Canada. He examined our Scandinavian passports with their many stamps. Could he deport us? This was serious. Did he think we were spies? The man did not smile. He was grave and had all the power. Sonya and I remained dead quiet and didn't speak unless spoken to. It was tense. I think I held my breath a lot.

"Okay, you can go," he said at last.

We tried not to act nervous as we left the room in case he changed his mind. Once outside, I could finally breathe!

Mom drove us home to a joyful family reunion in Rosemere. My parents hugged us vigorously, happy to have me back for good and away from the "dangers of Africa."

That evening, my brother came for dinner to meet Sonya and me. I could see that sparks still flew between them and the look of love was there. They both seemed a little tongue-tied and hesitant to show their feelings; perhaps too many years had passed. For the sake of propriety, Sonya slept at my parents' home for the first two nights. After that, she stayed with my brother in the next town. They came home to us for dinners, more relaxed and gregarious than the first day. For Sonya, this was unfinished business. She needed to know if they had a chance at happiness, or to get closure so she could move on with her life. She had two weeks to find out.

⌒♪

One day while Viggo was at work, Sonya and I visited my sister Anna at her home on the Ste. Claire River just west of Montreal. She and her family lived in a two-story wooden house with a large balcony overlooking the water. After lunch, Sonya and I asked to use their little rowboat which was tied to the wharf.

We set out on the river, only to discover the boat was defective and could only row in circles. I've rowed before, so I knew it wasn't my fault that this boat only did circles. The predicament was hilarious and made us laugh. I rowed in circles to the middle of the river with Sonya draped on the back seat like a beautiful decoy. Her tanned slender legs were nicely exposed in a turquoise bikini while her long hair blew in the breeze. She was gorgeous. We looked like damsels in distress and it's possible that we were. But the situation was so comical that we couldn't take it seriously. The river patrol came by and asked if we needed help.

"No thanks, we're okay," Sonya said, flashing them a bright smile. At least three more boats with good-looking men offered to rescue us, enticed by the sight of Sonya displayed like a beguiling siren on the back seat.

The river current was getting stronger. I was afraid it might be too difficult to row in circles back to the house, so we accepted help from the last boat which came to rescue us. It was a medium sized yacht with a couple of middle-aged men on it. They towed our boat behind them and took us for a sight-seeing tour down the river. After twenty minutes of awkward conversation, we started to feel vulnerable out on the water with two strangers. We got an ominous feeling and asked to go home. The two men looked at each other.

"Aw, have a drink with us, ladies. Come on, stay with us. The night is young!" one of them cajoled.

"No thanks. We just want to go home."

We were both good swimmers and could have jumped from the speeding boat if we had to. They raced downriver with us for another five minutes. Then they spun their yacht around and dropped us and our dinghy close to the house. I was relieved they did as we asked. We hopped into our little vessel and rowed in circles back to the wharf. This had been an adventure. Our family saw us from their balcony and said they forgot to tell us that the boat was not quite right. But they thought we rowed in circles on purpose to get attention.

Sonya and Viggo enjoyed the two weeks they spent together. She told me that she would always love him, and I know he felt the same. But once again the dilemma of being first cousins would keep them apart; my brother couldn't get past that. And perhaps Sonya found him changed, I don't know. I wasn't privy to what took place in their private time. But I do know that he cherished those memories from her visit, and Sonya returned to Paris with the answer she sought. She could move on.

Job at Dunn's

After Sonya left, I searched endlessly for a job. Dad was pressuring me to pay him back for his portion of my plane ticket. I went to many unproductive interviews where companies asked me why on earth I'd want to tie myself down to office work after such interesting travels. Fed up with trying to get traditional work which was taking too long to find, I walked down Ste. Catherine Street in Montreal and knocked on restaurant doors. Mr. George, the elderly manager of Dunn's restaurant, greeted me at the entrance.

"I *really* need a job!" I said.

He surveyed me closely up and down. He asked no questions except my name, but nothing about previous experience. I had two legs and feet that functioned, a mouth which could talk, and I looked okay. I was hired and another woman was fired. That poor woman was sacked without notice to make way for me. She implored Mr. George to keep her on, tearfully explaining why things would be impossible for her without a job. But she was overweight and had trouble walking. It wasn't fair to fire her so suddenly. I felt it was my fault for showing up, but the boss didn't seem happy with her in any case. Waitressing is a precarious profession, in one day and out the next.

I was hired for the night-shift from 11 p.m. until 8 a.m. This shift allowed me to learn about the beings who lived by night. After the entertainment clubs and gay bars closed, they came to Dunn's for the most delicious smoked-meat sandwiches and cheesecake ever made. Strippers, night club performers and gay bar patrons---they all came during my shift. I'd never been exposed to this side of life, so it was a revelation. I took it all in stride and listened with amusement to the gays teasing each other. People forget that waitresses have ears. I tried not to react when they necked in the booths. Some of them even pretended to flirt with me to make their boyfriends jealous.

Then there was the drama between the cook and a waitress. He really liked her and pursued her in between orders. But she didn't feel the same and rebuffed him constantly. You could see the hurt in his eyes. He became sullen. But they had to find a way to work together without poisoning the atmosphere.

I gained a new respect for waitresses, those women who work at it all their lives. Everybody had a story. Some were single mothers trying to support their children. One waitress whose feet were bleeding, could take on a whole section of customers without letting on that she was in agony.

I enjoyed chatting with the customers but I was a slow server. Some patrons left because I took too long to get to them, although they were nice enough to apologize for leaving. After one long night in particular, it was time to serve breakfast. I was very tired. A young man ordered his breakfast and I brought him the bill after he'd eaten.

"Miss, I just want to say that this is not what I ordered," he said quietly after finishing his meal. "You brought me bacon and eggs but I asked for cereal and milk!"

I started to laugh. He was nice about it and paid anyway, such a good sport. He even left me a tip.

One thing I couldn't handle was working at the counter. It was too immediate. The customers were right there in your face with no space between us to let me think. I always panicked and wondered---was *he* the one that just placed the order, or was it the guy next to him? Darn, what did he order? I became a nervous wreck whenever they asked me to work there. But we all had to take turns to relieve the regular waitress on her breaks. She never waited tables because she couldn't walk fast or far. She loved serving at the counter and had ongoing friendships with the regulars who sat on stools right in front of her, much like a bar where clients confide in the sympathetic barmaid.

~

After working nights at Dunn's, I'd take the morning bus back to my parents' home in Rosemere. The trip took one hour. When I got home, I'd empty out my tips for the night and roll them in papers---quarters, nickels, dimes and pennies. A good haul was about $30 for a night. Then I'd close the curtains and stick an extra blanket on the window to block the sun. Physically exhausted, I'd lie there waiting for sleep and listening to the comforting sounds of my mother putzing in the kitchen.

On one bus ride home in late autumn, a young fellow sat beside me. He was about fourteen with a thin build, pale eyes and dish-water blond hair. He talked to me the whole time. I listened and asked the occasional question, not wanting to be rude. When I got off at my stop in Rosemere, he did too. I usually walked along a quiet road which ran parallel to the main street. It was peaceful, with trees on either side and old established family homes where my former classmates used to live. The boy took it upon himself to walk with me there. I thought he was a bit nervy, but saw no harm in it.

Half-way along that side road he pulled out a huge knife, brandishing it at me. He brought the knife closer and threatened me, directing me to the bushes beside the road. I looked at him in disbelief. This little shrimp came up to my shoulders, and now he thinks he's going to rape me because he has a knife? I could have toppled him easily, but that was a mighty big knife.

There was nobody on the road but us, nobody to help me. This was scary. I got that pang in the heart of impending danger and looked around for options. The Michener's house was not far away so I ran for it. My loud banging on the door brought old Mrs. Michener to the entrance, looking confused by the urgency.

"Help! A guy out here just pulled a knife on me!"

"Oh?" she said, looking around.

He'd disappeared. She let me into her kitchen and peered out the window. I'm not sure she believed me. Things like this don't happen in Rosemere on that quiet, picturesque road. I didn't dare leave and asked if I could stay a little longer. After ten minutes, I left by way of a shortcut through the golf course. I had jogged there often during my high school years and knew every path by heart. Arriving at the safety of my parents' home was a relief. I didn't tell them about that incident.

Letter from Jerome

That winter in Montreal was cold and snowy, the kind of winter that makes you long to be in the warm tropics. Mom seemed hesitant as she handed me a letter. The handwriting looked familiar... it was from Jerome! I felt my heart do a somersault. This was a huge surprise! He must have gotten my address from Yvonne. I tore it open, careful not to rip the precious contents.

I could hardly believe my eyes as I read his warm, loving words. He asked if we could try again to know each other better and build a lasting relationship. He said that he loves me. I wanted to melt with happiness. I always felt there was unfinished business between us. Surely if we had more time together, we could learn to love and appreciate each other. We were so well-matched otherwise, that I was certain the issue which gave us problems could be resolved with time.

Once again, we started a long-distance love affair through letters. As before, he expressed himself brilliantly and stimulated my mind. He had much to say in his letters which I looked forward to with great anticipation. Dad asked to read one "to examine the guy's angle," but I didn't let him. Jerome had no angle. He just loves me and wants me back, I was sure of it.

I eagerly counted my tips from the restaurant and

rolled them in papers. Soon I had enough saved from my salary and tips for an airline ticket to Mauritius. My motivation was sky-high as I'd shortly be joining the love of my life. I had no interest in meeting anyone else. Jerome was foremost in my mind, just like he had been before. Thoughts of love, weddings, babies and tropical weather were swirling in my head. He was all I could think about.

St. Mary's Church

The idea to become Catholic came to me... anything for Jerome! His faith was important to him and I wanted to share that with him. It didn't matter to me what religion I followed if it made Jerome love me more. I believed that God would look after me in whichever church I chose to worship Him.

St. Mary's was just down the road. I wanted to learn what was involved in becoming Catholic, and went to Mass that Sunday. I sat in the back row, the better to observe. It was a pretty church with a colourful statue of the smiling Virgin Mary holding baby Jesus. She had rosy cheeks and was dressed in a white robe with a sky-blue cape over her shoulders. A large statue of Jesus hung on a cross above the alter, and two angels with gold halos kneeled at his feet.

Sunlight streamed through stained-glass windows which showed dramatic scenes of devout people bearing the burdens of the world. Candles flickered in little glasses making everything cozy. I saw paintings of holy faces decorating the walls; perhaps they were saints. Organ music billowed from the second floor. Everything felt loving and welcoming. Yes, I could easily become Catholic amidst all this splendor.

After the sermon and singing of hymns, collection was taken. Then the seated people stood up one row at a time and walked to the alter. I didn't want to be the only one sitting, so I went up too. I'd seen the Sign of the Cross done in movies so I knew how to do it. When it was my turn in front of the priest, he gave me a wafer which I accepted and received his holy benediction. This felt so good.

After the service ended, I lingered in my seat to revel in all this righteousness.

"Are you a visitor here?" the priest asked, having crept up behind me.

"Yes," I said, my hopes dashed of not being noticed.

"You're not Catholic, are you?" he said, staring at me.

"No." I felt my face get hot as I averted his eyes.

"What did you do with the Host?"

"I ate it," I said, puzzled.

He looked horrified!

"You weren't supposed to eat the Host! Nor were you supposed to receive Holy Communion if you're not Catholic!"

I wanted to cry. "I'm very sorry. I didn't know."

"You should have crossed your arms like this and only received a Blessing, not Holy Communion!" His voice was stern.

I felt humiliated, and believed the Catholic church had rejected me. I would have kept them busy in Confession!

The Dentist

It was my birthday on that cold day in December. Christmas music played non-stop in the restaurant, while shiny red balls and flickering lights hung on evergreen boughs.

I just finished working the night shift with another waitress called Estelle, and sat myself down at the back of the room to transfer the overflowing tips from my uniform pockets to my purse. Customers tipped generously at Christmastime. I'll have plenty of money saved to join my darling Jerome in Mauritius.

Word got out to my boss Mr. George that it was my birthday. He insisted that Estelle and I join him and the night cook for a drink to celebrate my big day. I had a dentist appointment at noon, so I'd have to hang around the city for a couple of hours in any case. The four of us squeezed into a little booth and Mr. George poured whiskey from the bottle. Estelle and I drank lots of whiskey, smoked, talked, laughed and listened. The day staff brought over some delicious cheesecake in my honour. We sat there and celebrated my birthday for two hours. Finally, time came for me to take a taxi to the dentist. Estelle was confused about where she was and asked to come with me.

We arrived at the dentist's office jubilant, possibly even off balance. I'm sure we stank of strong whiskey and cigarettes. The good dentist lived on the same street as my parents in our fine suburb of Rosemere. He was a friend of my father's, and had been our family dentist since my childhood. Now here I was all grown up and very drunk. I felt no shame at that point, and sank into the comfortable padded dentist chair. He was going to insert a crown on that back tooth, the one that got the root canal in Mauritius.

I opened my mouth wide and fell asleep. Although still conscious, I remember trying to kiss his hands many times as he worked on my mouth. I think his assistant managed to fend off most of my kisses. The drills sounded like melodious little songbirds in the distance. I felt the dentist's solid body next to me moving very close as his strong steady hands pushed the crown into position. He worked with such strength. I always found his manliness attractive.

Then it was over and I had to wake up and stand. It all seemed like a nice dream, no pain at all. I paid five hundred dollars to the secretary and looked around for Estelle. Two receptionists walked her back to the office from the bathroom. She got very sick from all that whiskey and they had to babysit her. That was a day they will all remember.

The dentist himself accompanied me to the elevator. I regained my senses a little, but was still feeling very sensual. This was awkward, him standing with me in the foyer waiting for the lift. What did he expect from a woman who kept trying to kiss his hands during surgery? Perhaps he hoped for some kind of invitation. He stood there in all his masculinity and smiled at me. *Oh boy, what have I done?* By now I was truly embarrassed. He was a respectable family man and friend of my father's. After some small-talk with him, I escaped down the elevator with Estelle in tow.

We hailed a taxi on the street. Estelle stuck her head out the window for fresh air like a puppy dog. I was still drunk and afflicted by excessive sensuality. It's possible that

I may have groped her body which was encased in her thick winter coat. I probably shouldn't have done that. The cab dropped her off at her house and continued to the bus terminal for me. Next day at work, rumours had spread that I liked *girls!*

Telegram from Jerome, 1977

Our love letters continued across the miles. Jerome wrote that he loved me. My parents knew I was crazy about this man who broke my heart once before. Now here I was deliriously in love with him again, the photo of his smiling face displayed on my night table close to me.

Then things went quiet and no letters came. What was happening? There was nothing for a month and a half. The silence was driving me nuts. I was ready to leave winter behind and join my true love in Mauritius, but something was wrong. I decided to force his hand, and sent a telegram saying that I'll be arriving for his birthday in February. Almost immediately, a cable came from him:

"Do not come. There is a change of plans. Letter follows. Jerome."

I was devastated. The wire was sent to my sister Anna's address because I didn't want my father knowing everything that was going on in my love-life. She telephoned and read it to me. My heart sank. With those words, I knew it was over.

That winter in Montreal was frigid with three feet of snow on the ground. Mom drove me to Anna's house to pick up the telegram. My sister served us a snack of crackers and shots of 150 % proof Jamaican rum. Then she handed me the cable with Jerome's message. When I saw those typed words so cold on the page, I cried until there were no more tears left, sobbing wretchedly and getting very drunk on the rum. As we walked back to Mom's car, I collapsed in a snowbank. My brother-in-law lifted me out of the snow and helped me to the car. I slept all the way home.

A week later came Jerome's explanation in a letter. He chastised me for taking the decision to travel without first consulting him. The reason he hadn't written was because he'd met someone else and it wasn't the right time to try to make our relationship work.

That was it! As I read his words, I realized we had reached the end. I had to get over him. I didn't reply to his letter. Rather, I took the deliberate decision to spend my airline money on furniture for a new apartment in downtown Montreal. In my mind, Jerome was over for good.

Mom helped me look for an apartment. We found a nice one-bedroom suite in a high-rise on Milton Street near McGill University. She proposed that we go halves on the rent so she could stay over sometimes after work during a snowstorm instead of driving to Rosemere. Winter storms in Quebec can be wicked. I knew she hoped that I would settle down in Canada and not succumb to wanderlust again. She thought it might be easier for me if I lived in Montreal rather than with her and Dad in Rosemere. I agreed. Besides, my parents fought too much, just like they did in my childhood.

It was a pleasure to spend my money on furniture, starting with a comfortable rust-coloured corduroy love-seat. Next, an easy chair and a bed. Mom brought over a table, chairs, and a desk. We made it cozy. The apartment had a balcony with a scenic view of Mount Royal. There was even a swimming pool in the building. I felt at peace after finally accepting that it was over with Jerome. I could move on.

A Swanky New Job

An old classmate from my high school years saw me working at Dunn's and thought I should have a better job. He had become a lawyer, and knew of a job at a prestigious law firm where they needed a receptionist to replace a woman on maternity leave. *Fantastic!* He made the arrangements and I went for an interview. Their fine offices were located in one of the towers in Place Ville Marie, the heart of Montreal's business district.

The firm's modern offices were impressive. Anyone could see this was a first-class establishment. I wore Mimi's light green dress for good luck. My hands were sweaty from anxiety by the time I met the boss and office manager. In fact, they were dripping wet. I had to shake people's hands; it was mortifying! Everyone was so proper. One secretary wiped her hand on her skirt after shaking my hand, yet she managed to keep smiling. I wanted to die! The underarms on my dress were wet from perspiration. I hadn't worked in a proper office for years. In spite of the sweat, they hired me to answer the switchboard and receive clients.

My telephone in reception had lots of extensions and buttons that lit up. I'd never seen such a complicated phone and felt terribly backward. The last phone I worked on professionally was that large old-fashioned board with plug-in cords in Cape Town. I didn't want to seem stupid or ask too many questions, but I should have. When they asked me to make a couple of Xerox copies, the machine spewed out hundreds of them! And sometimes the young girl-Friday asked me to hand her this or that lying on my desk, but I didn't know what it looked like or what I was supposed to give her. She shook her head as if wondering what planet I'd come from. Once I handled a phone call from the Prime Minister of Canada and accidentally put him on hold. I got heck for that.

I soon realized this was a highly esteemed legal practice and believed that our fine lawyers were the most prominent in Canada. One of the tall, dark-haired partners sometimes wore a spectacular black cape to work and swung it off dramatically to hang it up. This maneuver was impressive to witness. He was going to spend the day in Court, so perhaps this performance was a prelude. Even the breadth of his shoulders was intimidating.

Another time a wife called her lawyer husband and I told her he'd left for the day. She immediately got suspicious and quizzed me about where he could have gone, presuming he had a girlfriend. Realizing my blunder, I said he likely went out for cigarettes, which was a plausible guess.

A man came into reception one day asking to see one of our lawyers. He had striking blue eyes, but I didn't recognize him.

"Who shall I say is calling?" I said.

"John Turner."

Five minutes later, three of the secretaries scurried to my desk, awestruck by this famous man and how good looking he was. I should have recognized him but for my absence from the country these past seven years. He would become Canada's Prime Minister one day.

I was walking on eggshells here. These distinguished

lawyers and their secretaries were conservative, proper and self-controlled. Everybody was serious. My three-month term of employment with the Law Firm ended; they did not keep me on. Instead, they referred me to another legal office where I accepted the position of receptionist.

This new place needed a telephonist to sit in a tiny cubicle and answer phone calls. The walls in that cubicle were painted harsh white with no pictures hanging on them, no view or anything to look at. A glaring neon light hung in the ceiling. There was only enough room for my chair, a small desk, and a telephone with a few extensions. It was so different from the sophisticated law practice where I'd just been working. As soon as I answered the phone at this new place, the company's three lawyers were already listening on their extensions. It felt so sleazy, so desperate for business. I couldn't stand it.

I soon realized that the secretary was having an affair with the owner of the firm. His office door was often locked with him and that woman inside. A "Do Not Disturb" sign hung on the door, and I had instructions to hold all his calls. She eventually came out a bit dishevelled, but I pretended not to notice. She didn't seem happy about the situation. He also made her go shopping for him---gifts for his wife or kids. The goings-on in that place did not sit well with me.

When I returned to the prestigious office to pick up my last paycheck, I was surprised to see the secretary of my present employer there. She was talking quietly to my former office manageress. They obviously knew each other. She was crying and wiped her tears with a tissue. I thought perhaps she was unhappy about being forced to have sex with her boss in order to keep her job. I made a mental note never to let that happen to me.

I did not like my new job, and hated to waste precious time and energy in that place. To relieve the stress after work one day, I craved a drink in a pleasant setting around congenial people. There was a fine hotel on Sherbrooke Street not far from my apartment. I walked there and sat in one of the plush green chairs in the lounge, feeling a bit awkward to have come alone. But I needed a drink, and was comforted by the subdued lighting and soft music playing in the half-filled room. Patrons talked quietly. It felt good to be in the company of others. I wanted something strong and ordered a Black Russian. I was starting to relax now.

About fifty feet away, a group of men were seated, deep in discussion. I was enjoying my drink and happened to glance over at them. One of those men kept looking at me.

"Are you a working girl?" he hollered across the room.

"Yes," I said.

"How much?" he asked.

It took me a minute to fathom what he meant. I started to laugh. *He thinks I'm a hooker!*

"I work as a receptionist," I said, still laughing.

Oops! The man said he was very sorry. He sent over a glass of cognac by way of apology. I lifted my glass to thank him, but thought about that incident afterwards. A woman can't go and enjoy a drink by herself like fellows do without appearing to be on the make. It wasn't fair.

Fridays, a popular pub in Montreal, lay just around the corner from my workplace. People went there after five to eat, drink and relax. I needed to unwind after yet another joyless day at the shady law office, and strolled over to the pub. Fridays was beautifully decorated with Tiffany-style lamps in the ceilings and sparkling clean glasses which hung upside down above the bar. I looked around at the well-dressed men and women who sat near me, absorbed in their conversations.

A tall, dark-haired man in his late thirties approached and asked if he could buy me a drink. His name was Mario, a commercial artist and very easy to talk to. He said that he worked for an art company a few blocks from there. I mentioned that I used to earn a living painting portraits. This seemed to pique his interest, and he introduced me to his buddies who were also artists. After another round of beer and friendly banter, they invited me to walk with them to their studio and show me the place. I felt at home with these people. They laughed and joked, and life was not so serious as in a legal office. These people suited me.

Mario and I met for coffee a few times after that. I told him about my plight of working in a restrained, sleazy environment. He thought this was against my nature as an artist.

"How'd you like to visit a commercial art studio different from mine and see what happens there?"

"Fantastic! I'd love to!" I jumped at the chance.

He said he'd call me next day at work with the details.

As promised, he phoned me while I sat in my tiny white cubicle.

"Everything's set for tomorrow, Eva. I have a friend who runs an art studio and you can see what they do there. I'll take you. Meet me in front of Ogilvy's at ten in the morning."

That uplifted my spirits. Early next day, I called my lawyer boss with the excuse that I was sick and couldn't come in. Of course, they'd been listening on their extensions to my conversation with Mario and knew all about what I'd be doing. They fired me when I came to work the day after, thank God for that. I couldn't have stood it much longer.

But now I needed another job. Mario kindly arranged for me to assist him with his commercial photo retouching. His boss put an extra table in his office for me and I was allowed to work as an apprentice on reduced salary while I learned the trade. Another artist shared our office and swore every time he made a mistake, which was often. It was amusing yet unsettling. I preferred harmony.

I close-cut photos for Mario which prepared them for publication. This was exacting work, the opposite of impressionistic painting. I learned about this new field from him and enjoyed it more than any other office job. Mario boasted to his clients that I could draw portraits, so we received a job to paint a French-Canadian western singer called Willie LaMotte for a magazine. I didn't know the singer but worked from a photo of him. The magazine's Art Director was thrilled with the result and so was Mario.

I enjoyed the art world and felt more at home with these spontaneous, crazy artists than with lawyers. Mario and I settled into a routine; we'd work in the mornings, go for lunch at midday, then back to work again until five.

Mom came to visit me at the apartment one evening. She wanted to hear about my new job in the art studio and was curious about this man I'd met. I loved my mom. She was always there for me my whole life. I wanted her to meet my mentor, so we invited Mario to come for coffee and cake. He brought along his guitar.

"You don't have to worry about me," he said to Mom as he strummed a tune for us. "I'm a married man."

Mom smiled and nodded.

⌒つ

Mario and I grew close over the next eleven months of working together. Over time, we became romantically involved. We got along well, never argued and knew only joy. Business was so good that he wanted to set up his own company with me as his assistant. When a studio came up for rent in the next building, he grabbed it. The space was large with high ceilings and lots of light streaming through the windows. There was plenty of room for art tables, chairs, shelves, and nitrogen tanks for the air brushes. We also bought hanging green ferns to make the environment homey.

Mario's wife and 12-year-old daughter came to the office a few times to bring him lunch. His wife seemed pleasant... gentle, slender and blond. She removed some of the dead leaves from the plants. I found her gesture touching.

Mario strode through the McGill campus every morning before work to fetch me. We usually met halfway through the campus and walked to work together. He said he'd recognize my walk anywhere as I bounced with each quick little step. We were always happy to meet.

But as time passed, I discovered that nobody is as possessive as a married man. He phoned my apartment every evening to make sure I was home. If I said that I'd be meeting someone for coffee, he'd ask me where. Then he'd be right there, parked by the sidewalk of the café to drive me home. I felt like a naughty teenager. It's as if I belonged to him and nobody else could have me. I guess it was flattering, but he became obsessed. Then he started talking about leaving his wife and daughter. I did not ask for that, nor did I want it.

His wife must have known he was distracted of late. She'd phone him with the silliest emergencies. Once she called him at work and told him their dog threw-up on the bed and asked what should she do? Other times she phoned and said she couldn't control their twelve-year-old daughter. Things were heating up for him at home. Mario told me that she'd gone through his pockets and found his address book, and phoned everyone in it to ask if they knew Mario. She even called my mother in Rosemere because her number was in his book too. Mom lied and said she didn't know anyone called Mario.

I understood that his wife was fighting to keep her husband. I would have done the same. It had not occurred to me that that my happiness with Mario would cause suffering. It made me sad that his wife felt threatened by someone who had no intention of taking her husband away.

Mario started coming to work with dark bags under his eyes. He was going through hell at home and not sleeping well. He said he was torn between the two of us.

"It's exhausting to service two women," he said.

What? His words surprised me, because he'd given me the impression that he had a hum-drum marriage and didn't love his wife, but stayed in the marriage for his daughter's sake. Confused, I looked at him as he searched for the right words.

"She still pours my bath at night, cooks my meals, washes my clothes and takes care of our daughter," he said quietly, averting my eyes.

That's when I realized he still loves his wife, and she obviously loves him!

He said she was sleeping on the couch nowadays, and that she cried and cried. He was afraid something bad would happen to her eyes from crying so much with her glaucoma. Our affair had reached a crisis point. Mario was a nervous wreck. Then he spotted his wife stalking us from behind a building near the office. She'd seen us go out for lunch holding hands. By now he'd become paranoid. His life was falling apart and he needed to take one direction or another.

I bowed out of the relationship and also stopped working with him. We ended our affair so he could concentrate his family. I didn't want to cause either of them more pain, nor did I want this man on my hands full time. We would be "friends only" from then on. He was a good man, but I felt a sense of relief to be free.

Concordia

While working all those months with Mario, I discovered that I enjoyed the commercial art field and wanted to learn more. It was already September when I applied to study graphic design at Concordia University. It was late in the application process, but I really wanted to get in. Hoping to speed up my acceptance, I made an appointment with the Head of the Graphic Design Department to show him samples of my artwork.

It was hatred at first sight. I detested his personality type and he sure didn't like me either. He was a red-faced, impatient, middle aged man with high blood pressure, a quick temper, and a thick accent from Russia or someplace like that.

"No, I cannot make room for you in the program. It's already full!" he said.

I pressed him harder saying that I *really* wanted to do this and was very good.

"NO, I will absolutely not make any exceptions or remove somebody to make place for you!" He slammed his desk drawer shut and caught his finger which started to bleed.

"Damn it!" he yelled, as he licked the blood off his finger. He motioned furiously to the door with his bloodied hand.

"You can go! Get out!"

I left his office, my hopes dashed for a career in graphic design. A few days later, a letter arrived from the Concordia Admissions Office. I tore it open and read that I'd been accepted after all, as my academic credentials had gotten me in. Such fantastic news! I jumped up and down and felt on top of the world. Thankfully the Admissions Office didn't know that I just had a fight with the Head of the Department and drawn blood. They gave me two years credit for the four years I spent at McGill, so I only needed to study two years at Concordia to earn a Fine Art's Degree.

The following Monday was registration day in the auditorium where I would choose my courses. That crisp autumn day was glorious as I walked to the venue; the sun shone, birds were singing, and I was going back to university to train for a career which should take me through the rest of my working life. Happiness propelled me with energy.

You could feel the excitement in the auditorium as hundreds of students decided on their courses. I found the table where I was supposed to register. But my heart sank when I saw who was sitting there with a bandage on his finger---that horrid Head of the Graphic Design Department! His face turned white when he saw me.

"So, you got in after all?" he muttered, after recovering from the shock of seeing me.

"Yes," I said, looking for another table to register, but this was it, no other choice. The only chair was in front of him. So, I sat down and leafed through the curriculum. There were so many courses to choose from; it was confusing. I asked him which ones would be best for me.

"How can they let somebody in who doesn't even know what she wants to study?" was his surly answer.

My head wanted to explode with rage. I had to keep

calm and not give him any reason to throw me out. He's lucky I didn't attack him because in my mind I wanted to kill him! I completed registration and left the auditorium, trying to shake the anger that man ignited in me. Thank God he would not be teaching any of my courses. I found out later that he was living with one of his former students, a gentle fluffy girl whom he could bully.

∾

The next two years flew by with lectures and assignments. Can you believe it, Jerome sent me a telegram after my first year asking me to return to Mauritius so we could try again. I felt some satisfaction that he wanted me to come, but mostly relief that I'd gotten over him and my heart didn't flutter. I found it hard to believe that he had the gall to ask me that, after what he put me through over a year ago. It meant that another of his romances didn't work out and I was his back-up plan. I telegraphed him saying:

"Sorry. Cannot come. Am studying art at university. Letter follows."

It felt good to say "letter follows," just as he said to me when I was ready to join him last year. Our correspondence ended with my letter explaining the situation---that I was busy with courses which occupied all my time and didn't want to abandon my studies.

∾

At school, we were given challenging assignments which I worked hard to complete. Sometimes I did homework well into the night. I bought one of those slanted art tables which stood near my window next to a massive spider plant that hung from the ceiling. It had thick green foliage with one hundred baby blooms cascading from it. I counted them because the plant was spectacular. It thrived in that bright corner where it received lots of light and love.

Some of my classmates had taken courses with my father who was enrolled as an art student the year before. Dad said those painting classes at Concordia University were the greatest enjoyment he ever had. He was a talented artist, but when he was a young man in war-torn Norway, his parents didn't consider being an artist a serious profession for a man. He waited until he turned sixty to study it here.

During those years at Concordia, Dad bubbled with enthusiasm, and painted endlessly in his home studio in Rosemere. He placed his big easel by the window and always had a landscape on the go. Other impressive oil canvasses were displayed around the room. He painted nature scenes reminiscent of his Norwegian homeland--- trees, waterfalls, rivers and snow-capped mountains. With his artistic talent and persuasive personality, he managed to get his landscapes into Montreal's finest art galleries. Wherever he went, he wore his Rembrandt cap and brown corduroy jacket, just like the famous Dutch artist himself. It made me smile to see him dress the part.

Mom, Viggo and I, went to his graduation. It was a proud moment when he marched up to the stage to receive his degree along with hundreds of young graduates. He was so pleased by this accomplishment and so were we. At the reception afterwards, he proudly introduced us to his fellow students saying that he'd like them to meet his family. It meant a lot to him that we came to share in this triumphant occasion.

❧

I majored in Graphic Design which was part of the Fine Arts program. With help from student loans and my mother, I completed my studies in two years. Mario also helped. If I needed any of my artwork photographed to make large transparencies, he made them at the art studio where we had worked together. Sometimes he surprised me, catching me half-way through the McGill campus to walk me to my class. It was always nice to see him, like meeting a trusted friend. Occasionally he invited me for lunch to talk about how things were going. I missed him, but we were never lovers again. He was a good man.

A Personal Ad

I was lonely. The Gazette came to my door every day, Mom insisted. A high mountain of newspapers had grown in one corner of the bedroom and become part of the furniture. One advert in the personal column attracted my attention. The ad read:

"A gentleman would like to meet a nice lady artist for friendship and possible relationship. Please write to me with your contact information so we can meet for coffee."

I wrote back to him saying that I'm an artist, and gave my phone number to set up a rendezvous. I felt excited. He wanted to meet an artist, and as such, he might like *me*. Maybe this was the love I've been waiting for. He received my letter and phoned me some days later. He had a thick German accent. We decided to meet at the Roddick Gates, the marble arches in front of the McGill campus. It's a landmark and everybody knows where it is.

"How will I recognize you?" I said.

"I'll have a camera around my neck. What about you?"

"I'll be wearing a red blouse with a white skirt, and I have blond hair."

I couldn't wait to meet him. Our rendezvous was set for two o'clock next day. I never answered a Personal Ad before, and felt exhilarated by the prospect of meeting the man who might be "The One."

Close to two o'clock next afternoon, I waltzed down to the Roddick Gates which was five minutes from my apartment. There was nobody there. I waited a few minutes and looked around. I bet he's hiding, I thought, and saw a telephone booth across the street. Somebody was inside. I waved, and a man with a camera around his neck was shamed out of his hiding place. *What a coward!* I guess he wanted to see what I looked like from a safe distance.

He crossed the street and I almost died of revulsion. He was short, around fifty, with a few strands of combed over brown hair. The worst thing were his teeth. They were brownish and sticking out in all directions. He was carrying something in a plastic bag. I felt like running away but that would be rude.

"Where would you like to go for coffee?" he said.

I tried to think of the darkest place where none of my friends would see me with him. I suggested the Pam-Pam on Stanley Street. We arrived at the basement café and I seated myself on a padded bench with my back leaning against the wall. He sat in a chair facing me. We ordered coffee and made small talk.

"Why did you want to meet an artist?" I asked.

"Because in my experience, artists are broad-minded and more liberal."

So, he's done this before, I thought, and wondered why he wants us to be liberal and broad-minded. Does he mean *easy?* I listened to his drivel but tuned out most of it. Then came the point in the conversation where he asked to see me again.

"Sorry, but I have a boyfriend," I said.

I lied, and worried that my rejection had upset him. He was quiet for a moment. Then he reached into his bag to pull something out. I thought for sure he was really angry and was reaching for a gun to shoot me. I screamed and ducked to my right to avoid the bullet. Nearby patrons looked over at us. But there was no bullet; he took out some magazines. Now I was even more scared of him. He knew that I didn't like him or trust him.

"I thought if you were a lonely young lady, you might enjoy some fashion magazines to look at."

He handed me the magazines. Then his eyes narrowed, hardening as he looked at me.

"Don't ever let me catch you between Guy Street and Mansfield Street," he said in a menacing growl.

The creep just threatened me!

I got up to leave and he followed. He paid for the coffees and we went out the door. I said goodbye and ran away as fast as I could, my heart was racing. My life had just been threatened! His magazines were burning a hole in my hand so I threw them in the nearest trash can as I ran.

My mother... I needed to hear my mother's soothing voice. Having run a safe distance from the Pam-Pam, I found a payphone and dialed her number. Hearing my distress at what happened, she listened calmly. Then she laughed and told me not to worry or do something so stupid again. We talked a little more and my fears floated away at the sound of her voice. My heart stopped pounding and I loved her for calming my fears. No matter how old I got, the sound of my mother's voice always reassured me that all was well.

Sam

I spotted Sam on the platform while waiting for a subway in downtown Montreal. Sam was a black fellow from Rhodesia whom I'd met at McGill many years before. I came to know a number of students from Africa who studied there. When you became friends with one of them, you got pulled into the whole group. I enjoyed their parties where they played African music and served authentic food such as spicy ground nut stew. It was like travelling to an exciting new country. I was on a culture binge during my first year.

I wasn't the only white person at those parties; there were several white couples who came. They had lived in West Africa and seemed to have open marriages. Both spouses had sexual liaisons outside their unions, and spoke freely about how uninhibited black lovers are. Those white wives were now enjoying sex with the African students who tried to be discrete but let it slip. I learned about this because those students were my friends.

Sam was studying social work back then. After my first year of university, he helped me get hired at a summer camp for emotionally disturbed children. I was thinking of becoming a psychologist, but the intensity of that job put an end to that ambition. I did however, learn about human behaviour and to question *why* people do what they do. The experience of working at that camp made me ultra sensitive.

It took me six months back in "normal" society to recover. In regular life, a person can present themselves as anything they want to other people; they can hide their vulnerabilities. But not at that camp where every staff member was actively analyzing behaviour.

Years had passed since that summer camp. Sam recognized me on the subway platform and walked over to say hello. He hadn't changed and still looked as good as he did years ago.

"Where've you been all this time?" he said, smiling and surprised to see me.

"South Africa," I said, almost embarrassed to admit this to a black Rhodesian who had been my friend.

Living in South Africa for six years had changed me. My stay in that country during Apartheid might explain why I was a little cooler than usual. I'd been conditioned to be more distant with other races. It was something I couldn't help. I hoped it would soon pass, and that I'd be my old self again. We continued talking, and he asked if he could walk me home from my subway stop.

Back in my apartment, I made us tea and warmed up some chicken legs with rice. We chatted about old times and our friends from West Africa, particularly the Gambian students. Those kids were the cream of the crop. They eventually returned to their country to take up important jobs in government or education. Our conversation bubbled, and before you knew it, Sam missed his last bus.

"Could I stay here for the night?" he asked, not sure how I would react.

"Okay," I said, "but you have to keep your clothes on!"

Sam agreed, and understood that South Africa had left its mark on me. Poor Sam. He lay on the only comfortable sleeping surface which was my bed. He remained fully dressed in his shirt and tie, trousers and socks. I lay on my side of the bed while he slept as far away as he could on the other side. I felt guilty that he didn't dare to remove his tie. *I'm sorry Sam, please forgive me.* In the morning, he took the bus back to his own place to change for work. This was the last time I saw Sam. He was a good man.

Ryan comes to Montreal, 1978

Surprise! A letter arrived from Ryan. He was in England, staying at his parents' home in Bognor Regis. He'd taken me there when I first met him in London. I remember that big white house with a thatched roof like you see in the countryside. The home was filled with souvenirs from his family's life in Kenya---zebra skins hanging on the wall, primitive African masks, Masai spears and colourful tribal cloths. Looking around, it was obvious their roots were in Africa.

I hadn't heard from Ryan for several years, ever since he abandoned Mimi and me at the casino in Swaziland. To be honest, so much had happened in my own life that I hardly thought about him at all. As I read his letter now, I grasped the words that he wanted to visit me in Canada, to "make things right."

I didn't trust him. What was he up to? I suspected he might be running away from something but felt I owed him hospitality in Montreal if that's what he needed. I had lived with him in London and South Africa, so it was only fair. Maybe he had legal problems in England and wanted to escape.

I wrote back and told him he could stay with me for two weeks as a friend, and that was it. I still had art classes to attend during the day, so he'd have to keep himself busy.

And he'd have to sleep on my sofa. It was up to him if he wanted to come under those conditions or not. He replied saying that he accepted my terms. Perhaps he thought he could soften my stance once he got here.

I picked him up from Mirabel airport. It was a friendly reunion, but it felt odd to see my former boyfriend out of his element. He used to be the formidable safari leader calling all the shots. Now he seemed tame and lost, the strength of wild Africa gone from his aura. He was still a perfect gentleman, but I felt no real excitement at seeing him.

We visited my parents in Rosemere where at long last they could meet my great white hunter whom they'd heard so much about. One evening, they invited us to a party at a nursing friend of my mother's where the disc jockey played the song "Beat the Clock," all night long. Dad loved that song. He kept singing and drumming to beating the clock. He was the life of the party. Ryan told me afterwards that my father had taken him aside and said with a smile:

"If you ever hurt my daughter again, I'll kill you."

Ryan repeated this to me several times and couldn't get over it. He thought it was a great thing for a father to say. Ryan knew me mainly as a woman with no relatives, entirely dependent on him. It was new for him that I should have a family who cared about me. He said that he now regarded me with newfound respect. I wonder how he regarded me before?

While I attended classes, Ryan was free to explore Montreal. He usually had dinner ready when I came home and even cleaned the apartment. He was trying hard to get on my good side, and proudly showed me that he'd scrubbed my bathroom faucets till they sparkled shiny silver.

"Why?" I said, puzzled.

"Well, I thought you should have clean faucets," he

said, surprised that I should ask.

One weekend we drove to a water-filled quarry near Montreal where people swam in the nude. It was a secret place that someone told me about. We saw other people with no clothes on, so we removed everything except our under pants, keeping our privates covered. I swam bare-breasted. It felt good.

"Let's swim across," I said, charging ahead while Ryan followed.

The cold water was exhilarating. Poor Ryan, he was not a relaxed swimmer and held his breath most of the way. That made him tense, and he was like a brick in the water. I think he swam across just to please me.

We didn't talk about our lives since we last met, but perhaps we should have. He never said a word about the years which had passed. Much later, I learned from his sister-in-law Amy who eventually married Ryan's youngest brother Stuart, that one of Ryan's girlfriends burnt down his quaint cottage in Swaziland so she could collect the insurance on her mink coat hanging in there. What else was he hiding from me?

One evening, he insisted on taking me for dinner to an intimate little restaurant where you could bring your own wine. He brought a bottle of Valpolicella and made a big show of serving the wine. Then he ordered escargots and a fine main course of beef bourguignon. He must have saved up all his pennies for this occasion. Halfway through our delicious meal he paused, took my hand, and positioned himself facing me to ask something important. He hesitated, then eventually came right out with it.

"Eva, I'm filling out some forms, and wonder if can I write on my immigration papers that I'm your fiancé?"

My jaw dropped. So that's why he came to see me, the

rascal. He wants to immigrate!

I'm sure my face turned white. I understood then that it wasn't because he wanted to marry me or "put things right" after all these years. He wanted to move to Canada! There was a lengthy silence as I struggled with how to answer him.

"I'm sorry, but I don't want to do that," I found the strength to say.

He looked at me for a long moment, then let go of my hand. We finished our meal saying very little.

The second week with my visitor was uncomfortable. Now I knew why he'd come... not because he loved me, but to get into the country. He had it all planned. He was still kind to me, but I no longer trusted his motives. I'm sure he was disappointed too, having come all this way. That same gloomy rain cloud came over me as when I lived with him long ago. In the days that followed, I didn't feel like going straight home to him after my classes, but instead visited with lighthearted friends who made me laugh.

I was not sorry to see Ryan leave. In hind-sight, perhaps it was harsh of me to let him stay for only two weeks. I suppose he had hopes of rekindling our love and immigrating to Canada, but it could never have worked. It was too late. I loved him deeply when we were part of each others lives. But too much had happened for us to pick up where we left off. We were just old friends now. I love him for who he was to me and the exciting life I shared with him in South Africa. Those years would remain in the realm of unforgettable memories.

A Job in the Arts, 1979

After graduating from Concordia in late May, my fellow classmates and I were highly motivated and out looking for jobs. We had so much confidence. I was lucky to get an interview with a well-known art studio downtown, and wore my most energizing red dress. My large black portfolio containing samples of artwork weighed a ton, but I had to lug it around with me.

The bus let me off at the beginning of a long sidewalk. I could see my destination---a sedate, concrete building. It took me eight minutes to walk there in the heat. I climbed the stairs to the front door which had a windowpane of tinted glass, perfect for checking my reflection. I straightened my hair and practise-smiled. After one last preening glance at myself, there was the boss's grinning face on the other side of the glass door. He had been watching me all this time! Still wearing a huge smile on his face, he opened the door for me. I felt like melting into the woodwork.

We sat down on the sofa to talk. He looked at my art which was mock-ready for print. He listened patiently while I prattled on, confidently explaining the different samples.

"This one is wrong," he said. "The overlay should be under that sheet."

"Oh," I said, "Are you sure? Well, it doesn't really matter. It's just a mock-up."

I tried to make light of my mistake and chattered on undeterred. The result was that I talked myself into a job; he put me in sales. I was hoping to be placed at a drawing board like the other artists, but the boss said that would come in time. Meanwhile, he liked my unbridled enthusiasm and hired me to drum up business for the company.

"Do you have all your cards?" he said.

I didn't understand what he meant by "cards," and learned that he meant credit cards. He expected me to wine and dine potential clients. I had none, but was forced to apply for one in my name. Nor did I have a car to visit customers.

"Find yourself a car," he said. "I'll pay the deposit and monthly installments, and put the car in your name."

Hardly believing my ears, I wasn't going to question him. Although I couldn't help wondering if there was some kind of catch. I didn't want to be beholden to him in any way. When I told my parents about the offer, they were skeptical too. But we decided to take the boss at his word. A salesperson needs a car!

Being a former salesman himself, my father helped me pick out a new car---a compact Chevrolet Chevette. Dad was very good at that sort of thing. He managed to bring the price down by telling the salesman that we first wanted to check out the Honda dealership across the street in case they could offer us a better deal. Our young salesman succumbed to pressure and dropped the price down to $12,000. I paid my boss's cash deposit of $200 and signed the papers. I had a brand-new car in my name. *Wow!*

⌒⌒

At work, I was given an office to make phone calls from. This revered room belonged to a moody Art Director who was away on mental health leave. His creative scraps of paper with brilliant ideas were scattered all over the desk and floor; the office was a mess! I couldn't work in somebody else's clutter, no matter how gifted that person was. I gathered the pieces of paper into one pile to make room for myself. The Office Manager was watching this from his desk beside my office.

"No, no! Nobody is allowed to touch the Art Director's papers!" he said, alarmed to see me tidying up the sacred mess. I carried on cleaning.

"Don't worry, I'm not throwing anything out," I said, and showed him all the abandoned paper scraps which I'd put in a big basket.

Next, I took a Montreal telephone book and started making cold calls to large companies, asking to show them our studio's art work with the aim of doing their advertising. I was excited to get my first appointment, and remember trying to get there. It was with a big important corporation. I had the address and a map, but couldn't get off the highway to reach it. The company's name was clearly visible on the other side of the freeway. I drove up and down that busy road but couldn't find the right exit. I called the client several times from payphones to tell them that I was on my way, and eventually that I was hopelessly lost and couldn't make it. Sad. I never had a good sense of direction.

⌒

After working at the art studio for a couple of months, we fell into a regular routine. I arranged appointments for my boss, our audio-visual man and myself, to give sales presentations to advertising agencies and other corporations. We put on a good show, complete with slides and music. Our goal was to convince them to give us work.

I made an appointment with the Art Director of one well-known advertising company. We waited in the lobby for him to return from lunch. I recognized him right away as he strolled in.

"Oh my God, it's *you* Alain!" I said.

We were both art students at l'Ecole des Beaux Arts fifteen years before. Now here he was, a pipe-smoking Art Director wearing an ascot and flanked on all sides by his creative team. Very artsy. He was just as surprised to see me. Big hugs and kisses on the cheeks all around. I imagine my boss was pleased that I knew the man and hoped sales would be easier. But they didn't bite.

One time the boss and I invited a big executive from a major paper company for drinks and dinner. We talked nicely to him and asked him caring questions. The boss plied him with drinks, and the executive started talking about his personal life. He softened with each whiskey. I had just witnessed the power of schmooze! By the end of dinner, he was putty in our hands and we would be doing work for him. But I felt this process was wicked and manipulative.

My boss asked me to drive to Ottawa and bring a manuscript to a woman who worked for the government in Women's Affairs. The two-and-a-half-hour drive to Ottawa was along a straight highway, so not much chance of getting lost. I found her--- an industrious black woman with long red nails and a forceful personality. I showed her my boss's quote for the work.

"Okay, but not one penny more!" she said, scrutinizing the quote.

Then she sat me down and made me do some proof-reading for two hours on something unrelated. I found it impossible to say no to her, she had that much authority in her voice. My boss said he loved women like her, that they energized him. It was evening by the time she let me leave.

Life in Ottawa was dead quiet after eight o'clock and streets were almost deserted. Heading back to Montreal on the highway in complete darkness was unsettling; there were no streetlights or cars to light the way. Slowly, my headlights started to dim and the car gradually lost power until everything went black. The engine stopped. I had just enough time to pull over to the side of the road. Nothing worked. I was alone in the night with no buildings around, only trees and thick forest. My heart sank. I was not prepared for this and had no flashlight, flares or road-side assistance. I got out of my car and popped open the hood. There was no smoke, no fire, nothing.

I was wearing my favourite red dress which must have reflected in the headlights of a big eighteen-wheeler truck. Thank goodness the truck stopped and the driver got out to help me. He searched for the problem with his flashlight and found it--- a severed grounding wire. Another massive truck passed us and honked; the drivers saluted each other. My driver provisionally reconnected the wire and said he could do a better job at the truck stop up ahead.

I followed behind him to the stop where he fixed the wire and invited me in for coffee and donuts. He was the strong silent type and hardly said a word. I'd never had coffee at a truck stop with a truck driver before, and didn't know what to talk about. After fifteen minutes, I thanked him for his help and was on my way again.

I reached the office in Montreal at around midnight to hand in the accepted quote with a few changes. The boss was waiting for me. It should have been a two-hour drive but I was delayed by four hours, including the extra time the woman made me stay to proof-read. I told him what had happened and how lucky I was to get help with the car.

"Do you wanna fool around?" he said, wearing a grin.

His question surprised me as I didn't think he found me attractive.

"I'm flattered, but no. I never get involved with my bosses," I said, not wanting to hurt his feelings.

This was true, because it would give the boss too much power over me. I preferred to choose whom I loved, and it would never be a boss. Besides, he was married, although he may have been separated. It seemed to me that the artistic professions were morally quite relaxed. Then I remembered my past with Mario and knew that I was no different.

The basement in the Art Studio housed the darkroom and audio-visual department. A slender man with dark hair and brown eyes worked in those serene quarters. He was quiet and had an Italian sounding name. I had a soft spot for Italians, but Bob was timid and didn't look directly at me. This was the shyest Italian I'd ever met. But he wasn't Italian after all. His father had dropped the "U" at the end of their surname and replaced it with "O" which made it sound Italian.

Over time, we got to know each other. We went for lunch with the other employees, and sometimes just the two of us. Everybody loved Bob. He was calm, patient, and encouraging. Stressed-out guys and gals alike sought his company. I had to compete with them for his time, stand in line almost. He was relaxing to be with, just what my volatile personality needed. I had a new credit card to wine and dine clients with, but the only one I ever took out was Bob. We enjoyed hors d'oeuvres, drinks and dinner at some of the finest restaurants in town. I didn't care. In his presence, I found peace.

One morning, I poured a cup of coffee to carry downstairs to Bob in the basement. There was a gentleman client standing upstairs in reception and we greeted each other in passing. I felt elegant in my sister's very high heeled shoes which she'd given me. But on the second step down I tripped and fell, banged into the wall and crashed down the first six stairs. I grabbed my head instinctively and kept on falling. I somersaulted around the bend, tumbled another six steps causing a thunderous rumble, and landed at the foot of the basement stairs. Hot coffee spilled all over my clothes and the walls. When I opened my eyes, there was the red face of the gentleman from upstairs who had rushed down and was evidently expecting the worst. The dear man was shaking with fear for my condition.

Bob stepped out of his darkroom when he heard the commotion. He was surprised to see me lying in a heap with a stranger standing over me. I got up slowly... no broken bones, and reassured them both that I was all right. After seeing I was okay, Bob couldn't help laughing.

"So, you really fell for me, eh?" he said.

The whole building must have shaken when I fell. My boss ran downstairs to find out what happened. He looked at me and seemed relieved that I wasn't seriously hurt.

"Take the rest of the day off and go home. You'll be sore tomorrow," he said, remembering his college football days. He was so right.

⌒〜

The boss came looking for Bob one day and found us cuddling in the dark-room. When the door opened, my knee-jerk reaction was to stop and pretend nothing happened. But Bob continued to hold my hand steadfastly in spite of the intrusion. I could see the surprise on our boss's face, as though he couldn't fathom that I would prefer an underling to himself.

I'd never met a calmer, kinder, more patient man than

Bob. Very easy to be with. He was so wonderful that he was almost not for real. And he definitely wasn't gay. Sometimes I heard him on the phone arguing with someone. He looked depressed for hours afterwards. He'd been fighting with his wife. I heard through the grapevine that things weren't going well for them and hadn't been for over a year. He spent most of his time working at the art studio because he didn't want to go home. They had two young children and always fought about money; there was never enough of it. It didn't matter to me that he had none. One day he came to work carrying a suitcase. He looked miserable. His shoulders were stooped and his eyes downcast.

"What happened?" I asked, sitting down beside him.

"I've left her for good. I'm never going back there," he said, slumped in his chair.

He had no place to stay and didn't know what he was going to do. He mentioned renting a room somewhere. I told him he could sleep on my couch for a week until he got his bearings.

That week went by quickly. Another week went by, then another and another. We drove to and from work together, and I made dinner for us when we got home. He wasn't a vegetable lover and seemed disappointed when he looked in my fridge and saw nothing but a garden growing in there---green salads, parsley, red and yellow peppers, carrots, and yogurt, but no cold cuts or Pepsi. He was a meat and potatoes guy. I soon learned what to buy. We got along well and he was comfortable to be with.

Our friendship eventually grew into something more, and he was soon in my bed. To my surprise, this man had a sensual, passionate side. I didn't know it was possible to be so kind and gentle yet so sexy. We'd arrive at work much too happy. It was difficult to leave the pleasure of our bed and go to work. This man enjoyed sex and couldn't get enough of me. It was entirely mutual. I was happy that he seemed content in my company and didn't have to rush out to the bar like Ryan did, or feel the need to be with other people like Jerome. We enjoyed peace and harmony in each other's presence.

Mom surprised us with a visit to the apartment one evening. She couldn't understand what Bob was doing there. In her eyes, he was too quiet and mild, unusual for a man. Mom preferred exciting, extroverted men like my father.

The art company we worked for wasn't doing well financially. Perhaps one of the two sales representatives (me) could have done a better job of bringing in work for the company. The boss never did make the monthly payments for my car and said I'd have to handle it myself. He said that he thought I would've bought an old car which didn't cost as much.

Bad news came at a staff meeting when the boss announced that money was tight. He asked all of us to work for half our salary until things improved. Some of his loyal employees had been through this before and stuck with him. They would do so again, but I was not one of them. I already earned very little, and half of that would be almost nothing. Bob wasn't happy either. We stayed for a few more weeks and saved our money. He wanted me to go to Toronto with him.

By this time, Bob's wife was receiving welfare cheques and mother's allowance which amounted to more than what he could give her. She had security. He didn't talk much about her except to say that he was unhappy. He felt guilty for his part in the failed marriage, and may have wanted to escape the whole sorrowful mess by moving to

Toronto. He saw his children a few times before we left and said it was painful for them and for him. They cried and he cried. It was heart-breaking for the kids and for him.

I was blissfully unaware that some people blamed me, although I never knowingly encouraged him or asked him to leave her. He said that he was unhappy in his marriage long before he met me, and would have left his wife with or without me in the picture. But I fear that I might have made it easier for him.

Toronto Bound, January 1980

My little Chevette was packed to the brim. We didn't get far on our first day of driving, only two hours across the provincial border to Cornwall, Ontario. Snow pummelled my windshield. It was impossible to see anything but a wall of white. I couldn't see the road, and blindly followed the red rear lights of a truck which exited at Cornwall. A wise idea, so I did the same. There was a cozy bed and breakfast place just off the highway where we spent our first night, using up $100 of our little slush fund. We slept-in and were sorry to leave our cozy room in the morning.

We must have been crazy. I can only blame it on the folly of youth. We had made no arrangements for where we'd stay or what we'd do when we got to Toronto. We just drove off into the great unknown, hoping to find jobs and a place to live. Bob didn't have his driver's license, so I did all the driving and kept dozing-off at the wheel. That straight boring highway was hypnotic. I had to stop at every rest area and splash cold water on my face to keep my eyes from closing.

We reached busy Toronto in rush hour traffic and got swept away in the flurry of cars. This was stressful! So many cars, one-way streets, loud noises and honking. Drivers kept yelling at me. Neither Bob nor I had a sense of direction. In a panic, I accidentally backed into a metal pole which broke the right tail light. Poor Bob had to stick his arm out the window in the freezing cold to signal whenever we had to turn. We pulled over to calm our nerves and gather our thoughts. I was completely disoriented. Looking around, we found ourselves right downtown near the Eaton Center.

"What do we do first?" I said.

"Let's find a place to live," Bob said, as eager as I was to put down roots somewhere.

We drove in circles, trying to spot FOR RENT signs. We found a place on nearby Mutual Street, a house with self-contained studio apartments. Relief at last. We paid first and last month's rent and settled in. The big room was furnished with a bed, fridge, stove and an enclosed bathroom. Clean enough, but with paper-thin walls.

Within one week, Bob miraculously found a job at a prestigious art studio. He was hired as a photographer. It was none too soon as our grocery money had almost run out. I stayed home and painted samples of commercial book covers, intending to knock on doors after I illustrated a few of them. Meanwhile, I walked to Bob's workplace to meet him at lunchtime for a couple of weeks until he felt more comfortable. It was reassuring for both of us to see a familiar face. Some evenings, we photographed artistic compositions on our table for Bob's private portfolio. Each slide created a little world of its own. He was a talented photographer with the soul of an artist. We spoke the same visual language.

But nobody hired me to do commercial art for the book publishers. So instead, I concentrated on looking for a job which I was good at, namely photographic retouching. I had done lots of it at the photo studio in Johannesburg. Next, I searched the Yellow Pages for portrait photographers in Toronto. The best one seemed to be Rodson Studios, located in a pleasant part of town. I decided to have a look.

The boss was an elderly gentleman with silver hair who greeted me warmly, possibly thinking I was a customer. I liked this place, and asked him for a job to retouch photographs.

"Sorry miss, we already have Mickey, our retoucher. He's very good," he said.

I tried to convince him that he could take in more work if he hired me too. No dice. I went back the next day, and the day after that. Still no dice. Finally, I broke through the barrier into the basement where the retoucher was working.

"You can't go down there!" the receptionist said as she ran after me.

"Let me show you what I can do," I said, rushing down the stairs to keep ahead of her.

Surprised by the flurry, Mickey looked up to see us invading his territory.

"I'd like to work here and need to show them that I can retouch photos!" I said to him.

Still stunned, he wasn't sure what to do and looked at the receptionist who reluctantly nodded her approval. He then fetched a photograph of an older woman who needed rejuvenating---wrinkles softened, lips enhanced, age spots removed and a twinkle put in her eyes for zest. He offered me a good selection of coloured pencils to work with. The two of them left me in peace, although Mickey looked over my shoulder occasionally to see the progress. The woman's photo turned out splendid, which seemed to worry him that he'd be replaced. I immediately put his fears to rest, saying that I desperately needed a job and we could easily cooperate. The boss finally hired me after I kept turning up for work.

☙

This fine photo studio was located on Avenue Road in a lush, tree-lined part of Toronto. It was a pleasure to go to work. Bob and I both had jobs now, but not a nice place to live. We saw homeless men drinking booze on the lawn below our apartment, and our place got steaming hot in the summer when the sun shone through the windows. I had to cover the glass panes with large pieces of cardboard to keep the place cool. We needed a better place to live.

Our walls were so thin that our love-making woke our neighbour up. He banged on our wall a few times. Bob gave me a lot of pleasure, and I suppose that I voiced my appreciation. I swear our neighbour recorded us and played it back from his apartment. He wanted to get even with us. Touché, we deserved that. His revenge made it even more important for us find a place with thicker walls.

⌒

By now, I was getting paranoid of being named as a correspondent if Bob's wife started divorce proceedings. I'd seen old movies where the married spouse's lover can be sued by the wronged party, so I rented a basement apartment closer to where I worked. It was furnished and painted very white. The windows were eye-level to the lawn and flower beds. It was okay, but I didn't like living underground, too dark and depressing for me. I felt like I'd become a mole.

The home owner gave a garden party one day where his friends seemed to be enjoying themselves. I could see their legs and heard their laughter as they ate and drank in the yard. But he didn't invite *me*. I was an outsider. I felt like a sucker, paying towards his mortgage but not good enough to hob-knob with his guests. Silly of me to expect an invitation, I mean... he didn't *know* me. Still, I didn't like the feeling which this exclusion caused. I slept there for a few nights, but my heart belonged with Bob. He had found himself a posh bachelor apartment in a high-rise on Bay Street, the heart of Toronto's business area. It even had a swimming pool on one of the floors.

I couldn't bear to be apart from him and spent most of my nights with him. I parked wherever I could find a vacant spot, and gathered up a slew of parking tickets---a big wad of them, but never had any money to pay them. Eventually there came a summons for me to appear in court to deal with the offending fines. The day came for my court appearance, or so I thought. I found the right courtroom, but my name was never called.

"What about me?" I asked the judge.

He peered into his paperwork and said my court date was scheduled for yesterday. I started to laugh. Details were never my strength. The judge was not amused---no sense of humour. He looked at me with a stony expression. I thought it best to leave the room.

Just so you know, these tickets were paid some years later when I tried to renew my driver's license.

～

Back at the photo studio, Mickey and I got along well and did good work together. After a couple of months, my boss asked me work at his second location, an elegant photo studio in the Eaton Center. It was much like the studio in South Africa, with similar duties like passport photos, business sittings and wedding bookings.

I sold a lot of weddings for the boss, most of them very expensive. He called me up one day sounding upset. I heard his wife in the background, equally upset.

"Eva, I got paid for a big wedding and now the couple broke up and cancelled," he said. "I can't afford to give them their money back. Can you *please* convince them to let me keep their money and give them family portraits instead?"

They had paid him for the whole wedding package in advance. It was a lot of money.

"Okay, leave it with me," I said, half flattered that he would entrust me with this difficult, dirty task.

I called the bride and almost felt guilty about taking advantage of her grief.

"I'm so sorry to hear about your problems," I said, and heard her starting to sniff. "But Mr. Rodson has already booked the photo venue at The Old Mill, invested in film and equipment, hired extra photographers and made other commitments. It's impossible for him to cancel all those arrangements without losing money himself."

I could hear her breathing and making understanding sounds.

"He proposes to take some beautiful portraits of you and your family in place of those wedding photos," I said, "does that sound reasonable to you?"

By now, I felt she was on the verge of succumbing. I felt so guilty.

"Yes, that's fine. Tell him I'm sorry we cancelled the wedding and caused problems. We'll take family portraits instead," she said quietly.

I phoned Mr. Rodson.

"She said okay, you can keep the money."

There was a silence of disbelief on the line.

"Thank you," he said, skeptical that it was really true.

He must have wondered what magic words I spoke to her.

An Unexpected Guest

When I returned to the photo studio one day after lunch, Lila the manageress motioned to me.

"You have a visitor," she said, mischievously.

I looked at the visitor's chair and there sat my old friend Ryan. What a surprise! Once again, he was out of his African habitat where he shone, and sat in an ordinary chair along the wall. He'd written no letters since we met in Montreal two years before. Now here he was with his carry-on luggage and wearing that worn black leather jacket which he was so fond of. Lila told me to take the afternoon off and tend to my friend.

He'd flown from England straight to Toronto. My parents must have told him where to find me. He still wanted to immigrate to Canada and look for a job here. I suspect he was relying on me for a place to stay since he hadn't booked a hotel. But I was completely involved with Bob; he couldn't stay with me. However, there might be another possibility.

I'd paid for two month's rent for my basement apartment but seldom stayed there. Most of my nights were spent with Bob, so that extra apartment wasn't needed. And it didn't look like detectives would be naming me as a correspondent in a possible divorce case. Besides, I learned from a brief lawyer's appointment, that fault was no longer based on infidelity; that was an out-dated notion. Perhaps I could give Ryan that apartment and move into Bob's place for good. My landlord agreed, and Ryan moved in there while I brought my things over to Bob's. He seemed happy to have me back with him. We belonged together.

⁓

It was the middle of summer in Toronto, really hot. Ryan asked me to meet him for lunch at a café to chat. He wore his suit and tie, and was out looking for work in the oppressive heat. The humidity was unbearably high. He called Toronto "the big sweat," those words coming from a man accustomed to living in equatorial Africa. He wiped the perspiration from his forehead and loosened his tie.

"I can't bloody well apply to immigrate from inside the country," he said. "I'd have to leave Canada to do it, and nobody will give me a job because I don't have a work permit or social insurance number!"

Poor Ryan. He seemed so frustrated. He had stayed in my basement apartment for the time it was paid for, but was now living in the suburbs with a woman he'd met on the airplane over from England. She was a divorcee who gave him a coffee maker shortly after he moved into my basement flat. They had obviously kept in touch. I didn't need to worry about him since this woman was looking after him now. He called me occasionally to talk.

Stranger on a Train

It was Mom's 62nd birthday in mid-October. I took a train to Montreal on my own to visit my darling Mom. It was always good to see my folks. She baked her traditional Swedish "Princess-torta," with fresh cream and marzipan. Mom and I talked in the kitchen over dishes. She washed the plates louder than usual, and it seemed like she was struggling to tell me something. Finally, she came right out with it.

"I don't think Bob is the right man for you," she said. "He has no money or ambition, he's not an entrepreneur, he's too quiet, too young, not lively, no get-up-and-go...."

The list of complaints was long. She hoped that I would meet someone else to settle down with, a more prosperous man who could give me security. I was sad to hear her opinion, but she gave me something to think about.

After my visit, Mom drove me downtown to catch a train back to Toronto. The coach was almost full except for one empty seat beside a pleasant looking middle-aged man. After a few minutes, he politely shook my hand and introduced himself as Chris Jenkins. We made small talk. He was originally from England, born of a British father and Chinese mother. The refreshment cart came down the isle and he asked if he could offer me a small bottle of red wine. Yes, thanks. We had one bottle, then another, and possibly some whiskey too, I can't remember. It was a six-hour ride.

We talked a lot, drank and ate, smoked cigarettes, and drank some more. He was mature and seemed to be in command of his life. I fell asleep from all the alcohol and rested my head on his shoulder. He held my hand in his big warm hands. They were fleshy and enormous. I must have given him my phone number at work.

Bob met me at the train station in Toronto. I tried to get away from Chris and didn't want Bob to see me walking with him. Maybe he saw, but he didn't say anything. It was good to see my Bob again.

Next day Chris called me at work. He'd booked a hotel nearby and would stay there while on leave. My mother's words came back to me, and I wondered if this man would meet with her approval. Chris asked to meet me for lunch at the food court in the Eaton Center.

"You're a very attractive woman," Chris said as he took my hand. "I'd like to know you better. I think we'd get along well."

It turns out that he was 48 years old, never married, and worked as a marine engineer. *Mom would like that*. He was interesting and talked a lot. He made me feel desirable and phoned me every day at work to invite me for lunch or for coffee if it was after five o'clock. I told him several times that I was living with my boyfriend, but that didn't seem to deter him. He charged full speed ahead. I felt pressured by this romantic tornado who turned my life upside down.

Chris assumed I wasn't happy with Bob, and that *he*, being single and prosperous, was a much better prospect. I was in turmoil; he didn't let up! One evening he invited me for dinner at a fine hotel in Toronto where Rita Moreno was performing. He ordered red wine, tasted it and sent the bottle back. He also gave the servers a hard time about our expensive meal not being properly cooked. Maybe he was trying to impress me by being fussy, I don't know. I didn't like his attitude, but Mom's words kept spinning in my head; Bob's not good enough, not a business man, no ambition or get-up-and-go. Chris Jenkins was everything she seemed to admire.

As our dates progressed, he insisted that I should quit my job because the boss didn't give me a raise when I asked for one.

"You deserve better than to work for peanuts. I want to look after you and surround you with beautiful things," he said on one of our lunch dates.

He caressed my arm and pressed my hand to his lips. He was moving so fast my head was spinning. I felt torn between two men. It was not pleasant!

"Let's look around tomorrow for a nice apartment for you," he said. "I'll sign the lease and you can move in right away. I'll buy some furniture and have it delivered. What do you say?"

This was a sudden proposal. I wasn't quite sure what to make of it. I guess he wanted access to an apartment so he could have someplace to stay when he came off the boats. He was so forceful and moving so damn fast that it made me dizzy.

"Okay," I said, "but I don't want you to have a key. You said it would be *my* place."

He hesitated, and looked around the restaurant for a minute.

"All right," he said, turning to me with a wily smile. "I agree to those terms."

⌒〇

I broke up with Bob when I got home that evening. He was waiting up for me. Feeling apprehensive, I told him.

"I've met a man who's seriously interested in me," I

said, after we sat down. "You're still married Bob, and you've made no arrangements to get divorced."

Bob was silent, hardly believing what he heard. I felt like I'd shot an arrow through his heart. I was sorry for it. He didn't get mad or yell at me. He looked down, and I saw his Adam's apple move as he swallowed.

"When did all this happen?" he asked. His eyes were moist.

"About two months ago," I said, angry that my mother didn't think he was good enough for me, angry that I'd hurt this gentle man who loved me.

"Chris wants to find an apartment tomorrow and I'm to move in there. He said it will be *my* apartment, so he's not getting a key."

Bob sat quietly as he processed this news. Then he reached for my hand.

"Let me help you when you find one," he said at last.

This man is so good!

Next morning I quit my job, giving the reason that the boss didn't offer me a raise when I asked for one. I sold so many expensive weddings for him and made him tons of money, that I deserved a better salary, so Chris said. After I quit, I learned that the boss gave all his other employees a raise in case they'd leave too.

I then phoned Chris at his hotel and we went apartment hunting. He was pressed for time as his boat was leaving early next morning for Sarnia. Everything was rushed, but we found a place in St. Jamestown in one of the many white apartment blocks. I had no idea it lay in a rough area of Toronto and neither did he. He signed the lease and gave me the key, after which we took a cab to the steamship in the harbour.

Chris worked on this vessel and wanted to show me

the ship and what he did for a living. He gave me a tour of his domain in the bowels of the boat. There I saw a world of pipes painted white which snaked everywhere, hissing machinery, valves, nuts and bolts. He explained that as a marine engineer, it was his job to make sure that everything ran smoothly. He even confessed to using bread to repair a leak sometimes.

I didn't know this is what a marine engineer did, and had imagined a more sophisticated office job perhaps because of the word "engineer." Then he showed me the cubby hole where he slept---a tiny little room with a single bed. I was disappointed with his workplace and felt that in our courtship he'd put on a big show of trying to impress me with his wealth and superior attitude.

"Here's some money to buy a bed, kitchen table and a couple of chairs," he said, handing me cash, "and get a phone installed so I can reach you."

We said goodbye. He intended to sleep onboard and sail out next morning. He told me that he'll contact me when he gets into town again. I felt disillusioned. This is not who I thought he was. I had met some of Chris's friends several weeks before who told me that he desperately needed a home and a woman to come home to. I guess that woman would be me. This whole situation didn't feel right somehow, too much pressure. My head ached and I felt pulled in two directions. This was happening way too fast.

∽

I slept at Bob's place that night. He seemed distraught that I was leaving him, but wanted to help me with whatever needed to be done. Perhaps he thought I deserved a man who was free to marry me. He had the weekend off and helped me pick out furniture and have it delivered to my new apartment in St. Jamestown. We also brought my clothes.

Chris and I were in such a rush when we looked at the place, that I hadn't noticed the holes in the wall or the dirty paint. Bob fetched some putty and paint from the superintendent and got to work fixing things up for me. He patched the walls beautifully and spent the weekend with me. He even returned on Monday night after he finished work, bringing hamburgers from McDonald's. We were in bed when the doorbell buzzer rang. It was late.

"Shhh, don't say anything," I whispered, "it must be Chris."

I didn't answer the intercom and did not want to let him in. What's more, I decided then that I didn't like Chris very much. He had put so much pressure on me to do this and like a fool I succumbed... possibly because I felt flattered that he wanted me so much, and because I thought my Mom would approve of him. He rang the buzzer for a long time. Bob and I lay in bed listening. I was scared. Next morning the phone rang. I dreaded speaking to Chris but knew that I had to. He was furious.

"I stood outside the building like an idiot ringing your doorbell for twenty minutes! I had a television set for you!" he said, exhaling smoke from his cigarette. "Is Bob with you?"

"Yes, he's been fixing the holes in the wall," I said, feeling like a criminal.

"In that case, I want you to leave. Pack your bags and get out! Go back to him! I don't want you and him living in the apartment that I'm paying for!"

"He's just helping me," I said, "but that's fine with me! I'll leave the key with the super." I slammed the receiver down.

Those were the last words we spoke. By now, I disliked him intensely, and couldn't wait to get out of there.

This had been a terrible mistake. We tossed my clothes back in my suitcase and took a taxi to Bob's studio apartment on Bay Street. I loved this wonderful man and never wanted to leave him again. I made a huge blunder thinking I could be happy with someone who suited my mother.

A Divine Surprise

Bob and I were happy. We had peace and harmony. But we made love so much that I ended up in the hospital, barely able to move with an injured lower back. The physician laughed when I told him the cause of my injury. I told him that I'd fallen, which I had... I'd fallen in love. He prescribed strong muscle relaxants, anti-inflammatory pills and bed rest.

Bob was wonderful. I lay flat on our bed until he came home during his lunch hour to take care of me. I looked forward to hearing his key turn in the door. He gave me juice through one of those bendable straws. I loved him for being so kind. It took me a week to recover.

But all that lovemaking came with a consequence. I missed my period. A positive pregnancy test from the pharmacy came as a shock. Bob wasn't divorced yet. He already had two young children and we had very little money. Our situation wasn't stable. There were more and more reasons why we shouldn't have a baby.

I made an appointment with an obstetrician at a Toronto hospital to discuss terminating the pregnancy. The doctor examined me and I was indeed pregnant. We talked for at least forty-five minutes about my frame of mind---that my situation wasn't right for bringing a child into the world, that I wasn't married but my boyfriend was.

"Take a week to think about it," the doctor said, and he booked me for another appointment.

I don't know what words of wisdom he spoke in those forty-five minutes, but during the week that followed, my heart was at war with my brain. I was confused and torn. There was a constant lump in my throat and I wanted to cry at the thought of ending this life growing within me. With each passing day I became more attached to it. By the end of the week, I yearned for my baby to hold and love. I wanted this baby so badly, and was ashamed for ever having thought otherwise. This child was conceived in love. Bob was okay with whatever I decided and was resigned to his fate. I was glad for that. He said that women get pregnant and it comes with the territory. Feeling lucid and happy in my thoughts, I went for my scheduled appointment with the obstetrician.

"How would you like to help me have a baby?" I said.

The doctor's face brightened when he heard that. I think he was happy that he'd saved another child and would bring it into the world. He hadn't told me what to do the week before, but it must have been how he talked and what he said to me. He'd spoken the right words to my heart and made me change my mind.

We called all our friends with the good news, even some old colleagues from the art studio in Montreal where Bob and I first met. I was surprised when the copy-writer asked how we could be so happy since we weren't married. Her comment didn't dampen my spirits, although it stayed in the back of my mind. We kept the news a secret from my parents, and wanted to tell them in person when we'd visit them in Montreal for Christmas. I wasn't sure how they'd react.

⇛

Christmastime at my parents' cozy home went well for us.

They pampered us with lots of goodies to eat in front of a crackling fire---chocolates, cold cuts, cheese and nuts of all kinds. The tree smelled of fresh pine as Dad chopped it down from the forest the day before. Christmas lights covered by angel hair created a magical ambiance, and the delicious aroma of ham baking in the oven filled the house. Mom always made her Swedish ham recipe with all the trimmings.

After dinner, we moved to the sofa and started opening gifts. I waited for the right moment to break the news. Bob and I looked at each other and he gave me a nod... here goes!

"Guess what?" I said, unable to hold it any longer. "We're expecting a baby!"

My parents both stared at me with open mouths and wide eyes. This was big news for them. They'd waited a long time for me to settle down, and didn't flinch about our not being married. They were thrilled to see me become a mother after so many years of wandering the earth. They may have been surprised by my choice of partner, but Bob was good for me. My father liked him and thought Bob was a marvellous conversationalist which made me laugh. Bob just listened to him talk. Dad couldn't stop smiling and was more attentive to me now that I was in a delicate condition. He didn't even dare to get drunk for fear of causing an argument which might upset the unborn.

Bob and I drove back to Toronto in good spirits. Christmas had gone well. We were both relieved that my parents seemed delighted by news of my pregnancy. Our hearts were happy.

That winter day was freezing with high snowbanks on either side of the major highway. We drove past several cars in the ditch. There must be patches of black ice on the road which you couldn't see.

"Oh no, *shit!* Hang on!" I said.

It happened so fast. Our car slid, swivelled around and careened into the ditch. This was bad. Our seat belts restrained us and helped with the impact. We sat there dumbfounded, not knowing what to do next. There was no way we could get out of there. Across the highway, three gigantic men jumped out of their car and ran towards us. I locked the doors, worried about what they might do to us.

"We'll help get you out!" hollered one of the men, seeing the fear on my face.

With a few strong coordinated pushes, they freed the car and put it facing the right way. We were grateful. I felt bad for misjudging them. Perhaps being pregnant makes a woman feel vulnerable.

Months passed. Bob and I were content. One day I got a surprise phone call from the woman Ryan was staying with. *So, he's still in the country.* She started by talking politely in circles, and eventually came right out with it.

"Could you possibly help me with Ryan?" she said. "My financial position is precarious. He smokes imported cigarettes which cost money every day, and he can't work in Canada. It's hard for me to support him on my own."

Her phone call caught me off guard. I hadn't thought about Ryan for a long time. I guess the woman believed he was partially *my* responsibility because he came to Canada to see me, even though I didn't invite him.

"I'm sorry, but I'm very pregnant and not working. We hardly have enough money for ourselves. I'm really sorry, but we can't help you."

She must have been desperate for money to call me. It made me sad to refuse, but it was impossible to share what little income we had. I don't know how long Ryan stayed in the country. I presume the woman drove him the airport when his tourist visa expired.

⌒

By the time summer came, my belly was huge. I went for daily walks in Queen's Park near the Ontario government building and sat on benches in the shade. The baby was pressing on my bladder so I couldn't stray far from a bathroom. Our baby was due in a few weeks. Bob saw a lawyer for a divorce, but it wasn't happening fast enough. We met with this lawyer and asked him to speed it up. He took one look at me and understood the problem.

"I see you have a dilemma," he said, stroking his chin. "It can be done, but it'll cost you an extra four hundred dollars to rush it."

We had no choice but to pay. We wanted to be married before the baby was born.

Bob's Divorce Certificate finally came in the mail. I rushed to the Registrar's Office with the precious envelope to get a Marriage License. Standing in line, I saw people snicker softly to one another as they looked at me. They all knew why I was there.

Then Bob's landlord informed us that we were living in an "adults only" building, and they don't allow babies--- too noisy. We'd have to find another apartment fast. Thankfully we found a two-bedroom in Willowdale, in the northern part of Toronto. Moving day would be on July 1st and our wedding was scheduled for July 3rd at the City Hall chapel. Things were moving quickly. I sewed my wedding outfit---a beige pleated maternity tunic and a white lace blouse. Sweet-smelling mauve freesias were pinned to my dress on the big day, and I bought carnation boutonnieres for the men. It was all a bit hux flux, but we were as ready as we could be.

My parents and brother Viggo came from Montreal to see us get married. We also invited two other couples who were artists from Montreal and now lived in Toronto. They'd become our good friends. One of those men served as Bob's best man and picked us up in his black Jaguar to take us to the chapel.

I was stressed out. When Bob tried to put his mother's gold ring on my finger during the ceremony, I became hysterical and started to laugh and cry because it didn't fit. My hands were swollen with pregnancy. Dad laughed and cried too. We managed to compose ourselves until it was over. I felt relieved that Bob and I were finally wed. Our child would be born to married parents. That was important to me.

The reception was held at our new apartment which we'd moved into two days before. The décor was sparse, but Mom helped with refreshments, wine and champagne. Everyone seemed happy enough, and spilled onto the balcony to sit in the cool evening air. We lived on the fourteenth floor with a marvellous view of Toronto's glittering lights in the distance. My parents and brother stayed overnight at the splendid Prince Hotel and would soon be on their way back to Montreal. It was slowly sinking in for me that Bob and I were husband and wife. I felt grateful it had all worked out.

On July 15th. Bob was laid off from work. This was not a good time to lose his job. He started searching desperately for another one. Then on July 22nd. I went for my regular appointment with the obstetrician and waited in a room filled with patients, many of them big like me.

"I've been leaking water all week," I said casually to the doctor.

He looked alarmed.

"How much water?"

"About a full pad per day," I said, thinking this was normal.

He grabbed some litmus paper and tested the liquid. It was amniotic fluid.

"How fast can you get back here?" he asked. "You've got to deliver as soon as possible!"

The doctor cancelled most of his appointments for the day while Bob and I drove home to pick up my suitcase. I wanted to believe that the doctor took a special interest in this baby, having saved it nine months ago.

Once back at the hospital, we parked in the indoor parking. I was placed on a gurney and wheeled into a room. My doctor tried to induce me for hours, but injections didn't work and neither did the balloon method. I wasn't dilating.

"Do you feel that contraction?" He said, sounding concerned. "You should be feeling it!"

"No, hardly anything."

The contraction only felt like those tensor treatments on my stomach which gave me a six-pack for Jerome. I felt no real pain then or at anytime. That wonderful doctor tried every method. He stayed with me all night, and periodically went to sleep in a room reserved for medical staff. The nurse who admitted me the day before returned to work twenty-four hours later.

"What, you're still here?" she said, surprised that I hadn't given birth yet.

My baby was in distress. The doctor decided to do a Caesarian section. I was prepped and whisked to the operating room. The anesthetist gave me an epidural block which froze my lower half and meant that I'd be awake for the surgery. But she overcalculated and gave me too much freezing. I was breathing but couldn't feel myself breathe. She had to remain with me the entire time to give me oxygen. She was being called away to surgery next door, but stayed with me. Then they cut me open and my baby came out---a healthy, strong baby boy!

"Ten out of ten," the doctor said triumphantly, and put him to my breast. But I was still frozen up to my neck from anaesthetic and couldn't feel anything or move my arms. I looked at my baby when they laid him on my chest. He was beautiful.

I stayed in the hospital for a week. Admissions thought my married name was Italian, so they reckoned I'd fit in well with three Italian mothers on the maternity ward. It was hell. As much as I love the warmth and passion of Italians, those women couldn't keep quiet for one minute. They talked to each other constantly, and when there was a lull in the conversation, they'd telephone somebody and talk some more. I closed the curtains around me, covered my eyes with a cold cloth and tried to get some peace.

The first time the nurse brought my baby to me in the ward, he reacted to my voice right away and looked straight at me. He was adorable... peach coloured skin and blond hair, the most precious baby in the world. It was love at first sight!

He was brought to me for feedings, first with sugared water because it takes three days for a mother's milk to come. In between feedings, he lay in a bassinette in the nursery along with a roomful of other newborns, all crying simultaneously for food. I was captivated by love for my beautiful baby who was part of me. Having him was the best experience of my life, and the most rewarding. We bonded immediately, and so did Bob. He came to visit us every day.

After a week in the hospital, my nightgown smelled of sour milk. I couldn't wait to go home. The car had been in the hospital parking lot the whole time. We had to pay a hundred dollars to get it out, a lot of money for the newly unemployed.

Once home, we gave that baby so much love. I held him and hugged him for hours. He was everything to me. Occasionally we had to read Dr. Spock to find out "why do babies cry?" and learned it's quite normal.

Bob eventually found a new job with an art studio downtown. When he left for work, I'd be holding the baby. When he came home, I'd be holding him again. Sometimes we'd go downstairs to greet Bob in the lobby when he got back from work.

At long last I found what I had been craving all those years---a man to love who gave me peace, stability and happiness. And he gave me our wonderful baby boy. I finally experienced the joy of motherhood, a great husband, and a cherished son to raise in love. I feel blessed, and am happy to say that Bob and I just celebrated our forty-third wedding anniversary. He is a good, good man.

ACKNOWLEDGMENTS

Thanks to my husband Bob for his love, encouragement and patience with me through the years, and to our wonderful son who allowed me to experience the journey of motherhood.

To Donna Davey for her motivation, Joanne Edwards for her help with editing, Maria (Mia) for always cheering me on, and to the men and women who inspired this memoir.